Gopī-gīta

OUR WEBSITES

www.purebhakti.com
for news, updates, and free downloads of books, lectures, and *bhajanas*

www.purebhakti.tv
to watch and hear, or to download, classes online

www.harikatha.com
to receive, by email, the lectures and videos of Śrī Śrīmad Bhaktivedānta Nārāyaṇa Gosvāmī Mahārāja on his world tours

www.bhaktistore.com
www.gvpbookdistribution.com
www.mygvp.com

FOR MORE INFORMATION

If you are interested to know more about the books, lectures, audios, videos, teachings, and international society of Śrī Śrīmad Bhaktivedānta Nārāyaṇa Gosvāmī Mahārāja, please contact the secretary at **connectwithussoon@gmail.com**

YOUR COMMENTS AND FEEDBACK

We humbly invite our readers to submit any errors they may find in this publication at **www.purebhakti.com/gvp**

There were many contributors to the completion of *Gopī-gīta*, in the form of translators, editors and Sanskrit editors, typists, proof-readers, artists, designers and typesetters. Their names are listed here: Śrīpād Bhagavat Mahārāja, Śrīpād Mādhava Mahārāja, Śrīpād Nemi Mahārāja, Śrīpād Tridaṇḍī Mahārāja, Śrīpād Vaikhānasa Mahārāja; Acyuta dāsa, Acyutānanda dāsa, Akhilesa dāsa, Ānitā dāsī, Bhadrā dāsī, Brajanātha dāsa, Gaṅgā dāsī, Harṣarāṇī dāsī, Jāhnavā dāsī, Jānakī dāsī, Kānta dāsī, Keśava-kānta dāsī, Kṛṣṇa-kāminī dāsī, Kṛṣṇa-kānta dāsa, Mādhavendra Purī dāsa, Prahlādānanda dāsī, Prema-prayojana dāsa, Rādhikā dāsī, Rāgalekhā dāsī, Ratna Stone, Śyāmala-sakhi dāsī, Śāntī dāsī, Sulatā dāsī, Śyāmarāṇī dāsī, Vaijayantī-mālā dāsī, Vasanti dāsī, Veṇu-dhara dāsī, Vicitri dāsī, and Vraja-sundarī dāsī.

Cover and design graphics: Vikāśa Ṭhākur
Design concept: Mañjarī dāsī

Special thanks to the artists who contributed to the completion of the line drawings and paintings: Bakula dāsī, Dhaniṣṭhā dāsī, Gaurahari dāsa, Keśava-kānta dāsī, Kṛṣṇa-vallabha dāsī, Mañjarī dāsī, Nandī-mukhī dāsī, Nīlāmbarī dāsī, Premavatī dāsī, Sarasvatī dāsī, Śyāmarāṇī dāsī, Sat-prema dāsa, Sundarī dāsī, and Viśvambhara dāsa.

Special thanks to Śrīpāda Bhaktivedānta Muni Mahārāja for organizing the instrumental backgrounds to the sound recording of Śrīla Mahārāja's chanting of the Gopī-gīta verses, as well as to Śrīla Mahārāja's lecture sound files on the subject.

Gopī-gīta

The Gopīs' Song of Separation

Śrīmad-Bhāgavatam

Canto Ten, Chapter Thirty-one

With Commentary by
Śrī Śrīmad Bhaktivedānta Nārāyaṇa Gosvāmī Mahārāja

Vṛndāvana, Uttar Pradesh, India.

ISBN: 978-1-935428-06-0

First printing: March, 2009 (5,000 copies)
Second printing: Kartika 2015 (2,000 copies)

Cataloging in Publication Data--DK
Courtesy: D.K. Agencies (P) Ltd. <docinfo@dkagencies.com>
Puranas. Bhāgavatapurūṇa. Gopīgīta. 10. skandha.
Gopī-gīta = The gopis' song of separation : Śrīmad Bhāgavatam canto ten, chapter thirty-one / with commentary by Śrī Śrīmad Bhaktivedānta Nārāyaṇa Gosvāmī Mahārāja.
pages cm
English and Sanskrit (Sanskrit in roman and Devanagari).
Portion of Bhāgavatapurūṇa; Sanskrit text with English translation and commentary.
ISBN 9781935428060
1. Puranas. Bhāgavatapurūṇa. 10. skandha. Gopīgīta.--Commentaries. 2. Krishnmla (Hindu deity)--Poetry. I. Puranas. Bhāgavatapurūṇa. 10. skandha. Gopīgīta. English. II. Title. III. Title: Gopis' song of separation.
BL1140.4.B4342G66 2015 DDC 294.5925 23

Śrī Śrīmad Bhaktivedānta Nārāyaṇa Gosvāmī Mahārāja

Śrī Śrīmad Bhaktivedānta Vāmana Gosvāmī Mahārāja

Śrī Śrīmad Bhaktivedānta Svāmī Mahārāja

Śrī Śrīmad Bhakti Prajñāna Keśava Gosvāmī Mahārāja

Śrī Śrīmad Bhaktisiddhānta Sarasvatī Ṭhākura Prabhupāda

Śrīla Jīva Gosvāmī

Śrīla Viśvanātha Cakravartī Ṭhākura

Table of Contents

Preface

The Sanskrit word *veda* means 'embodiment of all knowledge, both spiritual and material.' The highest and most sublime wisdom is found in Vedic knowledge, which has been passed down to modern times from the beginning of creation through an unbroken chain of self-realized spiritual masters and disciples.

We learn from the great sages and saints of India that the transcendental literature called *Śrīmad-Bhāgavatam* is the essence of all this timeless Vedic knowledge, and it was manifested in this world by Śrī Vyāsadeva, the literary incarnation of God Himself. The all-cognizant and fully independent source of creation, maintenance, and destruction is described in the first verse of *Śrīmad-Bhāgavatam* as Śrī Kṛṣṇa, and that Supreme Absolute Truth is present on each page of this great epic.

The sages teach that *Gopī-gīta* is one of *Śrīmad-Bhāgavatam's* five most important chapters. We are therefore first presenting to the respected reader the miraculous, magical effect of reading or hearing *Śrīmad-Bhāgavatam*, and then we present the benefit of reading or hearing *Gopī-gīta*.

The glory of *Śrīmad-Bhāgavatam* is given in the *Bhāgavatam* itself:

> The material miseries of the living entity, which are superfluous to him, can be directly mitigated by the linking process of devotional service. But the mass of people do not know this, and therefore the learned Vyāsadeva compiled this Vedic literature, which is in relation to the Supreme Truth. (*Śrīmad-Bhāgavatam* 1.7.6)

> Completely rejecting all religious activities which are materially motivated, this Bhāgavata Purāṇa propounds the highest truth, which is understandable by those devotees who are fully pure in heart. The highest truth is reality distinguished from illusion for the welfare of all. Such truth uproots the threefold miseries. This beautiful *Bhāgavatam*, compiled by the great sage Vyāsadeva (in his maturity), is sufficient in itself for God realization. What is the need of any other scripture? As soon as one attentively and submissively hears the message of *Bhāgavatam*, by this culture of knowledge the Supreme Lord is established within his heart. (*Śrīmad-Bhāgavatam* 1.1.2)

As mentioned above, *Gopī-gīta* is one of *Śrīmad-Bhāgavatam's* five most important chapters. In his discourse on Verse Fourteen of *Gopī-gīta*, Śrīla Bhaktivedānta Nārāyaṇa Gosvāmī Mahārāja reveals one of the benefits of reading or hearing it:

> There are others, who can hear about Kṛṣṇa's pastimes. They hear that Kṛṣṇa is playing His flute and that all human beings, animals, birds, and other creatures in Vṛndāvana are hearing His flute-song. As a result of listening to narrations of His pastimes, these persons, too, develop the ambition to hear His flute. They will certainly give up all desire to taste the forms and qualities of this world. They will never want Svarga or even liberation from birth and death.

The Sanskrit words *gopī-gīta* mean 'the beautiful song of the *gopīs*.' We learn from the ancient Vedic literature and from our lineage of spiritual masters that the *gopīs* are the transcendental expansions of Śrī Kṛṣṇa's inherent inconceivable power, His pleasure-giving potency, Śrī Rādhā. It is by the influence of this internal power that the Absolute Truth Śrī Kṛṣṇa exists in four features: His personal form as the supreme cause of all causes and supreme relisher of all transcendental mellows; His incarnations along with Their abodes and infinity of divine pastimes; all living entities; and the unmanifest state of material nature.

We read in the Vedic scripture, *Śrī Brahma-saṁhitā* (Verse 37):

> Śrī Kṛṣṇa, who is all-pervading and who exists within the hearts of all, resides in His abode known as Goloka-dhāma along with Śrī Rādhā, who is the embodiment of His pleasure potency and the counterpart of His own spiritual form. She is the epitome of transcendental *rasa*, and is expert in sixty-four arts. Śrī Rādhā and Śrī Kṛṣṇa are accompanied by the *gopīs*, who, as expansions of Śrī Rādhā's own transcendental body, are infused with blissful, spiritual *rasa*. I worship that original personality, Śrī Govinda.

Our predecessor spiritual master, Śrīla Jīva Gosvāmī, writes in his commentary to this verse:

> The function of the Supreme Lord's own pleasure potency, in the form of His beloved *gopīs*, is non-different from His intrinsic form and nature. Thus, the *gopīs* are manifestations of His personal

potency and also embodiments of the most elevated amorous mellow.

Gopī-gīta is sung by these very *gopīs*, and the magic of their song is praised in *Śrīmad-Bhāgavatam* thus: "When these *gopīs* loudly chant the glories of Śrī Kṛṣṇa, the vibration purifies the three worlds."

We pray that our readers will derive the greatest pleasure and benefit from Śrīla Bhaktivedānta Nārāyaṇa Gosvāmī Mahārāja's discourses on this divine song.

Aspiring for the service of Śrī Guru and the Vaiṣṇavas,

the editorial team
Gaura-pūrṇimā, March 2009

A Note from the Editors

In the early 1990s, a small group of *sannyāsīs* and other devotees were regularly visiting Śrīla Bhaktivedānta Nārāyaṇa Gosvāmī Mahārāja for guidance and instruction. Seated sometimes in his quarters in Vṛndāvana and sometimes in Mathurā, Śrīla Mahārāja answered their questions and explained to them the deep inner meanings of *Śrīmad-Bhāgavatam* through the writings of our Gauḍīya Vaiṣṇava *ācāryas* (spiritual masters). One of the main topics of discussion was *Gopī-gīta*, the *gopīs'* song of separation from Kṛṣṇa, which they sang piteously after He had left the *rāsa*-dance arena.

Five thousand years ago, the great sage Śrīla Śukadeva Gosvāmī mercifully revealed the *gopīs'* divine song during his recitation of *Śrīmad-Bhāgavatam* to the saintly King Parīkṣit, as they sat together on the banks of the Gaṅgā, surrounded by numerous sages and self-realized souls. Those *Gopī-gīta* verses later manifested as *Śrīmad-Bhāgavatam's* Canto Ten, Chapter Thirty-one.

A most elevated, sacred, and confidential subject, *Gopī-gīta* is far beyond the comprehension of conditioned souls. Therefore, with deep compassion, certain recipients of the *gopīs'* mercy have written commentaries on its verses. Śrīla Nārāyaṇa Gosvami Mahārāja explains, "Śrī Caitanya Mahāprabhu respected Śrīla Śrīdhara Svāmī's commentary. Using that as a foundation, Śrīla Sanātana Gosvāmī established Mahāprabhu's beautiful mood of *bhakti* in his own commentary on Canto Ten. Śrīla Jīva Gosvāmī gave further light to that explanation with his *Vaiṣṇava-toṣaṇī* commentary. Then, accepting both commentaries as remnants, Śrīla Viśvanātha Cakravartī Ṭhākura extracted their ambrosial essence and composed his own."

These *ācāryas'* commentaries were carefully handed down and taught by the self-realized spiritual masters in disciplic succession, all of whom were immersed in the sublime truths therein. Then, in 1966, Śrīla Bhaktivedānta Swāmī Mahārāja, famous throughout the world as Śrīla Prabhupāda, carefully carried the ancient Vedic culture to the West. He did this for the purpose of creating a worldwide platform upon which the troubled people of this Iron Age of quarrel and hypocrisy could access these hidden truths. In his summary-study of Canto Ten of *Śrīmad-Bhāgavatam*, called *Kṛṣṇa, the Supreme*

Personality of Godhead, he introduced the verses and commentaries of the *gopīs'* song in English, and also translated over sixty volumes of Vedic literature. He did this in order to bring his worldwide audience to its gradual understanding.

Then, in order to further illuminate this divine topic, Śrīla Bhaktivedānta Nārāyaṇa Gosvāmī Mahārāja gave elaborate explanations of the *ācāryas'* contributions in his series of English discourses in the early 1990s. These discourses were unique because, although Śrīla Nārāyaṇa Gosvāmī Mahārāja, had previously spoken in Hindi on this subject, to his senior students in Vṛndāvana and Mathurā, this was the first and only time he spoke about it so extensively in English. He stated in his discourse on Verse Two: "Some of this explanation is from Śrīla Viśvanātha Cakravartī Ṭhākura's commentary. There are also points that he has not explained, and in those cases I have taken the explanation from Śrīla Jīva Gosvāmī's commentary and also from my heart."

Śrīla Nārāyaṇa Gosvāmī Mahārāja's English audience consisted of disciples of Śrīla Bhaktivedānta Swāmī Mahārāja, and he revealed something to them of his own service to their Gurudeva. "I feel that I am serving him," he told them. "I feel this in my heart. Therefore I do not care for my own time. I take it as my *bhajana-sādhana* that I am helping you all. I pray that he will bestow his mercy upon me, and that he will tell my Gurudeva also to bestow his mercy – because they were bosom friends."

When some of the devotees in his audience suggested that a book be compiled of his wonderful discourses, he agreed, and he added that although the book would be available to all people and everyone would benefit, it would be especially precious to qualified persons.

Several years later, in 2005, while the editors were preparing the manuscript of his discourses, Śrīla Mahārāja began his formal Hindi *bhāvānuvāda* translation[1] of the Sanskrit commentaries of Śrīla Śrīdhara Svami, Śrīla Jīva Gosvāmī and Śrīla Visvanatha Cakravarti

---

[1] Śrīla Nārāyaṇa Gosvāmī Mahārāja's translation is not a literal one. It is a *bhāvānuvāda*, an explanation of the moods of Śrīla Śukadeva Gosvāmī and the *ācāryas*. It is an explanation of the deep meaning hidden in the commentaries of Śrīla Śrīdhara Svāmī, Śrīla Jīva Gosvāmī, and Śrīla Viśvanātha Cakravartī Ṭhākura.

Ṭhākura on *Rāsa-pañcādhyāyī*. These five chapters, which describe Śrī Kṛṣṇa's *rāsa* dance and other related pastimes with His *gopī* beloveds, are considered to be *pañca-prāṇa*, the five life-airs of *Śrīmad-Bhāgavatam*. The editors had the fortune of being able to read the English translation of Śrīla Mahārāja's pre-published manuscript of the commentaries of *Gopī-gīta*, which is one of those five chapters, and that helped a great deal in preparing this presentation of his lectures.

Śrīla Śrīdhara Svāmī's commentary is entitled *Bhāvārtha-dīpikā*, which means "Illuminations on the Inner Meanings of the Moods." Śrīla Jīva Gosvāmī is the author of the *Vaiṣṇava-toṣaṇī* commentary, which means "Bringing Satisfaction to the Vaiṣṇavas;" and Śrīla Viśvanātha Cakravartī Ṭhākura has given us *Sārārtha-darśinī*, meaning "Revealing the Essential Meanings." The editors asked Śrīla Nārāyaṇa Gosvāmī Mahārāja if he would kindly give a name to the written form of his own discourses, his spoken commentary, and he named it *Bhāva-prakāśika Vṛtti*, meaning "The Commentary That Illuminates the Mood."

Śrīla Mahārāja has used many Sanskrit terms in his commentary, which are usually explained in English, either in the text or in a foot-note. Where you find the explanation insufficient, you are invited to turn to the glossary. Where a footnote does not include a specific reference cite, it has usually been taken from one of the glossaries of Śrīla Mahārāja's other books. Following the tradition of our spiritual preceptors, we use standard diacritical markings to indicate the pronunciation of the Sanskrit words. Pronounce *ā* like a in father, *ī* like ea in neat, *ū* like oo in root, *ṛ* like ri in rip, *ṁ* and *ṅ* like ng in hung, *ś* and *ṣ* like sh in shy, and *c* like ch in chap.

A recording of Śrīla Mahārāja singing the nineteen verses of *Gopī-gīta*, as well as the first two verses of the next chapter that describe Śrī Kṛṣṇa reappearing to the *gopīs*, is available at *https://soundcloud.com/srila-bv-narayan-maharaja/sets/gopi-gita*. Before singing, Śrīla Mahārāja speaks three sanskrit verses as an auspicious invocation (*maṅgalācaraṇa*) and gives a short Hindi introduction to the song. You can find the translation of both in the appendix at the end of this book. On *https://soundcloud.com/srila-bv-narayan-maharaja/sets/gopi-gita* you can also find two audio lectures given by Śrīla Mahārāja in English, which elaborate on some of the pastimes and philosophical truths surrounding *Gopī-gīta*. Special thanks to Śrīpāda Bhaktivedānta Muni Mahārāja for organizing the instrumental backgrounds to Śrīla Mahārāja's chanting of the *Gopī-gīta* verses, as well as to Śrīla Mahārāja's lecture sound files on the subject.

We humbly beg you to forgive any mistakes made by us in compiling Śrīla Bhaktivedanta Nārāyaṇa Gosvāmī's Mahārāja's presentation.

Introduction

Upon seeing Kṛṣṇa dancing with all the other *gopīs* and at the same time dancing with Her, Rādhikā left the *rāsa* dance in a sulky mood.

Introduction

Gopī-gīta is part of *rāsa-pañca-adhyāyī*, the five chapters of *Śrīmad-Bhāgavatam* that relate *rāsa-līlā*.

The body has five kinds of life-airs (*pañca-prāṇa*) residing in the heart, and among these five, one is most vital. The twelve cantos of *Śrīmad-Bhāgavatam* are likened to twelve parts of a body. The tenth canto is the heart of that body. Within that heart, the five chapters that constitute *rāsa-pañca-adhyāyī* are its five life-airs, and among them, *Gopī-gīta* is the foremost.

We begin our discussion of *Gopī-gīta* by remembering the chapter in *Śrīmad-Bhāgavatam* that describes the *gopīs*' worship of the goddess Kātyāyanī-devī to attain Kṛṣṇa as their husband. The first verse of this chapter states:

hemante prathame māsi
nanda-vraja-kamārikāḥ
cerur haviṣyaṁ bhuñjānāḥ
kātyāyany-arcana-vratam
Śrīmad-Bhāgavatam (10.22.1)

During the first month of the winter season, the young unmarried girls of Gokula observed the vow of worshiping goddess Kātyāyanī. For the entire month they ate only unspiced *khichrī*.

The *gopīs* who observed the vow to worship Kātyāyanī were young and unmarried. What, then, was Śrī Kṛṣṇa's age at this time? Kṛṣṇa had left Gokula at the age of three and a half. According to Śrīla Vyāsadeva and Śrīla Śukadeva Gosvāmī, He was seven years old when He lifted the mountain, Girirāja Govardhana, on the little finger of His left hand. After He lifted Girirāja, all the elders and their priests gathered together and told Nanda Bābā, "You should not treat Kṛṣṇa as if He were your son. He is actually not your son. He may be a demigod, or perhaps He is God, or someone like God. We have heard that Nārāyaṇa Himself has come in the form of Kṛṣṇa, and perhaps it is true. So you should not treat Him like an ordinary boy. Do not bind His hands, and do not chastise or punish Him. He is only seven years old, and yet He lifted a mountain like Govardhana. How is that possible? This is indeed mysterious."

"Oh," Nanda Bābā laughed. "I have heard that *gopas* only become mature and intelligent at the age of eighty. They cannot properly decide anything before then, because their minds are not fixed. Kṛṣṇa is just an ordinary boy.

"God has far more good qualities than even the perfected saints. Such saints do not become angry, and they are not disturbed by hunger, thirst, or any other material distress. They do not steal or tell lies.

"Kṛṣṇa tells lies. He weeps and becomes angry. He plays tricks on people, and He is naughty in so many other ways. He sometimes cries for butter and sugar candy. If He does not get what He wants, He becomes furious and hurls all the items in our home onto the ground, and then scatters them here and there.

"This is conclusive proof that He is not God. In any case, even if you would insist that He is God, He is still my son, so I will admonish and punish Him and treat Him as a father should treat his child."

Nanda Bābā continued to laugh at the notion that Kṛṣṇa is God; then Yogamāyā came, and by her influence, everyone present forgot this idea.

This incident took place during the month of Kārtika, when Śrī Kṛṣṇa was seven years old, and it was just after Kārtika that the *gopīs* worshiped Kātyāyanī.

There were two groups of *gopīs*, married and unmarried. Although it was the unmarried *gopīs* who worshiped Kātyāyanī, the married *gopīs* like Lalitā, Viśākhā, and Śrīmatī Rādhikā also had *pūrva-rāga* (the *gopīs*' tender love for Kṛṣṇa before their first intimate meeting with Him). This is because, although they had met with Him so many times, they always felt the excited anticipation of a first meeting.

The unmarried *gopīs* were somewhat younger than the married *gopīs*. Śrīmatī Rādhikā is thirteen and a half years old, and Kṛṣṇa is fourteen. Lalitā is twenty-seven days older than Śrīmatī Rādhikā, and Viśākhā was born on the same day as Rādhikā. Rūpa Mañjarī and Rati Mañjarī are a little over twelve years, so they are about one and a half years younger than Kṛṣṇa. This means that when Kṛṣṇa was seven years old, the *gopīs* who were engaged in the worship of Kātyāyanī-devī were about six; but they already had love and affection for Him. Their love for Kṛṣṇa was not *kāma*, amorous affection, because *kāma* is not possible at such an age. They loved Him deeply, but without *kāma*.

Kṛṣṇa told those *gopīs* engaged in worship, "Next year, during the autumn season, I will fulfill your desires." Then, a year later, when Kṛṣṇa was about eight years old, He played His flute to call the *gopīs* to the *rāsa* dance.

It is said that Kṛṣṇa was in Vṛndāvana until He was ten years old, and within that time He performed *rāsa-līlā* as well as all His Vṛndāvana pastimes. In other words, He appeared to be fourteen years old when He was actually only ten, and the *gopīs* also appeared to be older than they were. Speaking in a humorous mood, typical of the playful nature of a maidservant of Śrīmatī Rādhikā, Śrīla Viśvanātha Cakravartī Ṭhākura has said that they grew up very quickly because they used to eat so much butter and sugar candy. In actual fact, the reason they appeared to be teenagers is because of the influence of Yogamāyā.

In their previous births, some of the young unmarried *gopīs* had been personified Vedic scriptures called *śrutis*, and they are known as *śruti-cārī gopīs*. Some had been personified Upaniṣads, and are known as *upaniṣad-cārī gopīs*.[1] Some had been sages from the Daṇḍakāraṇya forest (*daṇḍakāraṇya-ṛṣis*), some had been princesses (*rāja-kumārīs*) from Janaka-purī, and some, daughters of the demigods (*deva-kanyā*).

Among the *gopīs*, some had the association of the *nitya-siddha gopīs*, and they also had *pūrva-rāga*. These *gopīs* easily entered the *rāsa-līlā*, whether they were married or not. [The unmarried *gopīs* were already betrothed, and therefore they also thought of Kṛṣṇa as their beloved in a paramour mood.] On the other hand, the married *gopīs* who had *pūrva-rāga* but did not have the association of *nitya-siddha gopīs* were stopped from entering. The *gopīs* described in the above mentioned verse from *Śrīmad-Bhāgavatam* (10.22.1) had association with the *nitya-siddha gopīs*. We know this because at the end of the month they invited Rādhikā, Lalitā, Viśākhā, Citra, and all other such *gopīs* to join them in their worship. This means that they had the association of those *gopīs*, and consequently they could easily enter the *rāsa* dance.

This is confirmed in the *Śrīmad-Bhāgavatam*. The *nitya-siddha gopīs* and those who had their association entered the *rāsa-līlā* without difficulty, whereas the married *gopīs* with sons or daughters were checked by Yogamāyā. Even though they had *pūrva-rāga*, they could not go. It appeared that it was their husbands who had obstructed them, but actually it was Yogamāyā who did so. She had entered the minds of their husbands, fathers, mothers, and other relatives, influencing them to prevent the *gopīs* from going.

If Yogamāyā had wanted them to join the *rāsa-līlā*, she would have made duplicate forms of those *gopīs*. In this way the real *gopīs* would have been able to leave their homes unnoticed and enter *rāsa-līlā*. However, she could not help these *gopīs*, because they had some traces of a consciousness that was not favorable for fully

---

1 The *śruti-cārī gopīs* and *upaniṣad-cārī gopīs* also performed austerities to attain perfection (*siddha*). Since they originally manifested from *śabda-brahma*, the transcendental sound vibration of Vedic scriptures, they are not *kāya-vyūha*, or direct expansions of Śrīmatī Rādhikā. In other words, they did not originally manifest from Goloka.

developed paramour love in relationship to Kṛṣṇa (*parakīya-bhāva*). They still had the conception: "This is my husband, and these are my children." Their affection was not solely for Kṛṣṇa but was shared with many others.

We are now beginning the devotional process. If our eternal spiritual form is that of a *gopī*, we will develop an increasing taste to serve as a *gopī*. We will gradually be able to perform *sādhana* like Śrīla Rūpa Gosvāmī and Śrīla Raghunātha dāsa Gosvāmī, and in this way we will develop a yearning to be like the *gopīs*.

Now, in our present situation, by reading books on this subject, we must clearly define our goal. Success is sure if, as we read and remember, we long to attain that goal: "I must have that mood one day. I will not accept any other goal." We must be completely uncompromising, not accepting any other goal, no matter who offers it. We should think, "Even if Kṛṣṇa Himself comes and wants to offer me an alternative goal, I will not accept it." Who can be so determined? Only those with the *svarūpa* (intrinsic spiritual nature) of a *gopī* can act in this way.

Almost all the associates of Śrī Caitanya Mahāprabhu have this kind of *svarūpa*, although there are a few exceptions, such as Murāri Gupta, who is Hanumān in the pastimes of Lord Śrī Rāmacandra, and Anupama, another eternal associate of Śrī Rāma. Hanumān and other elevated associates whose *svarūpa* is different from that of the *gopīs* have no taste for this subject matter, even if they hear about it.

The same is true of Śrīla Haridāsa Ṭhākura, because he was Brahmā. According to the descriptions of his character in the pastimes of Śrī Caitanya Mahāprabhu, his *svarūpa* was not that of a *gopī*. Brahmā is the original *guru* in our *sampradāya*. In the tenth canto, fourteenth chapter of *Śrīmad-Bhāgavatam* he prayed to attain the dust from the lotus feet of the Vrajavāsīs, but he did not state clearly that it should be the *gopīs*' lotus foot-dust. Uddhava, on the other hand, specifically prayed for the dust of the *gopīs*' feet. We see in *Brahma-saṁhitā* that Brahmā performed worship by means of both the *gopāla-mantra* and *kāma-gāyatrī*, but that was only to gain power for creation, not to attain *gopī-prema*.

One year after Kṛṣṇa made His promise to the *gopīs*, on the full-moon night in autumn He looked at the moon and began to play His flute. He considered, "Our forefather, the moon, has a beloved other than his wife, Rohiṇī. His beloved is Pūrva-diśā, the eastern horizon."

The most erudite Śrīla Vyāsadeva, who knew how to apply all literary metaphors and ornaments (*alaṅkāra*), marvelously described this scene as follows:

Kṛṣṇa was thinking, "The hands of our forefather, the moon, are smeared with *kuṁkum*. Those hands, his rays, are decorating the face of his beloved Pūrva-diśā without any difficulty, and she is shyly accepting that reddish ornamentation. Why should I not do the same?"

In other words, the reddish rays of the moon radiated throughout the forest, bathing the trees and the rivers and everything else in it in a red light.

In that ambrosial atmosphere, thoughts of the *gopīs* came to Kṛṣṇa's mind, and He remembered His promise to fulfill their innermost desires. He pondered, "By diffusing the reddish hue of his gentle rays and by glowing with the effulgence of newly applied vermilion, Candra (the moon) has reminded Me of My promise and has placed within My heart the inspiration to fulfill it. This is the perfect moment for Me to do so."

Then, on that full moon night of the autumn season, He played a beautiful melody on His flute and the *gopīs* came running to Him. But when they arrived, He told them to return to Vraja. "A lady should serve her husband," He said, "regardless of his qualities. Her husband may be poor or plagued with diseases, but she should serve him under all circumstances."

At first the *gopīs* did not say anything in reply, but within their minds and hearts they questioned, "Does He really mean it or is He joking with us?" They observed Him closely as He tried to cleverly hide His real intention. It seemed that He was honestly expressing Himself in a straightforward manner, but in fact, He was not.

Finally, the *gopīs* said, "You are our *guru* and, as such, You are giving us so many instructions. We know that even in the presence of God, a person should serve his *gurudeva* first, so let us first serve You, our *gurudeva*, before we return to serve our husbands."

In *Bhagavad-gītā*, Kṛṣṇa says:

ye yathā māṁ prapadyante
tāṁs tathaiva bhajāmy aham
mama vartmānuvartante
manuṣyāḥ pārtha sarvaśaḥ
Bhagavad-gītā (4.11)

> As all surrender unto Me, I reward them accordingly. Everyone follows My path in all respects, O son of Pṛthā.

Śrī Kṛṣṇa was instructing the *gopīs* and also telling them, "I am God, so you should obey Me".

The *gopīs* replied, "We agree that if You are God we should certainly obey You, but our first duty is to serve our *gurudeva*. When we have executed that order, we will obey Your instructions to serve our husbands.

"Our second consideration is this. We know that God is our father, God is our real husband, and God is everything; so if You are God, then You are both our husband and our *guru*. In every way, if You do not accept our service You will be guilty of acting against the principles of religion. You are giving us instructions on religious principles, but You should practice this Yourself."

At last, *rāsa* began. Kṛṣṇa danced with Śrīmatī Rādhikā in the center of the circle of *gopīs*, and at the same time He danced with each of the *gopīs* comprising the circle. It is not that He expanded into as many manifestations of Himself as there were *gopīs*, because in Vṛndāvana, all His pastimes are free from the mood of opulence (*aiśvarya*). Rather, He danced so quickly, like a firebrand orbiting in a circle, that it simply looked as if He were constantly and simultaneously dancing with each and every *gopī*. Had He expanded into many manifestations of Himself, this pastime would have been *aiśvarya-līlā*. Instead, He was engaged in human-like pastimes (*nara-līlā*).

Many commentators have written that Kṛṣṇa manifested His *kāya-vyūha*, direct expansions of His personal form, when He was dancing in the *rāsa-līlā*, but Śrīla Viśvanātha Cakravartī Ṭhākura says that this is not so. He refutes the idea that the expansions of Kṛṣṇa's form performed this pastime, asserting that if His expansions had done so, it would be a *līlā* of Vaikuṇṭha. He explains that in fact, only Kṛṣṇa's original form (*svayaṁ-rūpa*) performed this transcendental pastime. We thus conclude that Kṛṣṇa moved like a lightning flash from *gopī* to *gopī*, dancing with each one in turn.

Śrīmatī Rādhikā saw that Kṛṣṇa was dancing with Her. Then, as She cast Her gaze over all the other *gopīs*, She saw that Kṛṣṇa was dancing with each of them as well. Each *gopī* thought, "Kṛṣṇa is dancing only with me." Śrīmatī Rādhikā alone could see Him with each and every *gopī*.

Kṛṣṇa's performance of *rāsa-līlā* in this way – manifesting no *aiśvarya* by bringing forth expansions of His form, but in fact whirling from *gopī* to *gopī* – was certainly miraculous. Moreover, He performed many varieties of activities with the *gopīs* as they danced together. He asked one *gopī* if she were fatigued, He gently wiped drops of perspiration from the face of another, and He fastened ankle-bells on the ankles of another. With each and every *gopī* He engaged in various interactions, and thus each *gopī* became maddened in their love for Him.

The *gopīs*' madness here, in which they were intoxicated by their own good fortune, is called *saubhāgya-mada*. In this regard *Śrīmad-Bhāgavatam* states:

tāsāṁ tat-saubhaga-madaṁ
vīkṣya mānaṁ ca keśavaḥ
praśamāya prasādāya
tatraivāntaradhīyata

Śrīmad-Bhāgavatam (10.29.48)

> Lord Keśava, seeing the *gopīs* too proud of their good fortune, wanted to relieve them of this pride and show them further mercy. Thus He immediately disappeared.

It is stated here that the *gopīs* as an entire group exhibited both *saubhāgya-mada* and *māna*. However, if we take a closer look at the meaning, it becomes apparent that *māna* was only exhibited by Śrīmatī Rādhikā. Only She could see Kṛṣṇa dancing with the other *gopīs*. The other *gopīs* did not see this, and thus they were intoxicated by their good fortune in which they perceived Kṛṣṇa dancing with them alone.

When a hero (*nāyaka*) is controlled by a heroine (*nāyikā*), the heroine thinks herself to be the most fortunate beloved. This fortune is called *saubhaga* and, as it evolves, it brings her to *saubhāgya-mada*. Generally *mada* means intoxication through drinking, but *saubhāgya-mada* means intoxication from the pride of thinking, "In all of Vraja, there is no one equal to me in good fortune."

In this state, the *gopīs* became so proud that if they had been aware of Kṛṣṇa's dancing with other *gopīs*, they would have developed *māna*. Then, in that angry and sulky mood, they would have been completely unable to continue participating in *rāsa-līlā* with the other *gopīs*. Instead, each *gopī* was convinced that she had Kṛṣṇa fully under her control, that He was captivated and controlled by her and obedient to her every command.

Kṛṣṇa understood this and considered, "I have decided to sport with all the *gopīs* and fulfill all their most cherished desires, but there is no hope of that happening unless they change their mood. Somehow their pride must be removed."

He then saw that Rādhikā was no longer there in *rāsa-līlā*. In Her *māna*, She had abruptly left that place and was going elsewhere. Then, suddenly, Kṛṣṇa also disappeared, and all of the *gopīs* began their search for Him.

Some commentators say that Kṛṣṇa became invisible, but Śrīla Viśvanātha Cakravartī Ṭhākura explains that He did not. Rather, He went to a nearby *kuñja* and hid there.

There were four kinds of *gopīs* present in the *rāsa-līlā* on the bank of Yamunā: *svapakṣa*, those in Rādhikā's own (*sva*) group (*pakṣa*); *vipakṣa*, those in the rival group of Candrāvalī; *suhṛd-pakṣa*, those who are friendly toward Rādhikā; and *taṭastha-pakṣa*, those who are neutral to Her party. Actually, *svapakṣa* can refer to either Rādhikā's group or Candrāvalī's group. For those in Rādhikā's group, Candrāvalī is *vipakṣa*, and for those in Candrāvalī's group, Rādhikā is *vipakṣa*.

Syāmalā is friendly toward Rādhikā, which means she is neutral to Candrāvalī. Bhadrā, on the other hand, is friendly toward Candrāvalī and neutral to Rādhā.

Within these four main groups of *gopīs*, there were hundreds upon hundreds of sub-categories, and all were searching for Kṛṣṇa. The *gopīs* in Rādhā's group could not see their *yutheśvarī* (group-leader), Śrī Rādhā, so they were searching for Her as well as for Kṛṣṇa. All the other *gopīs* were searching only for Kṛṣṇa.

Śrīmad-Bhāgavatam's Canto Ten, Chapter Thirty describes the *gopīs*' search for Kṛṣṇa, and how they all became *tadātmikā* with Him. This means they became so absorbed in remembering His characteristics, such as the way He walked and how sweetly He talked, that they began to think that they themselves were Him.

The *gopīs* became like mad persons, asking the trees, creepers, rivers, deer, and peacocks if they had seen Kṛṣṇa. They asked the Tulasī plant, but when Tulasī did not respond, the *gopīs* thought, "Oh, Kṛṣṇa has warned her not to tell us where He is, and because she is His beloved, she refuses to utter a word." They asked the trees, but when they did not reply, the *gopīs* thought, "These trees are male and therefore they are Kṛṣṇa's friends. He has no doubt told them not to tell us where He is. This is why they are remaining silent." When the *gopīs* saw the creepers laden with flowers, they thought, "Kṛṣṇa has touched these beautiful creepers with His fingers, and now they are so happy that they have no awareness of anything external. They cannot speak because they have taken leave of their external senses altogether."

At first the *gopīs* concluded that Kṛṣṇa was not to be found anywhere and that He would not return to them. They were somewhat consoled, however, when they finally noted His footprints. They followed His footprints for some distance until, to their surprise, they saw another set of footprints.

The *vipakṣa gopīs* (the rivals of Śrīmatī Rādhikā) were trying to guess whose footprints these were. They could see that the second set of footprints belonged to some *gopī*. They guessed that this *gopī* must have worshiped God, and as a result She had become so dear to Kṛṣṇa that He took Her with Him and left the *rāsa* dance. They did not think that Her good fortune was the result of Her worshiping Kṛṣṇa, but worshiping God. Thus they spoke the following words:

anayārādhito nūnaṁ
bhagavān harir īśvaraḥ
yan no vihāya govindaḥ
prīto yām anayad rahaḥ
Śrīmad-Bhāgavatam (10.30.28)

> Certainly this particular *gopī* has perfectly worshiped the all-powerful Personality of Godhead, since He was so pleased with Her that Govinda abandoned the rest of us and brought Her to a secluded place.

When Śrīmatī Rādhikā's *svapakṣa gopīs* saw those footprints, they immediately recognized them, as they were accustomed to serving Her lotus feet and knew the symbols on them. Therefore, seeing Her footprints next to Kṛṣṇa's overwhelmed those *gopīs* with joy.

After tracing the footprints a short distance, the *gopīs* now saw only one set of footprints instead of two. They could not see the footprints of the *gopī*; they could only see Kṛṣṇa's footprints, which were now an inch deeper in the earth. They assumed that when Kṛṣṇa and this beloved *gopī* reached this spot, She had become tired and told Him, "I cannot walk any further." He therefore took Her up in His arms and carried Her.

Further on, the *gopīs* noticed that in one spot, the upper parts of the creepers were laden with blossoms, but that the lower part had far less, some having been scattered on the ground. From this they guessed that Kṛṣṇa had seated His beloved in that place and decorated[2] Her with flowers.

As the *gopīs* proceeded further, they beheld that very *gopī*. Alone, and completely unconscious of Her surroundings, She was rolling on the ground, bitterly weeping:

---

2 The Sanskrit word for 'decoration' is *śṛṅgāra*, and that place where Kṛṣṇa decorated Śrīmatī Rādhikā in Vṛndāvana became famous as Śṛṅgāra-vaṭa.

hā nātha ramaṇa preṣṭha
kvāsi kvāsi mahā-bhuja
dāsyās te kṛpaṇāyā me
sakhe darśaya sannidhim
Śrīmad-Bhāgavatam (10.30.39)

She cried out: O master! My lover! O dear most, where are You? Where are You? Please, O mighty-armed one, O friend, show Yourself to Me, Your poor servant!

Śrī Caitanya Mahāprabhu and Śrīla Mādhavendra Purī used to repeat this verse, and as they did so, their hearts full of *bhāva* (transcendental mood), tears would pour forth from their eyes.

All of the *gopīs* – *svapakṣa*, *suhṛd*, *taṭastha*, and *vipakṣa* – then approached Śrīmatī Rādhikā and expressed their sympathy, for it is the nature of women to feel compassion for someone weeping. Although Candrāvalī generally feels envy towards Śrīmatī Rādhikā, when she saw Rādhikā weeping and rolling on the ground, suffering more than all the other *gopīs*, even her heart softened.

Another reason Candrāvalī felt sympathy for Rādhikā is that she is Rādhikā's sister. Actually, they are cousin-sisters, as their fathers, Candrabhānu and Vṛṣabhānu, are brothers. Śrīmatī Rādhikā and Candrāvalī love each other, but there is also some rivalry between them. Candrāvalī is a little older than Rādhikā, but Rādhikā is more beautiful and qualified in every way.

Upon seeing Kṛṣṇa dancing with all the other *gopīs*, and at the same time dancing with Her, Rādhikā had left the *rāsa* dance in a sulky mood (*māna*). Yet, when She was alone with Kṛṣṇa in the forest, She wanted those *gopīs* to be with Kṛṣṇa and Her. This is an example of *vyabhicārī-bhāva*, in which *māna* and other *bhāvas* rise up and subside, and sometimes combine with each other. This is likened to one wave rising up and overtaking another wave, thus causing the water from both waves to merge. After that, the same process is repeated and new waves appear. This is similar to the way in which Rādhikā's *māna* disappeared due to Her being immersed in Kṛṣṇa's loving dealings with Her. She then thought that all Her *svapakṣa gopīs* should come together, but since all the *gopīs* were searching together, they all came.

When the *gopīs* found Śrīmatī Rādhikā in this condition, they sprinkled some water on Her lotus face. When She came to external consciousness, they asked Her, "What has upset You? Why are You so overwhelmed and weeping?"

"As I was wandering throughout the forest with Kṛṣṇa," Śrīmatī Rādhikā replied, "I told Him that I was no longer able to walk."

Why had She said that to Śrī Kṛṣṇa? It was not due to *saubhāgya-mada*, the pride in Her incomparable good fortune. Rather, Her deep contemplation was as follows: "My *sakhīs* have left everything for Me. They have no purpose other than to serve Me, yet I am here, enjoying Kṛṣṇa's company alone. This is not at all fair. If I arrange for all of them to come and join Us, we can all enjoy *rāsa* together. I should not be with Kṛṣṇa alone." In the meantime, the other *gopīs* had been gradually coming nearer and nearer.

Kṛṣṇa told Her, "Quickly! Come with Me."

"But I cannot see You!" Śrīmatī Rādhikā cried.

Rādhikā's condition at this time is called *prema-vaicittya*. Kṛṣṇa was actually sitting with Her and worshiping Her, yet She felt an intense mood of separation from Him. She was unable to perceive that He was sitting right beside Her.

As the *gopīs* came closer, Kṛṣṇa thought, "If they see Us alone together, they will become envious of Rādhikā and everything will be spoiled; there will be no *rāsa-līlā*. I cannot let this happen."

At that very moment, Kṛṣṇa disappeared from that place and hid Himself in a *kuñja* somewhere in the darkness. Rādhikā fell to the ground in distress and it was then that the *gopīs* found Her. "What happened to You?" they now asked.

Somewhat hiding Her real *bhāva* of selflessly wanting them to also dance with Kṛṣṇa in *rāsa-līlā*, She simply told them. "I became maddened with the pride of My good fortune, just as you did. Now He has left Me as well."

Then, as one collective party, the *gopīs* began to search for Kṛṣṇa. Finally they decided that the only way He could be found would be through *saṅkīrtana*, chanting His glories in a mood of deep separation from Him. Thus, they returned to the bank of Yamunā and began to sing *jayati te 'dhikam*, the first verse of their Gop*ī-gīta*.

Verse One

O most beloved Kṛṣṇa, Your birth in this land of Vraja has made it exceedingly more glorious than Svarga, heaven, or Brahmaloka, the topmost heavenly realm in this universe. What to speak of the heavenly planets, Vraja has become even more glorious than the spiritual realm of Vaikuṇṭha.

Verse 1

गोप्य ऊचुः—
जयति तेऽधिकं जन्मना व्रजः
श्रयत इन्दिरा शश्वदत्र हि।
दयित दृश्यतां दिक्षु तावकास्
त्वयि धृतासवस्त्वां विचिन्वते ॥१॥

gopya ūcuḥ
jayati te 'dhikaṁ janmanā vrajaḥ
śrayata indirā śaśvad atra hi
dayita dṛśyatāṁ dikṣu tāvakās
tvayi dhṛtāsavas tvāṁ vicinvate

gopyaḥ ūcuḥ – the *gopīs* said; *jayati* – is glorious; *te* – Your; *adhikam* – exceedingly; *janmanā* – by the birth; *vrajaḥ* – the land of Vraja; *śrayate* – is residing; *indirā* – Lakṣmī, the goddess of fortune; *śaśvat* – perpetually; *atra* – here; *hi* – indeed; *dayita* – O beloved; *dṛśyatām* – may (You) be seen; *dikṣu* – in all directions; *tāvakāḥ* – Your (devotees); *tvayi* – for Your sake; *dhṛta* – sustained; *asavaḥ* – their life-airs; *tvām* – for You; *vicinvate* – they are searching.

Translation

The *gopīs* say, "O most beloved, because of Your birth in this land of Vraja, the entire area has become more glorious than Vaikuṇṭha and other planets. It is for this reason that Lakṣmī, the goddess of beauty and wealth, eternally decorates it with her presence. O beloved, in this blissful land of Vraja, it is only we *gopīs* who are not happy. We maintain our lives solely for Your sake, being extremely anguished in separation from You, and are wandering from forest to forest in search of You. Therefore, please appear before us now.

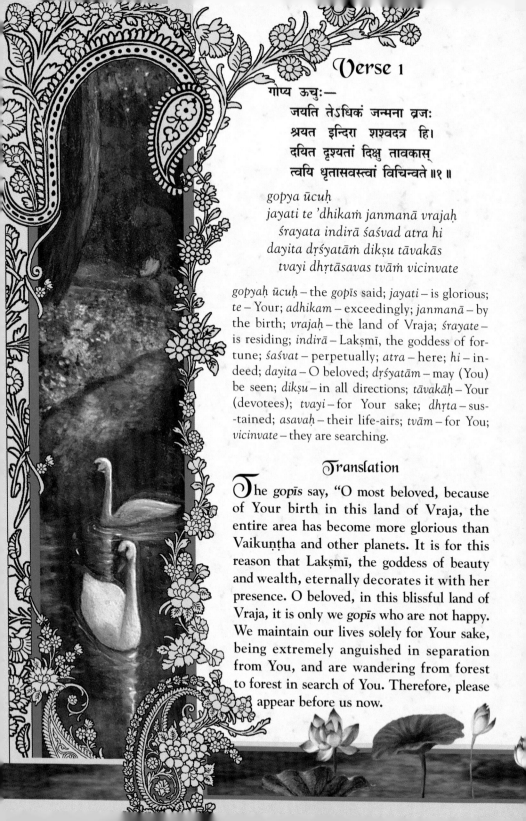

Bhāva-prakāśika Vṛtti

The Commentary That Illuminates The Mood

Śrīla Viśvanātha Cakravartī Ṭhākura begins his commentary on *Gopī-gīta* by offering prayers unto the lotus feet of Śrīla Sanātana Gosvāmī, Śrīla Śrīdhara Svāmī, and all the self-realized *ācāryas* in our disciplic succession, from whom he has received his transcendental moods. He also prays to Śrī Caitanya Mahāprabhu, who is Śrī Kṛṣṇa Himself covered by the mood and luster of Śrīmatī Rādhikā.

Śrīla Cakravartī Ṭhākura states that one cannot know the confidential sentiments of *Gopī-gīta* without receiving the mercy of the *gopīs*. He therefore prays to Śrīla Rūpa Gosvāmī, Śrīla Jīva Gosvāmī, Śrīla Kṛṣṇadāsa Kavirāja Gosvāmī, Śrīla Narottama dāsa Ṭhākura, and all the other *ācāryas*, first in their forms as *sādhakas* (practitioners of *bhakti*), and then in their *siddha* forms (their perfected forms as *gopīs*). In *Mādhurya-kādambinī* and *Rāga-vartma-candrikā*, he has explained that we should gradually approach a level of *bhakti* whereby we may practice *bhakti* in both our *sādhaka-rūpa* and *siddha-rūpa*.[1]

He prays for the remnants of these *ācāryas*, who are the very *gopīs* who joined the *rāsa* dance (*rāsa-līlā*). In other words, he humbly prays for their sublime moods to enter his heart. In truth, his heart is already imbued with their moods, and therefore he is able to reveal the wonder of the verses of *Gopī-gīta* in an astonishing way.

---

1 "On this path of *rāgānuga-bhakti*, the *sādhaka*, being enchanted by intense loving sentiments for Śrī Kṛṣṇa in the mood of any of Kṛṣṇa's beloved associates of Vraja, serves Him in two ways: In the *sādhaka-rūpa* (the present physical body) he follows the *sādhana* executed by the *rāgānuga-bhaktas*, our Gosvāmīs and Gauḍīya *ācāryas*. In the *siddha-rūpa* (the internally-perfected spiritual body suitable for directly carrying out one's longed-for service to Śrī Kṛṣṇa) he emulates the moods of Kṛṣṇa's dear most *rāgātmikā* associates, like Lalitā, Viśākhā, Rūpa Mañjarī, Rati Mañjarī, and so on" (*Rāga-vartma-candrikā*, First Illumination, Text 10).

Following his auspicious invocation, Śrīla Cakravartī Ṭhākura begins his explanation of *Gopī-gīta*.

The autumn *rāsa-līlā*, called *śāradīya-rāsa*, is described in *Śrīmad-Bhāgavatam*. It transpired in Vṛndāvana's Vaṁśīvaṭa, a vast forest where millions of *gopīs* gathered to dance with Śrī Kṛṣṇa. At that time Vaṁśīvaṭa looked completely different from the way it does now, for the branches of the massive banyan tree (*vaṭa*) under which Śrī Kṛṣṇa played His flute (*vaṁśī*) spanned a vast area.

In his commentaries on the previous chapter, Śrīla Cakravartī Ṭhākura described the *gopīs*' search for Kṛṣṇa after He left the *rāsa* dance. They sought Him everywhere, in every cave and *kuñja* (secluded grove) of Vraja, and despite feeling overwhelming hopelessness when their attempts failed, they continued their search.

Finally they came to the enchanting bank of the Yamunā River, where they became fully immersed in *saṅkīrtana* – a soulful entreaty to Śrī Kṛṣṇa by singing His names and pastimes – in the form of this *Gopī-gīta*. They wept as they sang, certain that only *saṅkīrtana* of this kind would ensure Kṛṣṇa's return to them.

The unique feature of this age of Kali is the extraordinary result of *saṅkīrtana*. Its practitioner, weeping in a mood of separation from Śrī Caitanya Mahāprabhu, or from Śrī Kṛṣṇa and the *gopīs*, and yearning from the core of his heart for their *darśana*, will certainly receive their mercy. Kṛṣṇa never fails to manifest Himself to such a devotee.

Each and every verse of *Gopī-gīta* contains the two distinct moods among the *gopīs* – submissive (*dākṣiṇya*) and contrary (*vāmya*) – and Śrīla Jīva Gosvāmī illustrates both moods in his commentary. The *gopīs* whose natures are submissive, such as those in Śrīmatī Candrāvalī's group, express the feelings of their hearts openly and directly, whereas those whose natures are contrary, such as Śrīmatī Rādhikā and the *gopīs* in Her group, communicate their emotions indirectly.

There are four groups of *gopīs* – *svapakṣa*, *suhṛt*, *taṭasthā*, and *vipakṣa* – each with different degrees of submissiveness and contrariness. Although the words of the *gopīs* in the different groups are ostensibly the same in the verses, the meanings and moods within each verse are diverse. While Śrīla Śukadeva Gosvāmī hid the various deep purports of these verses as he uttered them, they were later explained in the commentaries of our *ācāryas*.

For example, Śrīla Śukadeva Gosvāmī describes how, as the *gopīs* sing with tears gently rolling down their cheeks, they beseech Kṛṣṇa to place His lotus hands or feet on their heads or on their breasts. These verses are sung by all the groups of *gopīs*, but the meanings behind them differ.

An example of the mood of noncompliance expressed by the *gopīs* in Śrīmatī Rādhikā's group can be seen when Śrī Kṛṣṇa met with them just before *rāsa-līlā* began. "Actually, we have not come here to meet with You," they said. "We have come to this forest tonight only to behold its beauty when lit by the gentle rays of the full moon. We know that You are a very lustful male, but You should know that we are chaste young women who have vowed firm faithfulness to our husbands. We cannot delay here for a single second. You are trying to fill us with fear, telling us that the night is fearsome and wild beasts are roaming about, but we know this is not true. In an attempt to lure us to stay here, You implore us in various ways, but we do not care to hear Your pleas."

Because every verse of *Gopī-gīta* contains the moods of both the submissive *gopīs* and the contrary *gopīs*, each verse can be explained according to the direct meanings or the indirect meanings. Śrīla Jīva Gosvāmī and Śrīla Viśvanātha Cakravartī Ṭhākura reveal this in their commentaries.

Śrīla Jīva Gosvāmī and Śrīla Viśvanātha Cakravartī Ṭhākura give the example of this first verse of *Gopī-gīta* to indicate a poetic speciality found in several verses. Each of these verses consists of four lines (*padas*), and the first and seventh syllable of each line begins with the same letter. For example, in the opening line of this verse (*jayati te 'dhikaṁ*), the first syllable starts with the letter 'j' and the seventh syllable also starts with 'j' (*janmanā vrajaḥ*). In the next line, the first syllable is 'ś' (*śrayata indirā*) and the seventh syllable is also 'ś' (*śaśvad atra hi*). *Dayita dṛśyatāṁ* and *dikṣu tāvakās* both start with 'd,' and *tvayi dhṛtāsavas* and *tvāṁ vicinvate* both start with 't.'

The learned poet Vopadeva[2] has described such literary devices in his famous scholarly treatise *Muktāphala*. Vopadeva is also known as Līlāśuka, as is Śrīla Śukadeva Gosvāmī, the *śuka* (parrot) who recites the *līlā* (transcendental pastimes) of Śrī Śrī Rādhā and Kṛṣṇa in *Śrīmad-Bhāgavatam*. Some say that it was he, and not Śrīla Vyāsadeva, who wrote *Śrīmad-Bhāgavatam*, but this idea is incorrect.

Our *ācāryas* have informed us that *Gopī-gīta* contains many such specialities that will be revealed to us as we contemplatively study its verses.

We will now proceed to look carefully at the meanings, both general and hidden, of the various words and phrases in this first verse of the *gopīs*' appeal to Śrī Kṛṣṇa.

The *gopīs* sing, "*Jayati te 'dhikaṁ janmanā vrajaḥ*." *Jayati* means 'to become glorious or victorious.' When we call out, "Gurudeva *kī jaya ho*!" "Govindajī *kī jaya ho*!" or "Tulasī-devī *kī jaya ho*!" we are expressing our hope that they will have victory. The victory of one party automatically implies defeat of the opposing party. He who is conquered is captured and imprisoned by the victor and, having come under his full control, is bound to carry out his every order.

The heart and mind of a conditioned soul are in battle with Śrī Hari, *guru*, Vaiṣṇavas, Vṛndā-devī, and all other transcendental personalities. A conditioned soul who aspires to be a devotee laments his condition and prays, "My uncontrolled heart and mind are like demons, and therefore I have no desire to serve Kṛṣṇa, *guru*, and Vaiṣṇavas."

"Gurudeva *kī jaya*!" actually means, "O Gurudeva, please conquer my rebellious heart and mind so that they have no choice but to obey your every command. O Gurudeva, having conquered my heart, do as you please with me. Make me your servant; make me yours."

Jayati te 'dhikaṁ janmanā vrajaḥ: The word *adhikam* means 'exceedingly.' The *gopīs* tell Kṛṣṇa, "O most beloved Kṛṣṇa (*dayita*),

---

[2] Vopadeva was a grammarian who lived in the 13th century.

Your birth in this land of Vraja has made it exceedingly more glorious than Svarga, heaven, or Brahmaloka, the topmost heavenly realm in this universe. What to speak of the heavenly planets, Vraja has become even more glorious than the spiritual realm of Vaikuṇṭha."

Śrīla Viśvanātha Cakravartī Ṭhākura comments elsewhere that if Śrīla Śukadeva Gosvāmī had been in external consciousness when he spoke this verse to Parīkṣit Mahārāja, he would have tried to please him by stating that Śrī Kṛṣṇa took birth in Mathurā. Parīkṣit Mahārāja was born in the dynasty of Kṛṣṇa's relatives in Mathurā as the grandson of Kṛṣṇa's cousin, Arjuna, and therefore he would be most pleased to hear about Kṛṣṇa's intimate relationship with Mathurā. But here, Śrīla Śukadeva Gosvāmī did not say that Kṛṣṇa was born in Mathurā. Absorbed in internal consciousness, he revealed the actual fact by the words *janmanā vrajah*. This statement of the *gopīs*, emanating from his lotus mouth, is the most substantial evidence that Kṛṣṇa indeed took birth in Gokula, in Vraja.

Śrayata indirā śaśvad atra hi: The *gopīs* continue, "Because You have taken birth in Vraja, the goddess of fortune, Lakṣmī (also known as Indirā), has left Lord Nārāyaṇa in Vaikuṇṭha and has come to serve You here in Vṛndāvana. From the time You were born, she has been sweeping and decorating the residences of Nanda Mahārāja and Yaśodā-maiyā, and serving Girirāja Govardhana, Kāmyavana, Varṣāṇā, Caraṇa-pahāḍī, the banks of the Yamunā River, and all the narrow passageways and *kuñjas* of Vraja in the same way. She does so because she wants to serve the places of Your divine pastimes.

"Vraja is not only more glorious and opulent than Vaikuṇṭha because of the beauty of Lakṣmī's decorations, but it is more glorious in wealth and in every other way."

Śrī Brahma-saṁhitā (5.43) confirms that although Vaikuṇṭha (Hari-dhāma) is more glorious than all other realms, Goloka is still superior:

goloka-nāmni nija-dhāmni tale ca tasya
devī-maheśahari-dhāmasu teṣu teṣu

> The material world (Devī-dhāma) is located below all other realms; above it is the abode of Lord Śiva (Maheśa-dhāma); above Maheśa-dhāma is Lord Nārāyaṇa's abode (Hari-dhāma); and above all of them is Kṛṣṇa's own abode, Goloka.

In this first verse, the *gopīs* utter the words *vrajaḥ* and *atra*, which mean 'here in Vraja.' Thus, another reason Vraja is more glorious than Vaikuṇṭha is that Kṛṣṇa took birth in Vraja, whereas no one takes birth in Vaikuṇṭha.

These words also indicate that Śrī Kṛṣṇa's birth in Vraja is not the sole reason for its glory. The word *vraja* also means 'that which moves around,' and by using it in this verse, the *gopīs* imply, "In Vraja, You wander freely, running and frolicking here and there as You perform Your countless loving pastimes. You cannot do this in Vaikuṇṭha. In Vaikuṇṭha You have no parents, whereas here in Vraja, You are the son of Nanda Bābā and Yaśodā-maiyā. Moreover, here You honor numerous persons as fathers and mothers; You are not satisfied with just one mother and father."

This truth is illustrated in the pastime of Lord Brahmā stealing Kṛṣṇa's friends and calves. When Brahmā stole the cowherd boys and calves, Kṛṣṇa manifested Himself as all the cowherd boys and tasted the parental love of many fathers and mothers. He also manifested Himself as all the calves, and thus millions of cows became His mothers. His appetite for parental affection was still not satiated, however, and therefore He went from door to door, playfully stealing butter and yogurt from each house in order to elicit further motherly love from the elderly *gopīs*. Sweet pastimes such as these never take place in Vaikuṇṭha.

In Vraja, Śrī Kṛṣṇa takes the cows out to graze in the forests and pasturing grounds, whereas no such pastime occurs in Vaikuṇṭha. In Vraja He plays with unlimited cowherd boys, but in Vaikuṇṭha there is no sporting with loving friends. In Vraja, millions of Lakṣmīs (*gopīs*)[3]

---

[3] "I worship Govinda, the primeval Lord, who is always served with great reverence and affection by hundreds of thousands of Lakṣmīs or *gopīs*" (*Brahma-saṁhitā*. 5.29).

"According to expert opinion, Lakṣmī, the goddess of fortune, is a subordinate expansion of Śrīmatī Rādhārāṇī. As Kṛṣṇa has numerous expansions of *viṣṇu-mūrtis*, so His pleasure potency, Rādhārāṇī, also has innumerable expansions of goddesses participate in *rāsa-līlā*, while in Vaikuṇṭha there is only one Lakṣmī and no *rāsa-līlā*. In Vraja there are endless forests and other places of enchantment, whereas in Vaikuṇṭha we do not see such beautiful places. It is not described anywhere that Vaikuṇṭha has fragrant flowers comparable to those in Vraja – either in the forests, or in the Yamunā River, or on Girirāja Govardhana. For these reasons and more, Vraja far exceeds the excellence of Vaikuṇṭha.

Śrayata indirā: As mentioned earlier, Indirā is another name of Lakṣmī, the beloved consort of Lord Nārāyaṇa. The word *indirā* refers to both wealth and the goddess of wealth, Śrī Lakṣmī, and the *gopīs* thus indicate that both are present in Vraja. They say, "Brahmā, Śaṅkara (Śiva) and all other demigods worship Indirā, the mistress of Vaikuṇṭha, in order to receive her blessings. Yet in Vraja, this queen of Vaikuṇṭha takes it upon herself to perform countless menial services."

In truth, it is not possible for Lakṣmī-devī to enter Vraja, but the *gopīs* speak in this way because they are intoxicated with *prema*. They are simply describing Vṛndāvana, which is so sweet and fragrant that Vaikuṇṭha, the realm of majesty and opulence, cannot compare to even a particle of its dust. This is the purport of their statement, *śrayata indirā śaśvad atra hi*.

In the madness of *prema*, the *gopīs* continue, "In Vṛndāvana, Indirā is always present and continually giving her abundant blessings. Thus, all the Vrajavāsīs, including the birds, animals, creepers, trees, as well as the men and women, both old and young, sink deeply in the ocean of bliss.

"In the midst of this boundless happiness, we *gopīs* alone endure unbearable heartache and weep. No one in the past has ever felt the distress that we feel now; at present, no one is as distressed as us; and, in the future, no one will ever be as distressed.

"Often someone says, 'You *gopīs* are dearer to Kṛṣṇa than anyone else,' and we also consider ourselves to be so. Why, then, have You left us weeping? This, we cannot begin to understand. We implore You to

---

of fortune. Therefore the goddess of fortune, Lakṣmījī, is eager to be elevated to the position of the *gopīs*" (*Kṛṣṇa, the Supreme Personality of Godhead*, Chapter 46).

return and delight us all. We are Your *gopīs*. You have accepted us as Your very own, and we see ourselves as Yours (*tāvakāh*)."

It may seem that this verse, which expresses the words 'we are Yours,' is spoken by the *gopīs* in Candrāvalī's party. Ordinarily, Śrīmatī Rādhikā and the *gopīs* in Her party never feel they belong to Kṛṣṇa and thus never speak like this. Rather, they see that Kṛṣṇa is rightfully theirs. Yet, a careful analysis of this verse reveals that in the anguish of separation from their beloved, Śrīmatī Rādhikā and Her *gopīs* may speak like this as well.

The word *dṛśyatām* has two deep meanings, both of which are hidden. According to one interpretation, *dṛśyatām* means, "Please come before us so that we can see You." Alternatively, according to another interpretation, it means, "You must look at us and see us, just once. We pray that You will."

Kṛṣṇa asks them,[4] "Why are you praying to Me in this way?"

"Because we are dying," the *gopīs* reply.

"Why are you dying?"

"Because You have not seen such *gopīs* as us. You should see us, and thus make Your eyes successful."

"Why?"

"Seeing us will fulfill the purpose of Your having eyes, and You will consider, 'Oh, I have never before beheld such a wondrous sight.' "

In a previous chapter of *Śrīmad-Bhāgavatam* (10.21.7), the *gopīs* expressed this same mood in their glorification of Kṛṣṇa's sweet flute-song. At that time they told Him, "The eyes of one who witnesses You casting sidelong glances at us, as our eyes simultaneously perform *arcana* of You, are fully successful. You wistfully gaze at Śrīmatī Rādhikā as She plays Your bamboo flute and looks toward You with

---

[4] In their commentaries on *Gopī-gīta*, Śrīla Jīva Gosvāmī and Śrīla Viśvanātha Cakravartī Ṭhākura sometimes write, 'If Kṛṣṇa says...,' 'Kṛṣṇa may say...,' or even 'Kṛṣṇa says...,' as if He is speaking with the *gopīs*. It is understood by such wording that the *gopīs* are not with Kṛṣṇa directly. Rather, they are so absorbed in meditating on Him in their mood of separation that they actually see Him before them and converse with Him. He actually appears to them in their hearts. It is very difficult to understand this mood of the *gopīs* unless we receive their mercy" (Śrī Śrīmad Bhaktivedānta Nārāyaṇa Gosvāmī Mahārāja. Airport *darśana*. Hong Kong, July 4, 2006).

sidelong glances. As those glances strike and bewilder You, You nearly fall to the ground in a faint, Your peacock-feathered crown totters and falls, and Your yellow shawl slips as well."

Now again, in *Gopī-gīta*, the *gopīs* tell Kṛṣṇa that by seeing them He will make His eyes successful. To this He replies, "What is so special about seeing you today? I can see you tomorrow or the day after, or at any other time."

"No," the *gopīs* reply, "our youthful beauty may leave at any moment, never to return."

It is written in Śrīla Bhaktivinoda Ṭhākura's *kīrtana* named "Śrī Rādhā-Kṛṣṇe Vijñapti" (Verse 6), "*gelo je divasa nā āsibe āra, ebe kṛṣṇa ki habe upāya*." Absorbed in the mood of the *gopīs*, he indicates, "Today we are fit, lovely, sweet, and beautiful to the extreme, and our bodies are soft and fragrant. But this youthful splendor can leave us at any time; it may be gone by tomorrow."

The last word in this verse is *vicinvate*, which means 'search.' The *gopīs* tell Kṛṣṇa, "We have been searching for You, overwhelmed by unendurable separation."

"Why are you searching for Me?" Kṛṣṇa asks.

"Only to show ourselves to You," the *gopīs* reply. "No one in this world is as beautiful and sweet as we are. If You see us just once, Your eyes and You Yourself will have attained full success."

Kṛṣṇa questions further, "Why do you speak like this?"

"We have accepted You to be our very own," they say, "and You have taken us to be Yours; so we are feeling pain for You, not for us. Soon the most precious treasure of our incomparable youthful beauty will be gone, and if we have not shown that beauty to You before it disappears, we will die. We are Yours, but You have not yet seen us. This is why we are feeling such intense separation from You."

"You have all become madwomen (*unmādinī*)," Kṛṣṇa replies. "Why else would you speak in this way?"

There is a world of difference between the madness of an ordinary person of this world and the *unmāda* of the *gopīs*. The heart of a mad person is completely empty, whereas the *unmāda* that takes place in the hearts of the *gopīs* is caused by waves of ever-fresh, transcendental love for Kṛṣṇa as it rises in their hearts.

"If we have become madwomen," the *gopīs* say, "You are fully to blame. It is not our fault. It is You who have made us like this."

Kṛṣṇa asks, "If you are actually suffering and feeling as much separation as you say, why are you not dying?"

"Because of You," they reply. "We nearly die, but we cannot die. We are simply floundering – *chat-pat*, *chat-pat*[5]."

Kṛṣṇa then points out that in reality, true *prema* cannot exist in all the fourteen planetary systems created by Brahmā: "One who really has *prema* dies at once," He tells the *gopīs*. "Even if one who has it does not die, he becomes mad and useless in this world, so how is it that you remain alive? The fact that you are still living is conclusive proof that there is no *prema* in your hearts."

The *gopīs* reply with the word *dhṛtāsavaḥ*. *Dhṛta* means 'sustained,' and *asava* means 'life-airs.' "If we could die, we certainly would," they say, "but we have either given our life to You or You have stolen it. In any case, our life-airs are pleasantly residing in You, and that is why we do not die.

"It brings You full satisfaction to see us burning in the fire of separation and sorrow, and because our life-airs reside in You, they also feel complete happiness. Had they been in our own bodies, our life-airs would have been burnt long ago.

"Your sole purpose in going out of our sight was to see us suffer. Our suffering is what You want; this is what pleases You. If we were to die, You would receive no pleasure at all, for no one can suffer on Your account as we do."

As most of Śrīla Jīva Gosvāmī's commentary on this verse is similar to that of Śrīla Viśvanātha Cakravartī Ṭhākura, I will discuss only the specialities of his explanations.

Śrīla Jīva Gosvāmī explains the *gopīs*' use of the word *dayita*, which has several meanings. One meaning is 'beloved' and another is 'full of mercy.' The *gopīs* say, "The pangs of separation we are feeling from You are unbearable." With these words they imply the second meaning: "Seeing us in this condition, You should be merciful to us, for You are *dayita*; You possess the treasure of mercy (*dayā*)."

---

[5] The Hindi phrase *chat-pat, chat-pat* represents the sound of a fish or animal floundering in its death throes.

He gives yet another explanation of the word *dayita*, which he took from the poet Kṣīra Svāmī: "*Dayite cittam ādatte iti dayita* – one who takes another person's heart is called *dayita*." According to this meaning, the *gopīs* utter this word to imply, "You are *dayita* because You have taken our hearts. Please return that stolen property now." *Dayita* also means 'lover,' or 'one who can give up everything for his beloved.'

Śrīla Jīva Gosvāmī explains that as the *gopīs* sing this verse, they weep so that Kṛṣṇa will hear them and bestow His mercy upon them. Mercy especially comes to those who bitterly weep for it in this way. A child who cries with full feeling evokes the mercy of his parents, who stop everything and attend to his needs.

The *gopīs* do not sing their song of longing within the forest, where the trees and mountains would have obstructed the sound of their voices. They have come out of the forest and are sitting down on the bank of the Yamunā. Now, wherever Kṛṣṇa might be, He would hear them weeping; and certainly He would be unable to check Himself from coming before them.

This first verse of *Gopī-gīta* is the *gopīs' maṅgalācaraṇa*, their auspicious opening, and as their song continues, the extraordinary sweetness of their moods continually increases. Throughout the rest of their song, they will speak astonishing verses full of sublime, hidden meanings, and the person hearing or reading them will be able to grasp the purports in accordance with his realization, or qualification. By absorbing oneself in internalized devotional practices (*bhajana*), these meanings are revealed in one's hearts.

For a pure devotee, fresh realizations of these verses come to him every time he reads them. On one day, certain profound meanings come into his heart, and a few days later even more meanings and moods are revealed to him. At first sight, it may seem that these verses can only be explained in one way; but exalted, self realized devotees of Śrī Kṛṣṇa, who are constantly engaged in relishing service to Him, are able to derive the verses' many deep imports within their hearts. Śrīla Viśvanātha Cakravartī Ṭhākura is experiencing such ever fresh moods, and in fact no one can realize and explain this subject matter as he has.

Verse Two

Your eyes possess the wealth of beauty that they stole from the petals of the lotus. But Your eyes have an extra magic that make them unique, which is that they can steal the qualities of something just by looking at it.

Verse 2

शरदुदाशये साधुजातसत्
सरसिजोदर श्रीमुषा दृशा।
सुरतनाथ तेऽशुल्कदासिका
वरद निघ्नतो नेह किं वधः ॥२॥

śarad-udāśaye sādhu-jāta-sat-
sarasi jodara-śrī-muṣā dṛśā
surata-nātha te 'śulka-dāsikā
vara-da nighnato neha kiṁ vadhaḥ

śarat – the autumn season; *uda-āśaye* – in the reservoir of water; *sādhu* – excellently; *jāta* – grown; *sat* – fine, pure; *sarasi-ja* – of the lotus flowers; *udara* – in the middle; *śrī* – the beauty; *muṣā* – which excels; *dṛśā* – with Your glance; *surata-nātha* – O master of amorous pleasure; *te* – Your; *aśulka* – acquired without payment; *dāsikāḥ* – maid-servants; *vara-da* – O giver of benedictions; *nighnataḥ* – for You who are killing; *na* – not; *iha* – in this world; *kiṁ* –why; *vadhaḥ* – murder.

Translation

O Kṛṣṇa, master of amorous pleasure, O bestower of benedictions, we are Your unpaid maidservants. You are killing us by the glance of Your eyes that steal even the proud beauty of the whorl of supremely enchanting, high born lotuses that blossom exquisitely in ponds during the autumn season. Is killing by a glance not considered murder in this world?

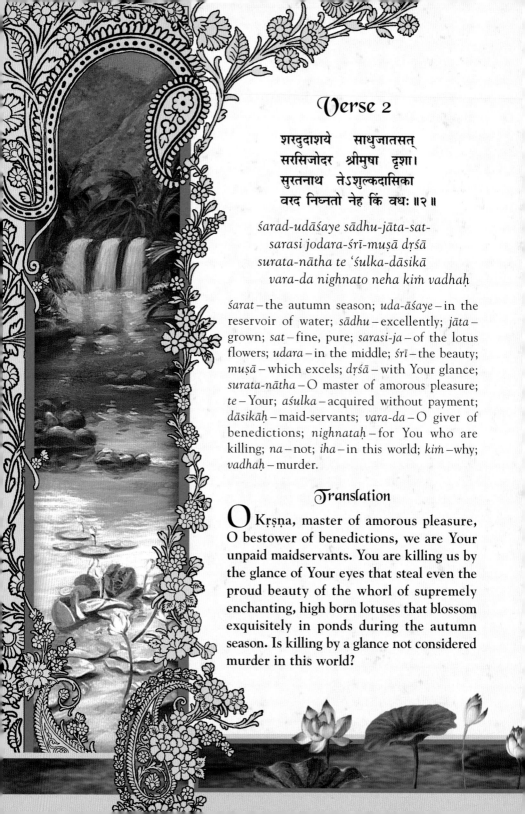

Bhāva-prakāśika Vṛtti

In the previous verse, the *gopīs* told Śrī Kṛṣṇa, "We have been searching for You, unable to bear the pain of separation from You and burning in the fire of amorous desires." He responded by asking, "What unhappiness or calamity have I caused you?"

Now, in this verse, the *gopīs* say, "You are not merely making us unhappy; You are killing us. Weapons are not the only means by which one kills. There are other means as well."

The word *dṛśā* refers to Kṛṣṇa's glance. The *gopīs* say, "With the glances of Your lotus eyes, You are killing us."

Kṛṣṇa may ask, "How am I killing you?"

The *gopīs* reply, "You are killing us simply by Your being *surata-nātha*.

The immaculate loving pastime of the hero (*nāyaka*) and the heroine (*nāyikā*) in their solitary meeting is called *surata*. *Su* means 'special,' and *rata* means 'intermingling with great attachment.' The intermingling of the transcendental *nāyaka* and the *nāyikā* is so complete and so extraordinary that they truly become one; any difference between them becomes indiscernible. There is a description of *surata* in *Śrī Caitanya-caritāmṛta* that issued from the lotus mouth of Śrīmatī Rādhikā Herself:

> *pahilehi rāga nayana-bhaṅge bhela*
> *anudina bāḍhala, avadhi nā gela*
> *nā so ramaṇa, nā hāma ramaṇī*
> *duṅhu-mana manobhava peṣala jāni'*
>
> *Caitanya-caritāmṛta* (*Madhya-līlā* 8.194)

> Alas, before We met there was an initial attachment between Us, brought about by an exchange of glances. In this way attachment evolved. That attachment has gradually grown, and there is no limit to it. Now that attachment has become a natural sequence between Ourselves. It is not that it is due to Kṛṣṇa, the enjoyer, nor is it due to Me, for I am the enjoyed. It is not like that. This attachment was made possible by mutual meeting.

> This mutual exchange of attraction is known as *manobhava*, or Cupid Kṛṣṇa's mind and My mind have merged together. Now, during this time of separation, it is very difficult to explain these loving affairs. My dear friend, though Kṛṣṇa might have forgotten all these things, you can understand and bring this message to Him. But during Our first meeting there was no messenger between Us, nor did I request anyone to see Him. Indeed, Cupid's five arrows were Our via media. Now, during this separation, that attraction has increased to another ecstatic state. My dear friend, please act as a messenger on My behalf, because if one is in love with a beautiful person, this is the consequence.

Śrī Kṛṣṇa is *rasika-śekhara*, He who is unsurpassed in relishing transcendental, amorous *rasa*, and Śrī Rādhikā is *mahābhāva-svarūpiṇī*, the very embodiment of *mahābhāva*, or the highest development of pure transcendental emotion. This verse refers to the meeting of *rasika-śekhara* Śrī Kṛṣṇa and *mahābhāva-svarūpiṇī* Śrī Rādhikā, in which They unite to become one in every respect – heart, body, and soul. Their uniting in this way is called *sambhoga-līlā*.[1]

The *gopīs* say, "With Your eyes, You create the inspiration within us for *surata*, and then You meet with us."

Nātha means 'lord,' so the general understanding of *surata-nātha* is 'the lord of *surata*.' But *nātha* also means 'to beg.' When explained in connection with the word *surata-nātha*, the word *dṛṣā* becomes *dṛṣaiva surata-nātha* – He who begs (*nātha*) for amorous union (*surata*) with His glance (*dṛṣā*). When the *gopīs* use this term to address Kṛṣṇa, they mean, "With Your sidelong glances You begged us for *surata*, and by doing so, You transmitted that same desire for *surata* to our hearts and we became mad. In that state we were deprived of any ability to discriminate between right and wrong, good and bad. We were ready to give You whatever You begged from us.

Śrīla Viśvanātha Cakravartī Ṭhākura describes this pristine *surata-līlā* in *Surata-kathāmṛta* and also in *Śrī Saṅkalpa-kalpa-druma*, which begins with the following two verses:

---

1 *Ujjvala-nīlamaṇi* describes *sambhoga* as follows: "The lover and beloved's sole purpose in meeting and embracing each other is to become filled with indescribable bliss. The escalation of this bliss is known as *sambhoga*."

vṛndāvaneśvari vayo-guṇa-rūpa-līlā
saubhāgya-keli-karuṇā-jaladhe 'radhehi
dāsī-bhavānī sukhayani sadā sa-kāntaṁ
tvaṁ alibhiḥ parivṛtam idam eva yāce
Saṅkalpa-kalpa-druma (1)

O Goddess of Vṛndāvana, Śrī Rādhā, O ocean of all youthfulness, virtue, beauty, pleasure-pastimes, good fortune, romantic love, and compassion. Please hear me, for there is something I want to tell You. I wish to become Your *dāsī*, to serve You and to make You joyful when You are with Your beloved Śrī Kṛṣṇa and surrounded by Your *sakhīs* and *mañjarīs*. I beg this of You.

śṛṅgārayāṇi bhavatīm abhisārayāṇi
vīkṣyaiva kānta-vadanaṁ parivṛtya yāntīm
dhṛtvāñcalena hari-sannidhim ānayāni
samprāpya tarjana-sudhāṁ hṛṣitā bhavāni
Saṅkalpa-kalpa-druma (2)

In this second verse, Śrīla Viśvanātha Cakravartī Ṭhākura describes the meeting of Śrīmatī Rādhikā and Śrī Kṛṣṇa. Although Rādhikā went to the forest only to meet with Kṛṣṇa, as soon as She saw Him She immediately turned around and began to return home. With a longing to serve Her, Śrīla Viśvanātha Cakravartī Ṭhākura prays, "I will clasp Your garments and forcibly draw You to Kṛṣṇa, the ocean of *surata*, and He will compel You to engage in Your beautiful *surata-līlā*."

Nātha means both 'master' and 'beggar,' and it also has a third meaning, namely 'giver of great calamities and distress.' Kṛṣṇa had communicated with His glance, "I can fulfill your desire for *surata*, and I also want *surata* from you." The *gopīs* now say, "You ignited our desire for this special meeting and we became maddened by that. Then, amidst our *surata-līlā*, You suddenly disappeared."

An example can be given of the disappointment a hungry man feels when, just as he is about to take a meal, a monkey comes and snatches his plate away. Similarly, the *gopīs* say that, bereft of their wisdom and sense of judgment, they were prepared to take part in *surata*, which Kṛṣṇa had begged from them with His sidelong glances. Then, just at that moment, He disappeared.

The *gopīs* conclude that the fault does not lie with Kṛṣṇa Himself, but with His beautiful eyes. From where had His eyes obtained their beauty? The *gopīs* express their realization of this with the words *śarad-udāsaye*. Śrīla Viśvanātha Cakravartī Ṭhākura has explained that, in their own way, the *gopīs* compare Kṛṣṇa's eyes with the beautiful petals of the lotus flower.

Śarat means 'the autumn season,' the season in which this pastime took place. *Ud* means 'water,' and *āśaye* means 'reservoir of water,' such as a pond, lake, river, or ocean. In this context, *udāsaye* means 'lake.' During *śarat*, the best of seasons, the water in the lakes is clean and pure. The word *sādhu* in this verse means 'pure, sacred, and possessing all kinds of virtue.' If a man has taken birth in a good family, a family of *sādhus*, we can generally conclude that a son or daughter born to him will also have a pious nature.

The *gopīs* tell Kṛṣṇa, "The beautiful lotus growing in the vast pond is fragrant, soft, and sweet. In the autumn season the water is pure, and therefore the lotus growing in that water is also pure. The petals on that lotus and the pollen on the petals are also completely pure. Every part of that lotus has manifested with purity, and as a result of purity. Without this purity, the lotus in all of its features would also be without beauty."

Śrīla Viśvanātha Cakravartī Ṭhākura and Śrīla Jīva Gosvāmī both explain that in comparing Kṛṣṇa's eyes with lotus petals, the *gopīs* say, "Your eyes possess the wealth of beauty that they stole from the petals of the lotus. But Your eyes have an extra magic make them unique, which is that they can steal the qualities of something just by looking at it. You simply glanced at the lotus, and in doing so You took away its loveliness. In this way You left the lotus reduced in magnificence, while the beauty of Your eyes increased.

"Then, after You stole the qualities of the lotus, You cast Your glance at us, and in doing so, You stole the contents of our hearts. You are such an expert thief that You can steal the beauty of the petals of a lotus, even of one that grows far from the water's edge where it is dangerous to venture and where it is surrounded by other lotuses.

"In fact, which of Your possessions have You not stolen? You stole the beauty of a new rain cloud and the dance of the peacock. From this we can easily understand that You are an expert thief.

"It is not easy to steal our hearts, because we are always protected by our relatives – our parents, brothers, husbands, sisters-in-law, mothers and fathers-in-law – and also by our shyness, patience, and chastity. Yet, You went straight into our hearts without any consideration, and You captured us. Actually, it was not You who entered our hearts; it was Your eyes. It follows, then, that Your eyes can easily steal the beauty of the lotus flower.

"Still, the qualities we see in Your eyes now are not those which we saw before. This is another difference between Your eyes and the lotus. The lotus always looks the same, but when we look into Your eyes, we see that they contain newer and newer allurements at every moment. In this way, through Your eyes You begged us for something, we became maddened, and ever-new waves from the ocean of transcendental *prema* then arose in our hearts. Simply because of the way You glanced at us and expressed Your desire for *surata*, we became Your unpaid maidservants (*aśulka dāsikā*). You accomplished this by glancing at us from the corner of just one of Your lotus eyes. When just one of Your eyes can so expertly express Your intention, what would have happened if You looked at us with two eyes?

"Why do we say we are Your unpaid maidservants? First of all, have You ever given us anything for our services? Never. Second, have our parents given us to You in marriage? No. Moreover, although we were never willing to marry You, our parents still could have given us to You in charity, thinking it would have been best for us; but they never did this.

"Third, even if we had wanted to marry You, but were not given to You by our fathers and mothers, we could have had a *gāndharva* style marriage whereby we would have simply exchanged garlands with You. But You have also not performed the *gāndharva* marriage with us. You have paid us nothing and given us nothing.

"We have become Your unpaid maidservants because Your eyes begged for our hearts. You have not begged, but Your eyes begged, again and again, and we fell silent." What was the meaning of the *gopīs*' silence? It signified their acceptance of His proposal.

The texts on literary theory called *alaṅkāra-śāstra* state that the moods of *prema*, or *kāma*, first arise in the heroine (*nāyikā*) and then in the hero (*nāyaka*). Yet, the heroine does not approach the hero to express her feelings; rather, the hero approaches the heroine and then she responds. In this case, however, the situation is reversed. Kṛṣṇa is not making any advances. Instead He is silent and has disappeared from the *gopīs*' midst, as if rejecting this special meeting. It is the *gopīs* who are repeatedly appealing to Him, without shyness.

"You begged us for this and we came to You," they say. "But then, when we began to dance with You and engage in our sweet pastimes, You left us. Now we are begging You to again perform those pastimes with us, even though we should not beg anything from You at all. We have disregarded all religious regulations and have forsaken all our family connections, duties, shyness, chastity, patience, and everything else for You. And now, in separation from You, we are dying.

"We want only that You come and see us. Without beholding us, Your eyes cannot be successful. In our extreme sorrow, we are not begging that *surata-līlā* from You for our own sake, but for Yours.

"First of all, from the corner of Your eyes, You beseeched us for the precious gift of *surata*, and in doing so You also created a wish for *surata* in our hearts. But now You have taken away our wealth, our most precious treasure. We had been keeping it in our hearts and protecting it very carefully, but then You stole our hearts and went away. We request You to come and cast just one glance upon us. And when You do, we pray that You will return to us all the valuable treasures You stole."

The word *nighnato* in this verse means 'You are killing us.' The *gopīs* say, "If You do not return our cherished treasure, we will die. It is sinful to kill a man, and it is even more sinful to kill a woman. We *gopīs* are far dearer to You than a wife is to a husband, so if You kill us, You will be performing a most heinous act. Furthermore, You would be responsible for killing not just one *gopī*, but millions of us. We want to protect You from the suffering that will come from this sinful act, so please come back and return the wealth of *surata* that You stole from us."

Some of this explanation is from Śrīla Viśvanātha Cakravartī Ṭhākura's commentary. There are also points that he has not explained, and in those cases I have taken the explanation from Śrīla Jīva Gosvāmī's commentary and from my heart. This subject will be precious to qualified persons, not to everyone.

Verse Three

Holding Girirāja Govardhana on the tip of Your finger, You protected us from Indra's inundation of rain, fierce tempest, and furious hurling of thunderbolts. In fact You not only protected us, You overwhelmed us with great happiness at that time.

Verse 3

विषजलाप्ययाद्व्यालराक्षसाद्
वर्षमारुताद्वैद्युतानलात् ।
वृषमयात्मजाद्विश्वतो भयाद्
ऋषभ ते वयं रक्षिता मुहुः ॥३॥

viṣa-jalāpyayād vyāla-rākṣasād
varṣa-mārutād vaidyutānalāt
vṛṣa-mayātmajād viśvato bhayād
ṛṣabha te vayaṁ rakṣitā muhuḥ

viṣa – poisonous; *jala* – by the water (of the Yamunā, contaminated by Kāliya); *apyayāt* – from destruction; *vyāla* – fearsome; *rākṣasāt* – from the demon (Agha); *varṣa* – from rain (sent by Indra); *mārutāt* – and the wind-storm (created by Tṛṇāvarta); *vaidyuta-analāt* – from the thunderbolt (of Indra); *vṛṣa* – from the bull, Ariṣṭāsura; *maya-ātmajāt* – from the son of Maya (Vyomāsura); *viśvataḥ* – from all; *bhayāt* – fear; *ṛṣabha* – O greatest of personalities; *te* – by You; *vayam* – we; *rakṣitāḥ* – have been protected; *muhuḥ* – repeatedly.

Translation

O crest-jewel among men, time and again You saved us cowherd maidens from the grip of death – from the poisonous water of Kāliya-hrada in the Yamunā where the serpent Kāliya resided, from the python Aghāsura, and from the rain and terrible storm of Indra. You saved us from the whirlwind demon Tṛṇāvarta, from the firing of Indra's thunderbolts, from the dreadful forest fire, from the bull-demon Ariṣṭāsura, from the son of Maya named Vyomāsura, and from every other kind of threat.

Bhāva-prakāśika Vṛtti

Weeping as they perform their *kīrtana*, the *gopīs* tell Kṛṣṇa, "In the past, You protected us from various kinds of dangers and from the devouring mouth of death. You rescued us so many times, so why are You now killing us with the arrows of Your glance? You are making us burn in the fire of love-filled desire, and in the fire of painful feelings of separation from You. Now, nothing can protect us. What, then, was the use of protecting us before?

"If someone plants a tree, that person develops some attachment for it as it grows. Even if it is poisonous and he is advised by others to cut it down, he will hesitate to do so. It seems that You have forgotten this principle. You are so cruel-hearted and merciless that You are cutting us down, although previously You protected us and watched us grow."

Viṣa-jalāpyayād: Viṣa-jala means 'poisonous water.' The *gopīs* refer to the serpent Kāliya, who poisoned the waters of the Yamunā River. They say, "With his virulent vapors, Kāliya polluted the water of Kāliya-hrada[1], making it boil and foam. But You protected us from that danger."

When Śrī Kṛṣṇa jumped into the poisoned water of the Yamunā River, it appeared that He Himself was dying. Why, then, do the *gopīs* say that He protected them? All the boys and calves had been playing on the bank of the Yamunā at Kāliya-hrada, and from the mere smell of that poison, they fell to the ground as if dead. Kṛṣṇa immediately restored their life by His glances, which are full of life-giving nectar. Determined to send Kāliya away, He then jumped into the Yamunā.

The *gopīs* continue, "If You had died, we would have also died, and Nanda Bābā, Mother Yaśodā, and all the Vrajavāsīs would have died. To protect us all, You subdued Kāliya and he left this place. The water became pure once more and everyone was safe."

1 The lake within Yamunā where the serpent Kāliya resided.

Vyāla-rākṣasād: *Vyāla* means 'snake,' and here the *gopīs* refer to Aghāsura, the great snake-demon who laid on the road with his mouth wide open, waiting to swallow Kṛṣṇa. The calves and cowherd boys were running and frolicking here and there, and gradually, as they played, they came closer and closer to the demon. "What a magnificent cave!" they exclaimed when they saw Agha's open mouth. "It looks just like a serpent, but it can't be! No serpent could be that huge. Still, even if it is a serpent, there is no harm in going inside; if he tries to swallow us all, then Kṛṣṇa will kill him immediately. And if it is a cave, then obviously there is no harm. We should go in and find out."

Kṛṣṇa was watching all this from afar. "Friends! O friends! Don't go in!" He cried out, but they did not hear Him and did not look back to check with Him. They walked into the mouth of the demon, who kept his mouth open as he sat and waited for Kṛṣṇa to enter.

That day was Baladeva's birthday, so He had not gone out to herd the calves with Kṛṣṇa. His mother, Rohiṇī-devī, had kept Him at home and told Him, "Today we will perform ceremonies for purification, give cows in charity, and busy ourselves for the occasion."

Śrī Kṛṣṇa creates situations like this when it is necessary for the performance of His sweet pastimes. If Baladeva had been with Him, He could not have performed the *brahma-vimohana-līlā*, His divine pastime of bewildering Brahmā. The pastime with Aghāsura was the prelude to this pastime, which took place later that same day. Baladeva would not have been able to keep the event secret. He would certainly have told Mother Yaśodā and Nanda Bābā that Kṛṣṇa had expanded Himself into all the cowherd boys and calves, and then all of Vraja would have come to know of it. If this had happened, a myriad of loving exchanges could not have taken place.

When Kṛṣṇa killed Aghāsura, Brahmā saw the glaring effulgence of Aghāsura's life-air come out from Aghāsura's head and remain suspended in the sky. Then, when Kṛṣṇa came out of Aghāsura's mouth, Brahmā saw that light descend and enter Śrī Kṛṣṇa's lotus feet. Brahmā was astonished. "How is this possible?" he thought. "Others intently try to attain liberation, without success, but this demon attained it just by taking Kṛṣṇa within his mouth with the purpose of killing Him." Brahmā then witnessed another of Kṛṣṇa's wonderful pastimes – His assuming the forms of all the calves and cowherd boys. Kṛṣṇa's primary objective in performing this transcendental pastime was not to bewilder Brahmā. Rather, within His heart he was aware that many of the elderly *gopīs* wanted to nourish Him as their son and that many of the cows wanted to nurture Him as their calf, and He thus made an arrangement to fulfill their desire. This was one of the several reasons that His *yogamāyā* potency inspired Brahmā to witness the Aghāsura pastime.

Now, in *Gopī-gīta*, the *gopīs* say, "If all the boys had died within the body of Aghāsura, everyone else in Vraja would have died as well, including us. We could have easily died. Why did You bother protecting us then, if you want to kill us now?"

The word *varṣa-mārutād* in this verse refers to Indra, the king of heaven. *Varṣa* means 'rainfall,' *marut* means 'tremendous windstorm,' and *vidyut* means 'thunderbolt.' The *gopīs* tell Śrī Kṛṣṇa, "By holding Girirāja Govardhana on the tip of Your smallest finger, You protected us from Indra's inundation of rain, fierce tempest, and furious hurling of thunderbolts. In fact You not only protected us, You overwhelmed us with great happiness at that time."

The word *analāt* means 'from fire.' Kṛṣṇa saved the Vrajavāsīs from two great fires, one of which took place in the forest near Bhāṇḍīravana. There, in the shade of a massive banyan tree known as Bhāṇḍīravaṭa, Kṛṣṇa was playing with His cowherd friends as the cows drank the water of the Yamunā and grazed on the lush, green grass. Gradually, the cows wandered away from Kṛṣṇa and the boys and entered Muñjāṭavī, a forest of prickly *muñja* plants that was some distance away. It was summer, and the scorching heat dried the forest, which was so dense that the cows lost track of the path by which they had come. Overwhelmed by thirst and heat, they became most perturbed.

The cowherd boys began to search for the cows and, in doing so, they left Kṛṣṇa and Balarāma. They entered Muñjāṭavī and, like the cows, became agitated by excessive thirst and intense heat. It was then that wicked Kaṁsa's servants, who had been hiding in the forest, set the grass and trees ablaze. Within a moment a wind flushed the fire throughout the area, leaving both the cows and cowherd boys caught in its center.

Seeing no other means of escape, they all began to cry out to Kṛṣṇa and Balarāma. Immediately upon hearing their distressed call, Kṛṣṇa and Balarāma came in their midst. "Close your eyes for just a moment," Kṛṣṇa told them, and in that moment He swallowed the terrible forest fire. The boys considered why Kṛṣṇa might have told them to close their eyes. "Kṛṣṇa must know a *mantra* for putting out fire," they thought, "and maybe that *mantra* can only be recited in a very secluded place. If we shut our eyes, He will feel that He is alone."

There was another reason why Kṛṣṇa told them to close their eyes. Once before, when He was still a baby, the boys had seen Him eating earth, and they had complained about it to Mother Yaśodā. So now He thought, "If they see Me eating fire, they will complain to Mother again, and she will punish Me. Besides this, if My friends see Me swallowing the entire fire, they will think that I will surely burn up, and their life-air will depart."

When, after a moment, the boys opened their eyes, they saw themselves once again standing with Kṛṣṇa and Balarāma in the cooling shade of Bhāṇḍīravaṭa, their cows peacefully lying nearby and chewing their cud. "Was that a dream?" they wondered in amazement.

Referring to this forest fire, the *gopīs* now say, "You protected us at that time." By these words they imply, "If all the cowherd boys had died in the fire, their fathers and mothers would have died also, from grief, and we *gopīs* would also have died. By protecting all of Vraja in this way, You protected us as well."

With the phrase *vṛṣa-mayātmajād*, the *gopīs* mention yet another instance of Kṛṣṇa protecting them. *Vṛṣa-mayātmajād* refers to two demons, Vatsāsura and Vyomāsura. The word *vṛṣa* refers to Vṛṣabhāsura (another name of Ariṣṭāsura), the gigantic bull demon, and the word *ātmajad* means 'son.' Conjoined with *vṛṣa*, *ātmajad* refers to the son of Vṛṣabhāsura, namely the calf-demon Vatsāsura. *Atmajad* is also conjoined with the word *maya*, thus referring to the son of the demon Maya named Vyomāsura, whom Kṛṣṇa killed in Kāmyavana.

When Kṛṣṇa first began taking the calves out to graze in Vṛndāvana, Vatsāsura appeared in their midst. As soon as Kṛṣṇa and Baladeva saw him, They understood that he was not one of Their calves but a demon in disguise, and They crafted a plan to kill him. They 'innocently' wandered over to him, and then Kṛṣṇa grabbed his two hind legs and whirled him around and around above His head. Vatsāsura then assumed his original, ghastly gigantic form, at which time Kṛṣṇa hurled him into a tree. Seeing Vatsāsura's enormous size, the cowherd boys became filled with fear and exclaimed, "He came in the shape of a beautiful calf, but just see his actual form!"

Vatsāsura's father, the gigantic bull-demon Ariṣṭāsura, was killed by Kṛṣṇa at Rādhā-kuṇḍa. Ariṣṭāsura was certainly sinful, so one may wonder how he could have entered the pristine area of Rādhā-kuṇḍa. He was able to do so only because Yogamāyā permitted him to enter, in order to facilitate Kṛṣṇa's pastime of killing him and subsequently intensifying the *gopīs' prema*. He had entered the village of Vṛndāvana when Kṛṣṇa was eager to perform *rāsa*. Kṛṣṇa killed him and protected all the *gopīs*, and then the *rāsa* dance began.

Kṛṣṇa also protected the *gopīs* from the demon Śaṅkhacūḍa, who tried to kidnap them by driving them along with a stick, as if they were she-goats, finally taking Śrīmatī Rādhikā upon his shoulders. One may wonder how it is possible for a demon to touch Śrīmatī Rādhikā, and the answer is that in order to facilitate Kṛṣṇa's human-like pastimes (*nara-līlā*), Yogamāyā arranges miraculous incidents. Actually, it was not possible for Śaṅkhacūḍa to touch Śrīmatī Rādhikā. Since Kṛṣṇa can do anything, the form of Śaṅkhacūḍa may have been a manifestation of Kṛṣṇa Himself. Sometimes, with the purpose of making Rādhikā run into His arms, He may frighten Her by assuming the form of a serpent. He performs unlimited pastimes such as these and, according to His desire, Yogamāyā makes all necessary arrangements.

Śrī Kṛṣṇa protected His associates from the horse-demon Keśī, the cart-demon Śakaṭāsura, the crane-demon Bakāsura, the ass-demon Dhenukāsura, and so many others. The *gopīs* continue, "*Ṛṣabha te vayaṁ rakṣitā muhuḥ* – You have shielded us from a myriad of calamities and from innumerable terrifying forms of death, but now You are killing us. If You desire to kill us now, why did You protect us on so many other occasions?"

In his *Sārārtha-darśini* commentary, Śrīla Viśvanātha Cakravartī Ṭhākura reveals the meaning of the *gopīs*' words: "We are dying due to the effects of Your five arrows. We have come to You for protection, but we find that Your five arrows have merely increased our *kāma* (divine passion) and the burning of our hearts."

Kṛṣṇa Himself is Kāmadeva, the transcendental Cupid. He has enchanted the *gopīs* by shooting at them the arrows of His lotus eyes, and by His mellifluous flute playing, His beautiful lips, His solitary talks with them, and His broad chest. He is addressed in the *kāma-gāyatrī mantra* as Puṣpabāṇa, He who shoots the flower-arrows that enamor the *gopīs*. This transcendental Kāmadeva can enchant the mind of the Kāmadeva of this world, and therefore the *gopīs* appeal to Him to extinguish the fire caused by Kāmadeva's five arrows.

The *gopīs* say, "At present, we see that You are *viśvāsa-ghātī*, a betrayer of another's faith." The inherent meaning of the Sanskrit word *viśvāsa-ghātī* is conveyed with the following words: "I slept with my head in your lap, fully trusting that you would protect me. But while I slept, you took a sword and killed me." In this mood, the *gopīs* are saying, "You protected us many times in the past, so we trusted that You would surely protect us now. Having given up everything we have and offering You our very existence, we came to You; but now You callously betray us. Even though we are dying, You do not protect us.

Śrīla Viśvanātha Cakravartī Ṭhākura says that some of the pastimes the *gopīs* mention here will actually take place after *rāsa-līlā*. We would expect the *gopīs* to talk about events that took place before *rāsa-līlā*, but how can they speak about future incidents?[2]

---

2 Śrīla Sanātana Gosvāmī reconciles this in his *Bṛhad-vaiṣṇava-toṣaṇī* commentary. He explains that even though the killing of Vyomāsura happened after *rāsa-līlā*, the *gopīs* were able to mention it because of their natural power of omniscience (*svabhāvika-sarvajñātā-śakti*). When the *gopīs* experience unbearable separation, *sphūrtis* (visions) of Kṛṣṇa's pastimes – past, present, and future – manifest

Śrīla Cakravartī Ṭhākura explains that these future events were common knowledge to the *gopīs*. They had heard about them long before, from Paurṇamāsī-devī, Gargācārya, Bhāguri Ṛṣi, and other sages. They had also heard from many persons about Kṛṣṇa's horoscope, and they are now repeating what they had heard.

Śrīla Jīva Gosvāmī says that Śrīla Śukadeva Gosvāmī, in his description of the *gopīs' pūrva-rāga* up to *rāsa-līlā* (*Śrīmad-Bhāgavatam* 10.21–33), was in a very *rasika* mood. Consequently, he related only Śrī Kṛṣṇa's sweet, loving pastimes. He did not relate Kṛṣṇa's pastimes of killing of demons which, by ordinary estimation, may be considered cruel or unpleasant. He recounted the *gopīs' pūrva-rāga*, Kṛṣṇa's beautiful pastime with the wives of the *brāhmaṇas* (*yajña-patnīs*), His lifting Girirāja Govardhana, and His pastimes with the cowherd boys and *gopīs* in autumn and summer. Śrīla Jīva Gosvāmī says that because of Śrīla Śukadeva Gosvāmī's deep mood, there were occasions when he rearranged the chronology of his narrations according to that mood. Consequently he recounted certain pastimes of Kṛṣṇa killing demons after he described *rāsa-līlā*, when in fact they took place beforehand.

The explanation given by Śrīla Jīva Gosvāmī seems to contradict that of Śrīla Viśvanātha Cakravartī Ṭhākura, but both explanations are correct. In different *kalpas*, or millennia, Kṛṣṇa performs His pastimes in different sequences.

As mentioned earlier, the *gopīs* accuse Kṛṣṇa of being a betrayer of faith (*viśvāsa-ghātī*). From ancient Indian history, I will now relate a story to illustrate the grief arising from betrayal of faith. The great Buddhist King Aśoka of India built a university, called Viśva Vidyālaya, in the very beautiful hilly region named Nalanda, near Patna. At that time Nalanda Viśva Vidyālaya was quite famous. Students came there from all over the world to study Vedānta and all the other schools of philosophy.

---

spontaneously in their hearts. This is how they came to know about the killing of Vyomāsura, which would actually take place in the future. Thus, due to their madness in separation from Kṛṣṇa, they refer to it as if it had happened in the past

One of the students was Kumārila Bhaṭṭa[3], who, from his childhood, had studied the Vedas, Upaniṣads, Smṛti, and other scriptures. He had also studied *karma-mīmāṁsā* philosophy, and now he wanted to study Buddhism, in order to defeat it. Knowing him to be very intelligent, the University authorities willingly admitted him. He studied there for twelve years and, by his final year, his scholarship was famous.

One day, as the Buddhist principal was teaching a class, he recited a verse from the Vedas and then explained it in a way that contradicted the actual meaning. He mocked the ideas of the Vedas, calling them bogus. When Kumārila Bhaṭṭa heard this, he began to weep. "He is crying!" the other students commented. "Perhaps he is a Vaiṣṇava or a member of some other sect. In any case, it is obvious that he is not a Buddhist."[4]

The principal of the school called for Kumārila Bhaṭṭa and asked, "Why are you weeping?"

"Your explanation is contradictory and useless," Kumārila Bhaṭṭa said. "This is not the actual meaning of the cited verse."

"Please give your explanation, then," the teacher said.

Kumārila Bhaṭṭa explained the verse wonderfully, but when he finished, his fellow students were resentful and conspired to kill him. Accosting him, they seized him and took him to the top of a tall building. "We are going to throw you off," they told him. "If your God is really true and if the Vedas are also true, you will be protected. Otherwise, you will simply die."

Kumārila Bhaṭṭa concurred. "You are correct," he said. "If the Vedas speak the Absolute Truth and if my God is real, then no harm will come to me."

---

3 Kumārila Bhaṭṭa was an 8th century Hindu philosopher and *mīmāṁsā* scholar from Prayāga. He is known to have defeated many Buddhist scholars of his time in philosophical debates.

4 The philosophical school called *karma-mīmāṁsā* (the science of fruitive work) explains the Vedas in ritualistic terms and defines pious fruitive or material work as the purpose of life, whereas Buddhism rejects the Vedas and preaches *ahiṁsā* (non-violence) and *śūnyatā* (voidism, extinction of the self) as the main goals of life.

They threw him from that building onto the ground below and then ran down, fully confident that they would find him dead. Instead, they saw him walking and talking, uninjured except for a broken finger. They firmly took hold of him and asked derisively, "If you were actually fully protected, why did your finger get broken?"

"I made the mistake of saying 'if' my God is real," he replied. "Had I not said 'if,' I would not have been injured at all."

Kumārila Bhaṭṭa soon preached so boldly against Buddhism that it was driven out of India into China and various other places. While Śaṅkarācārya's philosophy helped achieve this to some degree, the real credit for driving Buddhism out of India belongs to Kumārila Bhaṭṭa.

Despite his accomplishment, Kumārila Bhaṭṭa deeply grieved in his last days for what he saw as a grave mistake. "The principal of that university was my *guru*," he thought. "At the end of his life he was tormented by the thought that an insignificant disciple had defeated him, and he died of grief. I am *viśvāsa-ghātī*. I have betrayed my *guru*, who taught me so much. He helped me to make my life successful. He gave me the knowledge which I used to drive Buddhism out of India, and yet I betrayed him."[5]

Desiring to atone for what he considered to be his sin, he made a pile of rice husks and set fire to it. When rice husks burn, they smolder and look as though they are not burning; flames will only appear if the fire is fanned. Kumārila Bhaṭṭa lay down on that pile of smoldering rice husks and burned as if he were being slowly cooked. Although in extreme pain, he remained lying there. At that time Śrī Śaṅkarācārya's follower approached him and said, "I have come to beg something from you."

"What do you wish for?" Kumārila Bhaṭṭa asked.

---

5 Vedic culture has become corrupted in Kali-yuga. In ancient times, disobeying one's *guru* was only considered an offense if the *guru* was genuine. But as time passed, according to the distorted teacher-disciple ethics that were upheld by the *smārtas*, a disciple would honor the instructions and advice of his teacher, even if he were not bona fide. If he disobeyed his teacher, he would feel that he did wrong, regardless of whether the teacher was genuine or not. The disciple in the Vaiṣṇava culture is advised to reject any unqualified teacher without feeling the slightest guilt.

"I beg you to come out of this fire and debate with me on the new *advaita-vāda* philosophy[6] devised by Śaṅkarācārya, which is so beautiful. I want to defeat you, because you are a *smārta*[7] and you believe in the Vedas."

"I am dying now. I don't want to pollute my mouth with *advaita-vāda*," Kumārila Bhaṭṭa replied. "Please go away. I will not talk about this non-Vedic philosophy," he uttered, as his life slipped away.

This is an historical fact. It is not directly relevant to *Gopī-gīta*, but I wanted to take this opportunity to relate it. You should know this history because it will help you understand how the preaching of Vedānta developed.

---

6 *Advaita-vāda* – The doctrine of non-dualism and monism propagated by Śrī Śaṅkarācārya that propagates the fallacy that the living entities and God are one in all respects.

7 *Smārta* – An orthodox *brāhmaṇa* who rigidly adheres to the *smṛti-śāstras* and the codes of religious behavior, being overly attached to the external rituals without comprehending the underlying essence of the Vedic scriptures.

Verse Four

O crest-jewel of all neutral personalities, we now understand that You, the Supersoul, have taken birth in Vraja, but we cannot understand how or why.

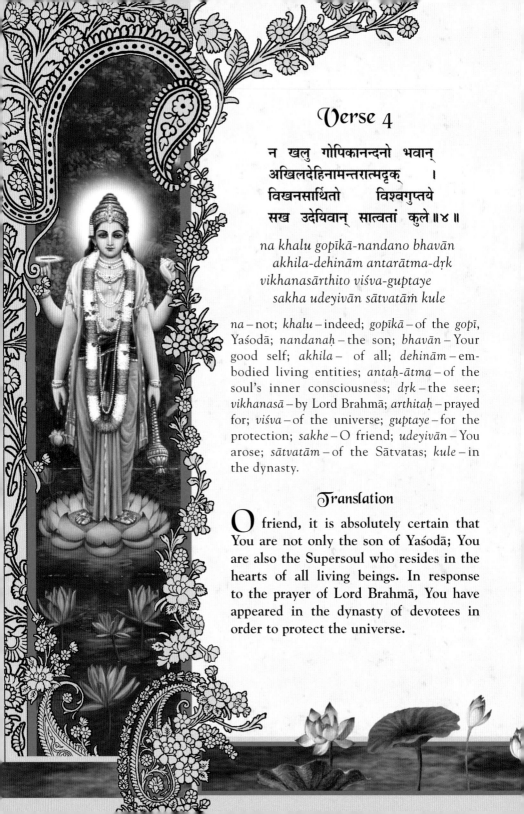

Verse 4

न खलु गोपिकानन्दनो भवान्
अखिलदेहिनामन्तरात्मदृक् ।
विखनसार्थितो विश्वगुप्तये
सख उदेयिवान् सात्वतां कुले ॥४॥

na khalu gopīkā-nandano bhavān
akhila-dehinām antarātma-dṛk
vikhanasārthito viśva-guptaye
sakha udeyivān sātvatāṁ kule

na – not; *khalu* – indeed; *gopīkā* – of the *gopī*, Yaśodā; *nandanaḥ* – the son; *bhavān* – Your good self; *akhila* – of all; *dehinām* – embodied living entities; *antaḥ-ātma* – of the soul's inner consciousness; *dṛk* – the seer; *vikhanasā* – by Lord Brahmā; *arthitaḥ* – prayed for; *viśva* – of the universe; *guptaye* – for the protection; *sakhe* – O friend; *udeyivān* – You arose; *sātvatām* – of the Sātvatas; *kule* – in the dynasty.

Translation

O friend, it is absolutely certain that You are not only the son of Yaśodā; You are also the Supersoul who resides in the hearts of all living beings. In response to the prayer of Lord Brahmā, You have appeared in the dynasty of devotees in order to protect the universe.

Bhāva-prakāśika Vṛtti

In his commentaries on the second and third verses of *Gopī-gīta*, Śrīla Viśvanātha Cakravartī Ṭhākura explained the *gopīs'* accusations and Kṛṣṇa's retorts. In the second verse the *gopīs* said, "Do not incur sin by killing millions of *gopīs* with the arrows of Your glances. If someone kills us outright, then so be it; but if we neither live nor die, the intolerable agony we feel is much worse than death itself." Then, in the third verse, they accused Him of being a betrayer of their faith.

Kṛṣṇa replied, "You have called Me a murderer of women and a betrayer of faith. You said that I want to kill millions of *gopīs*, and that if I do not come and meet with you, I will have to suffer all sorts of sinful reactions. Why do you speak such cruel words to Me? I cannot bear the anguish such piercing words cause Me. I am leaving this place immediately and will not return in this lifetime."

Seeing Śrī Kṛṣṇa's face so filled with pain, the *gopīs* feared He had become angry. "What will happen if He does not return?" they wondered. Their own anger subsided and they now speak the present verse. "It was our mistake to carelessly speak those words," they tell Him. "Really, You are our friend." They express a variety of moods to make Him pleased with them.

Na khalu gopīkā-nandano bhavān: *Khalu* means 'surely,' *gopīkā-nandana* refers to Yaśodā-nandana, the son of Yaśodā, and *bhavān* means 'You, Kṛṣṇa.' The *gopīs* say, "You are certainly not the son of Yaśodā."

Akhila-dehinām means 'for all beings,' and *antarātma-dṛk* means 'Paramātmā, the Supersoul, the partial expansion of Kṛṣṇa who is situated in everyone's heart.' As the constant witness of everyone's activities, Paramātmā awards the consequences of one's good and bad activities, and at the same time He remains completely neutral. He is not personally entangled in the good or bad results of anyone's activities.

Vikhanasārthito viśva-guptaye: *vikhanasā* refers to Lord Brahmā, *arthitah* means 'by the prayer,' and *viśva-guptaye* means 'for universal protection and welfare.' By uttering this phrase, the *gopīs* say, "Brahmā prayed for the welfare of all the inhabitants of the universe."

The *gopīs'* moods constantly change, rising and falling like waves in the ocean. When they address Kṛṣṇa as Paramātmā, or as their friend, they are in fact subtly criticizing Him.

Udeyivān sātvatāṁ kule: *Udeyivān* means 'arose like the sun.' With these words the *gopīs* imply, "You have come to this world." *Sātvatāṁ kule* has two meanings: 'the Yadu dynasty' and 'the pure devotees.' The *gopīs* have both meanings in mind when they say, "You have appeared in the dynasty of Sātvata."

"We know that You are the son of Yaśodā," they tell Śrī Kṛṣṇa. "We have firm belief in that. At the same time, when we perceive Your uncommon activities, we tend to accept what Gargācārya, Bhāguri Ṛṣi, and Paurṇamāsī have told us about You. You are certainly our friend, but You are not merely the son of Yaśodā-gopī."

"Well, who am I then?" Kṛṣṇa asks.

"You are the indwelling witness of all souls," the *gopīs* reply. "This has been told by the *ṛṣis* Bhāguri, Garga, Paurṇamāsī, and others. As the Supersoul, You reside perpetually in the hearts of all, where You witness everyone's deepest feelings and desires. You reside in our hearts as well, so You must know the depths of our sadness and the misery we feel in separation from You. Therefore do not be upset with us; kindly be pleased."

"You tell Me that I am Paramātmā and that I reside in everyone's heart," Kṛṣṇa says. "If this were true, how could I have come before you? I am here and you are seeing Me. The witness within everyone's heart is not seen by anyone."

"Lord Brahmā prayed to You and worshiped You for the protection of the entire world," the *gopīs* reply. "You became pleased with his worship and assumed a form for the world's protection, but actually You have no material form."

"O clever *gopīs* who are expert in *rasa*," Kṛṣṇa says. "If you know all these profound philosophical truths – that I am the Supersoul, the witness of all and He who bestows the results of everyone's fruitive activities – why have you spoken to Me with piercing words?"

"O *sakhā* (friend)," the *gopīs* reply, "Although You are the Supersoul, in response to the prayers of Brahmā to protect the world, You came here to Vṛndāvana and made us Your *sakhīs*. Having obtained a friend like You, we became so pleased that we sank in an ocean of bliss. The familiarity that comes from such intimate friendship blinded us to Your real identity, and that is why we spoke in this way. Please consider that we are also within this universe; protect us as well."

Here the *gopīs* imply, "We are burning in a great conflagration of separation from You. Please come and meet with us. We are Your dearly beloveds and You are aware of our affliction, but still You remain joyful. We have not seen or heard of anyone in this entire world – demigod, man, serpent, animal, or any other creature – who can remain happy in the face of his loved-one's distress. Rather, he himself will be overwhelmed by distress and try to relieve his loved-one of any suffering.

"It seems that You are different. You witness Your dear most *sakhīs* drowning in agony, but You remain peaceful. For this reason we think that You cannot possibly be the son of Yaśodā, who is renowned for her charitable and liberal nature. When she hears about others being even slightly aggrieved, she finds it intolerable. Her heart melts with compassion just to see a person, animal, or bird unhappy; she tries to console them and remove their misery. She is so soft-hearted that she could not possibly have given birth to one as cruel, harsh, merciless, ill-natured, and corrupt as You. We do not detect one single particle of her virtues in You."

"All right then. If I am not the son of Yaśodā and do not have a particle of her good qualities, who am I?"

"You are the Supersoul, the indwelling witness in everyone's heart."

"In what way am I the Supersoul?" Kṛṣṇa asks.

"The Supersoul lives in everyone's heart," the *gopīs* reply. "Even if someone is dying, bitterly crying, and rolling on the ground like a fish flapping on dry land, He remains detached and neutral, just like a judge. He will not give that person anything to help him, nor will He take anything from him; there is no exchange. Similarly, You remain content and indifferent to others' suffering, even if they are so miserable that they are dying. O crest-jewel of all neutral personalities, we now understand that You, the Supersoul, have taken birth in Vraja, but we cannot understand how or why. We have heard from three authorities, Gargācārya, Bhāguri Ṛṣi, and Paurṇamāsī, that Brahmā prayed to You to appear, but that is all we know."

Kṛṣṇa asks, "Why did Brahmā pray to the Supersoul and what was his prayer?"

The *gopīs* reply, "If You had manifested Your complete self in this world and thus revealed Your true identity, everyone would know that You are God and they would perform *bhakti* to You. Everyone would be liberated from this world and Brahmā's entire creation would be in vain. For this reason Brahmā has implored You to appear but to conceal Your identity, and because of this You have come in disguise.

"Now You have become a thief and a debauchee by mixing with others' wives and, having been well practiced from boyhood, You are also a cheater and a liar. When those who have some faith in God discover this about You, instead of practicing *bhakti*, they will become atheists. Jarāsandha and others are examples of this."

Jarāsandha, Karṇa, and Duryodhana were not demons originally. Jarāsandha was previously a righteous person and, like Karṇa, was adorned with the noble qualities of honesty, generosity, and kindness. Narakāsura was also not a demon at first, but by the association of Kālayavana and others he became a demon. All these demons had only two faults – they had no friendship with devotees and they were opposed to Kṛṣṇa. This makes one a demon.

Śrīmad-Bhāgavatam (5.18.12) states:

yasyāsti bhaktir bhagavaty akiñcanā
sarvair guṇais tatra samāsate surāḥ
harāv abhaktasya kuto mahad-guṇā
manorathenāsati dhāvato bahiḥ

All the demigods and their exalted qualities, such as religion, knowledge and renunciation, become manifest in the body of one

> who has developed unalloyed devotion for the Supreme Personality of Godhead, Vāsudeva. On the other hand, a person devoid of devotional service and engaged in material activities has no good qualities. Even if he is adept at the practice of mystic *yoga* or the honest endeavor of maintaining his family and relatives, he must be driven by his own mental speculations and must engage in the service of the Lord's external energy. How can there be any good qualities in such a man?

Devotees have twenty-six commendable qualities. If a person has twenty-five of these qualities but is not fully surrendered to Kṛṣṇa, he is still a demon to some extent, for demons can also possess many wonderful qualities. If someone simply surrenders to Kṛṣṇa, these other virtuous qualities are bound to come to him sooner or later; and, even if they do not come, there is no harm. This one quality alone – full surrender to Kṛṣṇa – is enough to make one a pure devotee.

Just as Lord Nārāyaṇa told Śaṅkara (Śiva) to preach in such a way that atheistic persons would neither know God nor perform *bhakti* to Him,[1] the *gopīs* say that Brahmā prayed to Kṛṣṇa to appear in this world but keep His identity secret, so that Brahmā's material creation would not come to an end."

They taunt Kṛṣṇa by saying, "You have appeared in the dynasty of the Yadus, the dynasty of saintly devotees (*sātvatāṁ kule*), yet You steal others' wives. This is evidence that You have abandoned the qualities belonging to the Supersoul. You have deviated from Your own nature." By addressing Śrī Kṛṣṇa as their friend, the *gopīs* actually tease Him, for they imply that it is His impiety and immorality – His

---

1 Since Śiva is so dear to Śrī Kṛṣṇa, Kṛṣṇa was able to give him the difficult task of coming to this world as a Māyāvādī – Śaṅkarācārya. At that time people were worshiping the Supreme Lord to fulfill their selfish purposes, thinking, "By our worship of God, He will be pleased with us and satisfy all our worldly desires."

Śrī Kṛṣṇa thought, "This situation is most dangerous." He called for Lord Śiva and instructed him: "Since false devotees will create substantial disturbances, I desire that you keep them far away from Me. Create a philosophy that teaches, '*brahma satyaṁ jagan mithyā* – the Absolute is true; this world is false,' and preach, 'All souls are *brahma*, the impersonal Absolute, and all are one. You are *brahma*. There is no need to worship an external God, for you yourself are the Supreme God' " (*Śiva-tattva*, Chapter 1).

meeting with other men's wives – that has made Him their friend. "So now You are our friend," they say. "Someone who is a friend will want to remove his friend's unhappiness somehow or other. But You are not doing anything to remove our painful feelings of separation; You are indifferent to our suffering."

Now we will look at some of the specialities of Śrīla Jīva Gosvāmī's *Śrī Vaiṣṇava-toṣaṇī*. There, Śrīla Jīva Gosvāmī states that this fourth verse explains the *gopīs*' mood in their glorification of Kṛṣṇa's extraordinary activities. In Verse Three they told Him, "You killed many demons, You lifted Govardhana Hill, and You gave salvation to Aghāsura." Now, in this fourth verse they say, "We have therefore decided that You are not an ordinary youth. You are certainly not the son of Yaśodā."

Śrīla Jīva Gosvāmī explains that with these words the *gopīs* may appear to be presenting Yaśodā as inferior, but this is not their intention. They know her as the crest-jewel of their community. They are merely implying that she, like them, is a *gopī*, the wife of a cowherd man, and therefore she cannot possibly be the mother of such an extraordinary personality as Kṛṣṇa. Kṛṣṇa cannot be the son of Yaśodā, or any other *gopī*.

In his commentary, Śrīla Jīva Gosvāmī gives some additional insights about the *gopīs*' addressing Kṛṣṇa as Paramātmā. They say, "As the Supersoul, You reside perpetually in our hearts. You certainly know all of our difficulties and calamities. There is no need to tell You the extent of our grief; no need to tell You how we are ablaze in the fire of separation from You. So You should certainly protect us."

By the words *vikhanasārthito viśva-guptaye*, they say, "Brahmā petitioned You to protect the entire world, and we also belong to the world, so Brahmā prayed for us as well. You are obliged to protect us."

It may seem that when the *gopīs* tell Kṛṣṇa, "You are the Supersoul," they are speaking in a mood of awe and reverence (*aiśvarya-bhāva*) and that they believe it; but this is not so. They are simply repeating the utterance of others; it is not their own idea. Whenever they refer to Kṛṣṇa as the son of Devakī or Vasudeva, or as Brahman,

Paramātmā, or the Supreme Personality of Godhead, as they did in *Bhramara-gīta* (*Śrīmad-Bhāgavatam* 10.47), they are only repeating the words of others. They personally know Him as the son of Yaśodā and nothing more.

Moreover, they only speak like this in the sorrow of separation from Him, not when they are feeling happy and satisfied. None of the inhabitants of Vraja speak like this unless they are grieving. For example, Nanda Bābā spoke like this when Uddhava came to Vraja. He did not believe that his son was God. Rather, he told Uddhava with sarcasm, "You say that my boy is God. He is God? If He is really God, He should try to give us salvation or some other boon. If in fact He is God, may He be pleased with us." In speaking these words, Nanda Bābā's mood is similar to that of the *gopīs*.

It is essential to know the distinction between *aiśvarya*, meaning the worship of Śrī Kṛṣṇa's opulent manifestation in a mood of awe and reverence, and *mādhurya*, intimate loving service to His sweet, human-like form. The Lord's pastimes in Vraja are always human-like (*naravata*), whether they display opulence or not. This is the criterion of *mādhurya*. On the other hand, whether or not there is a display of opulence, when His pastimes are beyond the limit of *nara-līlā*, then they are called *aiśvarya*.

The abounding opulence displayed by Kṛṣṇa in His *mādhurya* pastimes in Vraja does not even slightly impede the sweetness and intimacy of those pastimes, because the residents of Vraja are always without a tinge of awe and reverence towards Him. In the eyes of the *gopīs*, Śrī Yaśodā, His friends, and all the other Vrajavāsīs, He is an ordinary cowherd boy. Although all the Vrajavāsīs saw Him lift Girirāja Govardhana with only one finger, not one of them thought for a moment that He was God. Instead they thought, "Nārāyaṇa has come and lifted the mountain." They could not imagine that He had personally performed this feat. The cowherd boys held their sticks upright under the base of Girirāja Govardhana and considered that they themselves were lifting him.

There is far more *aiśvarya* in Vṛndāvana than in Vaikuṇṭha or Dvārakā, but in Vṛndāvana all *aiśvarya* is covered by *mādhurya*. For example, when Śrī Kṛṣṇa killed Aghāsura, it was not an insignificant act; that pastime contained much *aiśvarya*. Still, the Vrajavāsīs did not think Kṛṣṇa to be God. They simply thought, "Nārāyaṇa has performed this deed."

Śrīla Jīva Gosvāmī gives an additional explanation of *khalu* (certainly) in the first line of this verse, *na khalu gopīkā-nandano*. The *gopīs* say, "You are certainly the son of Yaśodā, and yet at the same time You are Paramātmā. How is this possible? Brahmā has prayed to You, Paramātmā, and You have therefore appeared in this world in the form of Yaśodā's son. He prayed to You to come and keep the world safe and nourished. We are also in this world, so You should protect and nourish us as well."

There is another speciality in Śrīla Jīva Gosvāmī's commentary, wherein he discusses the word *na* (not). He explains that *na*, which is seen only in the beginning of the first line, may be applied to all four lines as follows: "*Na khalu gopīkā-nandanaḥ* – You are not the son of Yaśodā. *Na akhila-dehinām antarātma-dṛk* – You are not the indwelling Supersoul of all living entities. *Na vikhanasārthito viśva-guptaye* – Brahmā has not prayed to You to protect the universe. *Na udeyivān sātvatām kule* – You could not have come in the dynasty of devotees."

With *na* common to all four lines, each line can be explained in this way: "*Na khalu gopīkā nandana* – You are not the son of Yaśodā, but the indwelling witness in the hearts of all entities. This is evident in Your cruelty and heartlessness. *Na akhila-dehinām antarātma-dṛk* – actually You are not Paramātmā. Paramātmā knows everyone's happiness and distress, but You do not know the extent of the pain in our hearts. *Na vikhanasārthito viśva-guptaye* – It cannot be true that Brahmā prayed to You to come and protect this universe. If You had come in response to his prayer, You would actually protect everyone, including us. *Na udeyivān sātvatāṁ kule* – You could not have appeared in the dynasty of devotees. Why do we say this? Because we see that You have none of the qualities of a devotee."

Verse Five

You are the brilliant sun that illuminates the lotus flower of the Yadu dynasty. Please place Your lotus hand on our heads.

Verse 5

विरचिताभयं वृष्णिधुर्य ते
चरणमीयुषां संसृतेर्भयात्।
करसरोरुहं कान्त कामदं
शिरसि धेहि नः श्रीकरग्रहम् ॥५॥

viracitābhayaṁ vṛṣṇi-dhūrya te
caraṇam īyuṣāṁ saṁsṛter bhayāt
kara-saroruhaṁ kānta kāma-daṁ
śirasi dhehi naḥ śrī-kara-graham

viracita – grants; *abhayam* – fearlessness; *vṛṣṇi* – of the Vṛṣṇi dynasty; *dhūrya* – O best; *te* – Your; *caraṇam* – feet; *īyuṣām* – of those who approach; *saṁsṛteḥ* – of material existence; *bhayāt* – out of fear; *kara* – Your hand; *saraḥ-ruham* – like a lotus flower; *kānta* – O lover; *kāma* – desires; *dam* – fulfilling; *śirasi* – on the heads; *dhehi* – please place; *naḥ* – of us; *śrī* – of the goddess of fortune, Lakṣmī-devī; *kara* – the hand; *graham* – taking.

Translation

O crest-jewel of the Yadu dynasty, O beloved, Your lotus hand grants fearlessness to those souls who, terrified by the cycle of birth and death, surrender to Your lotus feet. O fulfiller of our desires, please place on our heads that very lotus hand, which grants fearlessness and which accepted both the hands of Lakṣmī.

Bhāva-prakāśika Vṛtti

The *gopīs* say to Kṛṣṇa, "O crest-jewel of the Vṛṣṇi dynasty (Vṛṣṇi-dhūrya), O dear most beloved (Kānta), O You whose lotus hand fulfills all desires (Kāma-da). We are now extremely frightened (*viracitābhayam*)."

Those who are perplexed and frightened by worldly affairs approach the lotus feet of the Supreme Lord Śrī Kṛṣṇa to become free from the repetition of birth and death (*saṁsṛti*). In this cycle there are six phases of transformation: taking birth, existing, growing, producing byproducts (children), deteriorating, and death. After the age of fifty, all aspects of the body and mind gradually become 'worn and torn.' The eyes, teeth, ears, mind, mental faculties, and all the other senses become gradually decrepit. At that time one cannot even enjoy delicious foods, because he is not able to properly digest.

Śrīla Bhaktivinoda Ṭhākura has sung, "*Vṛddha kāla āola, saba sukha bhāgala, bhogābhāve duḥkhita* – I want to enjoy material happiness but I cannot, and this causes me overwhelming sorrow."[1] Śrī Śaṅkarācārya has written in *Bhaja Govindam* (Verse 22): "*Punar api jananam, punar api maraṇaṁ, punarapi jananī jaṭhare śayanam* – again birth, again death, again lying in the womb of a mother. This is *saṁsṛti*, traversing material existence."

The meaning of *saṁsṛti* also has relation to the word *vraja*, which means 'that which moves around.' But this type of *saṁsṛti* takes us toward Kṛṣṇa and the full happiness of Vraja. One *saṁsṛti* takes us to hell and complete destruction, and the other moves in the opposite direction and takes us to Vraja. Devotees

---

1 *vṛddha-kāla āolo, saba sukha bhāgalo, pīḍā-baśe hoinu kātar*
sarvendriya durbala, kṣīna kalevara, bhogābhāve duḥkhita antar

"Old age soon arrived, and all joys consequently departed. Subjected to the torments of disease, I am troubled and weak. All my senses are feeble now, my body is racked and exhausted, and my spirits are downcast in the absence of former sense pleasures" (*Śaraṇāgati* – First Principle of Surrender: *Dainya*/Humility, Song 5).

of Kṛṣṇa, who aim to loosen their attachment to the material world, circumambulate Gurudeva, Vaiṣṇavas, the Deity, and Tulasī in a clockwise direction. Those who are tightening their attachment, however, circumambulate in an anti-clockwise direction, such as in an Indian marriage ceremony, where the bride and groom walk counter-clockwise around the fire.

The *gopīs* say, "*Caraṇam īyuṣāṁ saṁsṛter bhayat* – If someone takes full shelter of the lotus feet of the Supreme Lord, He places His liberal hand on that person's head. Then, automatically, that person becomes fearless (*abhaya*). *Kanta kāma-dam* – O beloved, You fulfill all desires; so please keep Your lotus hand upon our head."

Now we will turn to the commentary of Śrīla Viśvanātha Cakravartī Ṭhākura. He has explained that in the previous verses, Śrī Kṛṣṇa heard everything the *gopīs* were telling Him. Thus, when they called Him a betrayer of faith and a sinful killer of women, He told them, "I am leaving this place immediately and will not return in this birth." The *gopīs* then became fearful. Therefore, in the fourth verse it is seen how they tried to appease Him by addressing Him as 'friend' and begging Him not to go.

Gratified by their appeal, Kṛṣṇa told them, "O *gopīs*, I have heard your words of sweet criticism. I know that they were not abuse, but an expression of your intimate feelings, spoken in the anger of pure love. While you were calling Me a cheat and a debauchee, I was standing nearby, eager to drink the nectar of your every word. I am so pleased with you that I will now offer you a boon. You may ask anything from Me. Tell Me what you desire and I will grant you that."

Now, gladdened by Kṛṣṇa's statement, the *gopīs* entreat Him in this fifth verse: "O most magnanimous personality in the entire Vṛṣṇi and Yadu dynasties, You are the brilliant sun that illuminates the lotus flower of the Yadu dynasty. Please place Your lotus hand on our heads."

Why do they ask for this? A man's love and affection for his subordinates, such as his child, disciple, junior, or anyone who comes to him for shelter, will be shown by his placing his hand on that person's head. By this he communicates, "I will give you whatever you want." We learn from *Śrī Bhakti-ratnākara* and *Śrī Navadvīpa-dhāma-*

māhātmya that Nityānanda Prabhu placed His lotus feet on the heads of Śrīla Kṛṣṇadāsa Kavirāja Gosvāmī and Śrīla Raghunātha dāsa Gosvāmī, and He also bestowed such mercy upon Śrīla Jīva Gosvāmī. He can do this because He is *guru*. He did not do this in His form as Śrī Baladeva, but as the all-merciful Nityānanda Prabhu, He placed His lotus feet on the heads of many devotees.

caitanya-nityānande nāhi esaba vicāra
nāma laite prema dena, vahe aśru-dhāra
Caitanya-caritāmṛta (*Ādi-līlā* 8.31)

> But if one only chants, with some slight faith, the holy names of Lord Caitanya and Nityānanda, very quickly he is cleansed of all offenses. Thus as soon as he chants the Hare Kṛṣṇa *mahā-mantra*, he feels the ecstasy of love for God.

We may live in Vṛndāvana and call out, "O Kṛṣṇa! Kṛṣṇa! Kṛṣṇa!" but tears do not fall from our eyes and our hearts do not melt. On the other hand, if we go to Navadvīpa-dhāma and cry out, "O Gaura! O Nityānanda! I am more sinful than Jagāi and Mādhāi and all other demons!" Śrī Gaurāṅga and Śrī Nityānanda Prabhu will surely bestow Their astonishing, causeless mercy upon us. We can beseech Nityānanda Prabhu in this way: "Jagāi and Mādhāi persecuted You, but You gave them Your mercy and they began to chant, 'Kṛṣṇa! Kṛṣṇa!' Both of them wept loudly and their hearts melted. But I am even more sinful than Jagāi and Mādhāi." Nityānanda Prabhu is our only true shelter. If we want *prema*, we need only approach His lotus feet. Nityānanda Prabhu comes to us through our *guru*, and He is the complete and undivided principle of Śrī Guru (*akhaṇḍa guru-tattva*). Therefore, Śrī Guru is a repository of the qualities of Śrī Nityānanda Prabhu. It is a great solace that our Gurudeva is His manifestation.

For example, in a marvelous way, *parama-pūjyapāda* Śrīla Bhaktivedānta Svāmī Mahārāja gave mercy to many drunkards and cheaters, who were disqualified in every way. He placed his hand on the heads of whoever came to him. He was so liberal that he even told them, "Oh, you want a wife? I will arrange everything." By his mercy he thought, "Somehow or other these people should come and taste the nectar of *kṛṣṇa-nāma*. By this, they will surely leave behind all their material attachments, if not in this birth then in two or three births from now. Thus, by the grace of Śrī Nityānanda Prabhu, they will become pure."

Now, in this fifth verse of *Śrī Gopī-gīta*, the *gopīs* implore Kṛṣṇa, "Your lotus hand can fulfill all of our desires, so please grant us fearlessness by placing it on our heads." What do the *gopīs* fear? They fear burning in the blazing fire of *kāma* because Kṛṣṇa is not with them. They think, "If Kṛṣṇa comes into our midst, we will be out of danger. He will certainly dance with us and perform all varieties of loving pastimes with us."

The *gopīs* ask Kṛṣṇa to place His hand on their heads, but in response He asks them, "How can I ever do that? It is not possible for Me to perform the sinful act of placing My hand on the heads of others' wives."

As mentioned above, the *gopīs* first address Kṛṣṇa as *kānta* (beloved) and then as *kāma-da* (He whose lotus hand awards the fulfillment of all desires, or He whose lotus hand gives *kāma*). In this way they say, "You told us we can ask a boon of You, and we know You have the power to give that boon. We have come to You because the five arrows of Kāmadeva have pierced our hearts, leaving us on the verge of death.

"The Supreme Personality of Godhead places His hand on the heads of those who take shelter of His lotus feet. All living entities who are bound up in the cycle of birth and death want freedom from the fear of remaining in that cycle. For someone who takes shelter of You, all his suffering disappears automatically and he becomes fearless, confident that he will never again become bound up in worldly enjoyment.[2]

"So we have surrendered unto Your feet, knowing that Your lotus hand will surely fulfill our desires. If You put Your hand on our heads, the burning fire of *kāma* will disappear from our hearts. But

---

2 Śrīla Bhaktivedānta Nārāyaṇa Gosvāmī Mahārāja's *bhāvānuvāda* of Śrīla Jīva Gosvāmī's commentary on this verse explains the *gopīs*' mood in this connection. There it is stated that although the *gopīs* have no knowledge of Śrī Kṛṣṇa's Godhood, they seem to be full of awe and reverence (*aiśvarya*) here, just as they seemed so in Verse Four.

not only that; we will no longer feel separation from You. We always fear that You will leave us. If You keep Your lotus hand on our heads, we will know for certain that You will never leave us and that we will always be with You."

Conditioned souls want to become free from the cycle of birth and death, but the *gopīs*' only desire is to be free from the fear of separation from Kṛṣṇa.

Kṛṣṇa may tell them, "You say you want Me to protect you from *kāma*, but *kāma* lives in the heart. If what you say is correct, why should I place My hand on your heads? Should I not place it where *kāma* is present? That desire is in Me, and I think you have the same desire."

In response to this they say, "*Śrī-kara-graham* – As You have taken the hand of Śrī, Lakṣmī, in marriage, which means that You will never leave Her, we want You to place our hands in Your hands; not what You suggest. Even if You want to place Your hand on the breast of Lakṣmī, she will not allow You to do so. Similarly, do not put Your hand on our bodies – only on our heads."

Verse Six

We have been pierced by Your five arrows, which are causing us unbearable pain and distress. If we see Your sweet, nectarean lotus face, this misery will completely disappear. Please, therefore, show us Your enchanting lotus face.

Verse 6

व्रजजनार्त्तिहन् वीर योषितां
निजजनस्मयध्वंसनस्मित ।
भज सखे भवत्किङ्करीः स्म नो
जलरुहाननं चारु दर्शय ॥६॥

vraja-janārti-han vīra yoṣitāṁ
nija-jana-smaya-dhvaṁsana-smita
bhaja sakhe bhavat-kiṅkarīḥ sma no
jala-ruhānanaṁ cāru darśaya

vraja-jana – of the people of Vraja; *ārti* – of the suffering; *han* – O destroyer; *vīra* – O hero; *yoṣitām* – of women; *nija* – Your own; *jana* – of the people; *smaya* – the pride; *dhvaṁsana* – destroying; *smita* – whose smile; *bhaja* – please accept; *sakhe* – O friend; *bhavat* – Your; *kiṅkarīḥ* – maidservants; *sma* – indeed; *naḥ* – us; *jala-ruha* – lotus; *ānanam* – Your face; *cāru* – beautiful; *darśaya* – please show.

Translation

O You who destroys the sorrows of the residents of Vraja; O best among heroes, the beam of whose mere smile shatters the pride of Your near and dear ones, which arises from good fortune, and from the sulky mood (*māna*) arising from that pride. O dear friend, please fulfill the desire of Your maidservants. At least this once, kindly show us helpless girls Your attractive lotus face and make us happy.

Bhāva-prakāśika Vṛtti

Before we begin, we should pray to Śrīla Śukadeva Gosvāmī and Śrī Parīkṣit Mahārāja, to Śrīla Vyāsadeva, then to the *gopīs*, and after that to Śrī Śrī Rādhā and Kṛṣṇa. Mercy is flowing to us through this line.

When we read, we should think that we are sitting in the assembly where Śrīla Śukadeva Gosvāmī is reciting *Śrīmad-Bhāgavatam* to Mahārāja Parīkṣit. Or, we should think that we are in Vṛndāvana, at the place where the *gopīs* are speaking with Śrī Kṛṣṇa. We should contemplate, "My heart, indeed my very self, is with the *gopīs* and also with Śukadeva Gosvāmī." We must yearn to have the same moods as they have, to be on the same platform as they are. The attainment of such absorption is called *samādhi*[1].

The *samādhi* of the *yogīs* is zero in comparison. The *yogīs* have no platform on which to stand – not for a second, or even for a millionth of a millionth of a second. The *samādhi* I speak about is situated on a very solid and perfect platform.

In the later chapters of *Śrīmad-Bhāgavatam*, Śrīla Viśvanātha Cakravartī Ṭhākura discusses Śrī Kṛṣṇa and the *gopīs*' feelings of separation from each other. He says that when Kṛṣṇa leaves Vṛndāvana, He does not take with Him His flute, His smile, or His Vraja attire. He keeps everything in Vṛndāvana, including His moods, which He leaves with the *gopīs*. He goes empty-hearted to Mathurā and Dvārakā, where He constantly weeps. We read in *Bṛhad-Bhāgavatāmṛta* how bitterly He weeps in Dvārakā, lamenting, "I have left everything of Mine in Vṛndāvana– My heart, My soul, and My mood."

At that time the *gopīs* also lament, "Kṛṣṇa has taken our minds, our hearts, our moods, and everything we possess. Moreover,

---

1 *Sama* means 'equal' and *dhī* means 'complete absorption of the intelligence.' In other words, a person in *samādhi* has the same level of consciousness as his worshipful Deity, and is doing service on that platform.

He has taken our closest, most devoted friends – sleeping and fainting. When we faint we get some temporary relief from our condition, and we also get some relief when we sleep, but Kṛṣṇa has taken them both, leaving us completely empty."

In separation from Kṛṣṇa, the *gopīs* feel His presence. They ponder every minute aspect of their meeting with Him, and in so doing, they experience Him fully. When they are with Him, they forget that experience. They lose that feeling of being united with Him internally. Withdrawing from external consciousness and associating with Him internally nourishes the desire for meeting Him, and also nourishes the actual experience of meeting Him. For this reason, the mood of separation is of extreme value to Śrī Kṛṣṇa and the *gopīs*.

If their moods of separation had not been revealed, we would have no idea of them; the world would have no idea of such elevated sentiments. This mood of separation between Kṛṣṇa and the *gopīs* is the main wealth of *rasika* and *bhāvuka*[2] *bhaktas*. *Śrīmad-Bhāgavatam* reveals these pastimes of separation:

nigama-kalpa-taror galitaṁ phalaṁ
śuka-mukhād amṛta-drava-saṁyutam
pibata bhāgavataṁ rasam ālayaṁ
muhur aho rasikā bhuvi bhāvukāḥ
Śrīmad-Bhāgavatam (1.1.3)

> O expert and thoughtful men, relish *Śrīmad-Bhāgavatam*, the mature fruit of the desire tree of Vedic literatures. It emanated from the lips of Śrī Śukadeva Gosvāmī. Therefore this fruit has become even more tasteful, although its nectarean juice was already relishable for all, including liberated souls.

Now, in their intolerable separation from Kṛṣṇa, the *gopīs* utter the words of this sixth verse beginning *vraja-janārti-han*. Ordinarily this means, "You destroy the sufferings of the residents of Vraja (*vraja-jana*), and the sufferings of people in general. Yet, although we are also *vraja-jana*, You are giving us distress. We have seen You remove the distress of everyone else in Vṛndāvana, so why not ours?"

---

2 *Bhāvuka* means 'one who is absorbed in *bhāva*, or transcendental emotions'.

In this verse, the word *vīra*, 'hero,' specifically refers to *gokula-vīra*, the hero of Gokula, and Gokula refers to Vṛndāvana, Rādhā-kuṇḍa, and all other pastime places of Śrī Śrī Rādhā and Kṛṣṇa. In this context, *vīra* does not carry its usual meaning, 'hero in battle.' It refers only to *madhura-rasa*, meaning Śrī Kṛṣṇa's transcendental amorous pastimes, and thus it indicates 'hero of *madhura-rasa*.' It specifically refers to Śrī Kṛṣṇa as *dhīra-lalita*, which *Śrī Bhakti-rasāmṛta-sindhu* describes as "the hero who is expert in the sixty-four arts and in amorous sports, always situated in fresh youth, expert at joking, devoid of anxiety, and controlled by the *prema* of His beloveds."

Yoṣitāṁ nija-jana-smaya-dhvaṁsana-smita: With these words the *gopīs* allude to their *kāma*, which is blazing like a fire, and thus they tell Kṛṣṇa, "By Your mere smile, You destroy the burning torment caused by Cupid's arrows."

Bhaja sakhe bhavat-kiṅkarīḥ: The *gopīs* continue, "We are Your *kiṅkarīs*, Your completely devoted maidservants, so please fulfill our desire." *Bhaj* means 'to serve,' so here the *gopīs* are saying, "You should serve Your *kiṅkarīs*." In actuality, however, they want Kṛṣṇa to fulfill their desire to serve Him. In this connection, the word *bhaja* implies that the devotees serve Kṛṣṇa and Kṛṣṇa serves His devotees. Kṛṣṇa says in *Bhagavad-gītā*, "*Ye yathā māṁ prapadyante taṁs tathaiva bhajāmy aham* – As they surrender to Me, I reciprocate accordingly." This is His promise.

Nija-jala-ruhānanaṁ cāru darśaya: The *gopīs* entreat Kṛṣṇa, "Please show us Your beautiful lotus face."

The above-mentioned explanations reveal the general meaning of the verse, whereas the commentary of Śrīla Viśvanātha Cakravartī Ṭhākura reveals what the *gopīs* are actually expressing: "For other persons, You destroy their various kinds of distress. For us *gopīs*, however, You annihilate the anguish caused by the arrows of Cupid; and only You can do this. You do not extinguish the burning pain caused by the *kāma* felt by the demigoddesses or other girls."

In order to explain the *gopīs*' words, Śrīla Viśvanātha Cakravartī Ṭhākura quotes a verse from *Yugala-gīta* (*Śrīmad-Bhāgavatam* 10.35.3):

vyoma-yāna-vanitāḥ saha siddhair
vismitās tad upadhārya sa-lajjāḥ
kāma-mārgaṇa-samarpita-cittāḥ
kaśmalaṁ yayur apasmṛta-nīvyaḥ

In the above-mentioned verse, the *gopīs* say that as the demigoddesses were sitting in their airplanes in the sky, embraced in their husbands' arms, they beheld Kṛṣṇa and heard His flute-song. As a result they became full of *kāma*, swooning unconscious into the their husbands' laps, with their garments loosened. Rather than become jealous at this display, their husbands became filled with admiration for them.

In *Yugala-gīta*, the *gopīs* simply point out that when the demigoddesses saw the lotus feet of Kṛṣṇa and heard His sweet flute-song, they became struck with wonder and fell unconscious in their husbands' laps. They do not say anything about Kṛṣṇa coming to pacify those demigoddesses.

Now, in this sixth verse of *Gopī-gīta*, the *gopīs* reveal why it is that Kṛṣṇa comes only to them. It is because no one experiences the agony they do, and no one else accepts Kṛṣṇa as the only doctor competent to treat them. They say, "We have been pierced by Your five arrows, which are causing us unbearable pain and distress; but if we see Your sweet, nectarean lotus face, this misery will completely disappear. Please, show us Your enchanting lotus face. O hero, You alone hold the power to eliminate this pain from our hearts."

There were two reasons Kṛṣṇa left the *rāsa* dance. The first was to remove the *gopīs'* pride in their own good fortune, and the second was to please Śrīmatī Rādhikā and assuage Her jealous anger. In this verse the *gopīs* give their opinion about His first reason: "You have used an atom bomb to destroy such a little thing. Your smile alone would have been enough to remove our pride. There was no good reason to have given us such pain by disappearing. This was a useless waste of energy." Thus they address Him as hero.

Upon hearing these words, Kṛṣṇa's heart melts. "Oh, you only want to see Me smiling?" He asks. "The loving words you speak give

Me so much happiness that I am ready to give you whatever you want. Tell Me immediately what you desire. Do not delay for a single moment."

In the *gopīs*' response, they address Him as friend (*sakhā*). In this way they tell Him, "It is true that we are Your completely dedicated maidservants (*kiṅkarīs*), but we are also Your *sakhīs*." With the word *bhaja*, they convey, "You should certainly serve us, but not just by appearing before us. You should also decorate us and give us betel nuts, as You did earlier, when we first came here to meet with You. At that time You asked us, 'What have you done? Why have you applied makeup to only one eye? Why not to the other eye as well?' Then, in a most charming way, You carefully and gently applied makeup to the other eye."

When Kṛṣṇa first called them for *rāsa-līlā* with His melodious flute-song, they had no time to adorn themselves properly. They had donned their ornaments haphazardly, having readied themselves in great haste before running from their homes. Their necklaces were on their waists and they had randomly placed their other ornaments. When they arrived at the spot where Śrī Kṛṣṇa was waiting for them, He very gently took their necklaces from their waists and placed them around their necks. He also straightened all the other ornaments on their divine forms. As He served them in this way, both He and they were overwhelmed with joy. Aware that His inner desire was to serve them, each *gopī* thought, "Kṛṣṇa should serve me like this every day."

Now, as they sing this *Gopī-gīta*, they say, "O *sakhā*, we order You to do what You did when we first arrived here."

"Why are you ordering Me in this way?" Kṛṣṇa asks.

"You are our *sakhā*," they reply. "A *sakhī* can give orders to her *sakhā*."

"Aren't you afraid to give Me orders?"

"No. Actually it is quite satisfying to give You orders. And if You carry out those orders, we will be delighted."

"Tell me, then, what should I do? How should I serve you?"

"The first thing You can do is to show us Your lotus face (*jala-ruhānanam*)." *Jala-ruha* means 'lotus' and *ānanam* means 'face.' "First come to us, and after that we will order You to do specific services."

A *rasika* and *bhāvuka* devotee silently contemplates these pastimes – Kṛṣṇa serving the *gopīs*, the pleasure He receives in doing so, and the simultaneous pleasure of the *gopīs*. The *gopīs* smile, and this is just what Śrī Kṛṣṇa wants to see. In fact, He wants to see their smiling faces more than He wants to smile Himself.

In this regard there is a passage in *Śrī Caitanya-caritāmṛta* (*Ādi-līlā* 4. 187-194): "The *gopīs* taste a pleasure ten million times greater than the pleasure Śrī Kṛṣṇa derives from seeing them. The *gopīs* have no inclination to act for their own enjoyment, and yet their joy increases; the joy of the *gopīs* lies in the joy of their beloved Kṛṣṇa. When Śrī Kṛṣṇa sees the *gopīs*, His joy increases and thus His unparalleled sweetness also increases. The *gopīs* think, 'Kṛṣṇa has obtained so much pleasure by seeing me.' That thought increases the fullness and beauty of their faces and bodies, the sight of which further increases the beauty of Kṛṣṇa. And, the more the *gopīs* see Kṛṣṇa's beauty, the more their own beauty increases. In this way a loving competition takes place between them, in which none of them acknowledges defeat."

Śrīla Kṛṣṇadāsa Kavirāja Gosvāmī thus describes the competition between Śrī Kṛṣṇa and the *gopīs*, which ended in a draw. Śrīla Kavirāja Gosvāmī 'whistled' and gave judgment that neither side had won. Actually, we Gauḍīya Vaiṣṇavas do not want this. We want the whistle to be blown to indicate Śrīmatī Rādhikā's victory. Rādhikā will be so happy, and we will applaud and celebrate.

This is the real mood of Śrīla Kṛṣṇadāsa Kavirāja Gosvāmī, Śrīla Raghunātha dāsa Gosvāmī, and Śrīla Rūpa Gosvāmī. If Śrīmatī Lalitā-devī is the mediator in a game, she will blow the whistle to say it is a draw, that no one has been defeated. But Śrī Rūpa Mañjarī will whistle to announce that Śrīmatī Rādhikā has defeated Kṛṣṇa.

It is Śrī Kṛṣṇa Himself who will experience the greatest pleasure when He is defeated, although His friends like Madhumaṅgala and others will not be pleased at all. Kundalatā-gopī will also be sorry that Kṛṣṇa has lost, and Dhaniṣṭhā-gopī may even faint. Kṛṣṇa's defeat causes such friends great distress, and His victory fills them with joy.

In his *Vaiṣṇava-toṣaṇī* commentary on this sixth verse, Śrīla Jīva Gosvāmī applies a rule of Sanskrit grammar. When a word starting with an 'a' is preceded by a word ending with an 'e,' the 'a' is dropped and replaced with an apostrophe. Thus, in this verse, the word *bhavat*, which means 'yours' may be read as *abhavat*, 'not yours,' and then the phrase will be *abhavat kiṅkarīḥ naḥ*. Accordingly, this line may read either *sakhe bhavat* or *sakhe abhavat*. Applying the latter interpretation, the *gopīs* say, "We are not saying that You should serve us. You can serve those who are not Your *kiṅkarīs*, like Kubjā and others. We are Your *kiṅkarīs* and they are not, so You should go to them and serve them."

Śrīla Jīva Gosvāmī also gives an alternative meaning to the words *naḥ jala-ruhānanaṁ cāru darśaya*. In this case, the *gopīs* say, "We do not want to see Your lotus face. You make us suffer from constant separation, not just once or twice, but always. So, there is no need to show us Your lotus face; we have now made a vow to die."

With the explanation of these alternative meanings, Śrīla Jīva Gosvāmī completes his commentary on the *gopīs*' sixth prayer.

Verse Seven

We see that Your lotus feet follow the cows as they run over the mountains to graze. They wander where there are grass shoots, edges of dry grains, and small sharp stones, yet Your lotus feet feel very happy there. Why, then, are You not able to place those lotus feet on our breasts, which are not nearly as rough and hard as those stones?

Verse 7

प्रणतदेहिनां पापकर्षणं
तृणचरानुगं श्रीनिकेतनम्।
फणिफणार्पितं ते पदाम्बुजं
कृणु कुचेषु नः कृन्धि हृच्छयम् ॥७॥

praṇata-dehināṁ pāpa-karṣaṇaṁ
tṛṇa-carānugaṁ śrī-niketanam
phaṇi-phaṇārpitaṁ te padāmbujaṁ
kṛṇu kuceṣu naḥ kṛndhi hṛc-chayam

praṇata – who are surrendered to You; *dehinām* – of the embodied living beings; *pāpa* – the sins; *karṣaṇam* – which remove; *tṛṇa* – grass; *cara* – who graze (the cows); *anugam* – following; *śrī* – of the goddess of fortune; *niketanam* – the abode; *phaṇi* – of the serpent (Kāliya); *phaṇa* – on the hoods; *arpitam* – placed; *te* – Your; *pada-ambujam* – lotus feet; *kṛṇu* – please put; *kuceṣu* – on the breasts; *naḥ* – our; *kṛndhi* – cut away; *hṛt-śayam* – the lust in our hearts.

Translation

Your lotus feet remove all the past sins of embodied beings who surrender to them, and they chase after the cows and calves that graze in the pastures. Those lotus feet are the abode of Lakṣmī-devī, the goddess of wealth and beauty, and You placed them even upon the hoods of a serpent (Kāliya). Please place those very lotus feet upon our breasts, and subdue our sufferings that have arisen from the lust in our hearts.

Praṇata-dehinām pāpa-karṣaṇam: *Praṇata* means 'surrendered,' *dehinām* refers to living entities in material bodies, and *pāpa-karṣaṇam* means 'removal of sinful reactions.' The *gopīs* tell Śrī Kṛṣṇa, "Your lotus feet remove all kinds of sinful reactions for those embodied beings who are surrendered to them." Again and again, they glorify the virtues of His lotus feet.

Tṛṇa-carānugam: *Tṛṇa-cara* refers to cows and all other animals that graze on grass, and *anuga* means 'following.' The *gopīs* say, "Your feet always follow behind the cows."

Śrī-niketanam: *Śrī* means 'beauty,' and it also refers to Lakṣmī, the goddess of fortune. In this way, the *gopīs*' statement has two meanings: "Your feet are exquisitely beautiful," and "Your feet are the abode (*niketana*) of Śrī, or Lakṣmī. She perpetually resides at Your feet and never leaves them."

Phaṇi-phaṇārpitaṁ te padāmbujam: *Phaṇi* refers to creatures with hoods (*phaṇa*). Here, *phaṇi* particularly refers to the hooded serpent Kāliya. *Arpitam* means 'placed,' and *te padāmbujam* refers to Śrī Kṛṣṇa's lotus feet. The *gopīs* say, "You placed Your lotus feet on the hoods of that serpent."

Kṛṇu kuceṣu naḥ kṛndhi hṛc-chayam: *Kṛṇu* means 'keep,' *kṛndhi* means 'cut away,' *kuceṣu* means 'breasts,' and *naḥ hṛc-chayam* refers to the disease of *kāma* in the *gopīs*' hearts. The *gopīs* pray, "Please place Your lotus feet on our hearts, and thus destroy our heart-disease of *kāma*."

Ordinary people imagine the *gopīs*' appeal to be born of mundane lust, and for this reason Śrīla Viśvanātha Cakravartī Ṭhākura eulogizes the divine nature of their immaculate love. Even a *sādhaka* who has attained the platform of a *madhyama-uttama adhikārī* has no such lust, what to speak of someone who has attained *svarūpa-siddhi* and thus realization of his eternal spiritual form. If someone has attained *vastu-siddhi* (one's own spiritual form) and thus complete liberation from matter, not the slightest trace of lust can be found in him.

Lust is the desire for one's own happiness, and the *gopīs* do not have a trace of such desire. Their attachment to Kṛṣṇa is called *samarthā-rati*, which means that, due to its total selflessness, it is fully capable of controlling Him.

Rati, attachment to Śrī Kṛṣṇa, is of three kinds: *sādhāraṇī*, *samañjasā*, and *samarthā*. *Sādhāraṇī-rati* is attachment to Kṛṣṇa for one's own enjoyment, and Śrīla Rūpa Gosvāmī has accepted the hunchback Kubjā as the only example of this *rati*. The moment Kubjā saw Kṛṣṇa, *sādhāraṇī-rati* entered her heart. She desired to enjoy Kṛṣṇa, not to give Him enjoyment, and this was the defect of her *rati*. Still, her lust was for Kṛṣṇa alone, not for King Kaṁsa or anyone else.

Samañjasā-rati is found in the queens of Dvārakā, such as Satyabhāmā and Rukmiṇī. Those imbued with *samañjasā-rati* may also occasionally desire their own happiness, but this is rare; a mood of service to Kṛṣṇa prevails. [Their desire for their own happiness has no connection with material happiness.] Sometimes the attachment is for Kṛṣṇa alone, and sometimes it is divided among many. The queens feel affection for Kṛṣṇa and also for their children. Each queen has ten sons and one daughter, so their love is divided among twelve. Their love is further divided because they also have affection for all the members of their household, including their maidservants. Kṛṣṇa may be controlled by this type of *rati*, or He may not; it depends on the circumstances. Ultimately, however, He is not controlled by it.

The *gopīs' prema* is *samarthā-rati*, and this *rati* is found only in Vraja. *Samarthā* means 'powerful' and 'competent,' which indicates that this *rati* surely controls Kṛṣṇa in every respect. The *gopīs* are selfless to the utmost degree and endowed with this pure *prema*. They never think about how they can be relieved of their own sorrow, nor do they worry for their personal happiness. They only want Kṛṣṇa's happiness, and that is why He is fully controlled by them.

The *gopīs* are *mahā-premavatī*, which means that they are situated in the highest stages of *mahābhāva*[1]. This is especially true of Śrīmatī

1 *Mahābhāva* is the highest stage of *prema*. It follows the stages of *sneha*, *māna*, *praṇaya*, *rāga*, and *anurāga*, and manifests when *anurāga* reaches a special state of intensity.

Rādhikā, who is eternally situated in *madanākhya-mahābhāva*, the pinnacle of selfless, ecstatic *prema*, and who is one of the *gopīs* speaking this verse. What to speak of the *gopīs*, even the *svarūpa-siddhi* devotee, who is situated on the level of *bhāva-bhakti* and who has realization of his eternal form, has no lust. Although he does not have the sense of intense possessiveness (*mamatā*) for Kṛṣṇa that the *gopīs* have, he does not have even a scent of lust.

Most devotees in this world practice *bhakti* because, in the core of their heart, they see it as a means to attain their own happiness and avoid distress. It is rare to find someone who only wants Śrī Kṛṣṇa's happiness. Only the *uttama-adhikārī*, like Śrī Prahlāda Mahārāja, has love of this caliber. Prahlāda's father, Hiraṇyakaśipu, cruelly tormented him because of his devotion. Still, he never prayed, "Please, God, remove my distress. Please make me happy." If Prahlāda did not do this, then what to speak of the *gopīs*, who do not have the slightest scent of desire to be free from distress and to taste their own happiness. They do not even desire to personally enjoy their loving relationship with Kṛṣṇa.

It is stated in the eighth verse of *Śrī Śikṣāṣṭaka*:

āśliṣya vā pāda-ratāṁ pinaṣṭu mām
adarśanān marma-hatāṁ karotu vā
yathā tathā vā vidadhātu lampaṭo
mat-prāṇa-nāthas tu sa eva nāparaḥ

> Let Kṛṣṇa tightly embrace this maidservant who has fallen at His lotus feet, or let Him trample Me or break My heart by never being visible to Me. He is a debauchee, after all, and He may do whatever He likes. Still, He alone, and no one else, is the worshipful lord of My heart.

Śrīmatī Rādhikā thinks in this way: "I know that Kṛṣṇa is a debauchee and that sometimes He wants to meet with other *gopīs*.

---

1 (continued) "When *anurāga* reaches its highest limit and becomes perceivable in the body, it is called *bhāva*. When the bodily symptoms are not very distinct, however, the emotional state is still called *anurāga*, not *bhāva*. When the ecstasy of *bhāva* is intensified, it is called *mahābhāva*. The symptoms of *mahābhāva* are visible only in the bodies of eternal associates like the *gopīs*" (*Caitanya-caritāmṛta*, *Madhya-līlā* 6.13, purport by Śrīla Bhaktivedānta Swāmī Mahārāja).

Despite this, I want only His pleasure; I do not want My own. If He hankers to reside in Mathurā or Dvārakā with His lady friends, He is perfectly free to do so. If I come to know that He desires to enjoy with a particular *sakhī*, I will go to her, serve her, and beg her to meet with Him. If He crushes Me with His feet, I will not ask Him why He is doing so, and if He becomes pleased by embracing Me, I will also become pleased. Everyone says that He is a debauchee and a cheat; nonetheless, I will always seek His happiness alone."

Śrīmatī Rādhikā and the *gopīs* are beyond even the level of the *uttamā-bhakta*, whose qualities are defined in the following two verses:

anya-vāñchā, anya-pūjā chāḍi' 'jñāna', 'karma'
ānukūlye sarvendriye kṛṣṇānuśīlana
Caitanya-caritāmṛta (*Madhya-līlā* 19.168)

A pure devotee must not cherish any desire other than to serve Kṛṣṇa. He should not offer worship to the demigods or to mundane personalities. He should not cultivate artificial knowledge, which is devoid of Kṛṣṇa consciousness, and he should not engage himself in anything other than Kṛṣṇa conscious activities. One must engage all one's purified senses in the service of the Lord. This is the favorable execution of Kṛṣṇa conscious activities.

Śrī Caitanya-caritāmṛta states: "*Ānukūlye sarvendriye kṛṣṇa-anuśīlana* – when one serves Kṛṣṇa favorably, with all his senses, that service is called *bhakti*."

anyābhilāṣitā-śūnyaṁ jñāna-karmādy-anāvṛtam
ānakūlyena kṛṣṇānu-śīlanaṁ bhaktir uttamā
Bhakti-rasāmṛta-sindhu (1.1.11)

Uttamā-bhakti is defined by the word *anuśīlanam*, which means service to Śrī Kṛṣṇa with one's body, mind, senses, words, intelligence, and all the sentiments of the soul. An elevated devotee entertains nothing that is detrimental to the development of his *bhakti*. Rather, his practices are exclusively favorable. Furthermore, his *bhakti* is continuous, performed without interruption, and is discharged under the guidance of a qualified *guru* and *rasika* Vaiṣṇava (*ānukūlyena kṛṣṇānuśīlana*). It is not tinged by impersonal knowledge (*jñāna*) or fruitive activity (*karma*), and it is devoid of any desire other than to please Śrī Kṛṣṇa (*anyābhilāṣita-śūnyaṁ*). When all these symptoms are present, that is *uttamā-bhakti*.

As mentioned above, the *gopīs* are not classified as *uttama-bhaktas*, even though they have all the qualities of an *uttama-bhakta*. They are the bodily expansions (*kāya-vyūha-rūpa*) of Śrīmatī Rādhikā, who is the personification of Kṛṣṇa's pleasure-giving potency, *hlādinī-śakti*.

The Vraja maidens, singing *Gopī-gīta* most expertly, reveal their youthful beauty and the pain of their separation from Kṛṣṇa, with the hope of arousing His desire to taste the bliss of *surata*. Because they know what He desires, they wish to inspire this in His heart by all the activities of their body, mind, and words. It is only for this reason that they sing their *Gopī-gīta*.

How do they know His desires? They heard His flute-song:

bhagavān api tā rātṛīḥ
śāradotphulla-mallikāḥ
vīkṣya rantuṁ manaś cakre
yoga-māyām upāśritaḥ
Śrīmad-Bhāgavatam (10.29.1)

Śrī Kṛṣṇa is the Supreme Personality of Godhead, full in all opulences, yet upon seeing those autumn nights scented with blossoming jasmine flowers, He turned His mind toward loving affairs. To fulfill His purposes He resorted His internal potency.

In the second verse of *Gopī-gīta*, the *gopīs* addressed Śrī Kṛṣṇa as *surata-nātha*, because He had begged them for the treasure of amorous pastimes. He had a taste for *surata*, and in order to satisfy that taste, He made up His mind to enjoy sweet pastimes with them. He wants this because He thinks that the *gopīs* want it. And the *gopīs* want it because He wants it. Kṛṣṇa and the *gopīs* try to please each other. The *gopīs* long to awaken in Śrī Kṛṣṇa's heart the desire for the happiness of *surata*, so that He will enjoy with them.

How did Kṛṣṇa know the *gopīs*' desires? In the previous year, the unmarried *gopīs* had performed austerities and worshiped the goddess

Kātyāyanī-devī in an effort to attain Him as their husband, and the married *gopīs*, like Śrīmatī Rādhikā and Her *sakhīs*, had joined them in the last day of their worship. At that time, Kṛṣṇa showed His eagerness and promised that He would fulfill their desires during the following year.

One year later, the *gopīs* heard Kṛṣṇa calling them to Him by the melody of His flute. Before leaving their homes, they made themselves look still more beautiful, desiring that He be controlled by their beauty. This is a symptom of their *rati*. Every aspect of their being – their form, youth, beauty, qualities, and desires – exists only to inspire *surata* in Kṛṣṇa's heart. They intentionally made themselves more beautiful, knowing that Kṛṣṇa would be controlled by their splendidly attractive appearance. They put an earring on one of their ears but not the other, and they put *kajjala* on one eye instead of two, knowing that it looks more sweet. This is a symptom of their *rati*.

In this way, fully aware of Kṛṣṇa's specific desires, the *gopīs* enhanced their charming beauty. They know the art of understanding and fulfilling His desires, and Śrīla Rūpa Gosvāmī also knows this art. Neophyte devotees, having no idea about the reality of this topic, can only repeat the subject matter like parrots.

Now, in this verse of *Gopī-gīta*, the *gopīs* again exhibit their ability to realize and fulfill Kṛṣṇa's desires. They openly beseech Him, "Please place Your lotus feet on our breasts."

Loving feelings and desires should not be spoken directly, and Śrīla Viśvanātha Cakravartī Ṭhākura illustrates this point with an example. Suppose a man receives a visit from his friend, and, in the happiness of wanting to welcome him, says, "O my friend, now that you have come here, I am going to purchase some ingredients to make you a delicious meal of *rasa-malai*, *malpurā*, and other delicacies." "No, no," his friend replies, "there is no need for you to do that." But the host insists, "I know that you are particularly fond of these delicacies, so I must prepare them for you." The host's expression of affection in this way only serves to reduce his love for his friend.[2]

---

2 Śrīla Viśvanātha Cakravartī Ṭhākura explains this principle in *Prema-sampuṭa*:

premā dvayo rasikayor api dīpa eva
hṛd-veśma bhāsayti niścalam eva bhāti

Similarly, if the *gopīs* were to say, "We know that You want to enjoy sweet pastimes with us, and we want to quench Your thirst for this enjoyment," their *prema* would be diminished. They do not verbalize their feelings and thus their *prema* is never reduced. Notwithstanding, because their love is absolutely selfless, even if they were to verbalize their feelings in such a way, still their *prema* would not be diminished. The *gopīs* are so clever in *prema* that they are able to defeat Kṛṣṇa. He cannot imagine the moods hidden in their hearts and it is for this reason that He left *rāsa-līlā* and followed them as they searched for Him. He had left them only to hear them weep and express their feelings.

When a devotee has the desire to serve Kṛṣṇa, Kṛṣṇa has the desire to receive that service. First, the *gopīs* desire to serve Him, and from this comes His appetite to be served. The root cause of their reciprocal exchanges is the *gopīs*' predisposition to serve. An idea comes into their minds; then, just like a sprout appearing from a seed, both Kṛṣṇa and the *gopīs* come to know each others' desires and want to serve each other.

Śrīla Rūpa Gosvāmī explains this topic in *Bhakti-rasāmṛta-sindhu*, and Śrīla Viśvanātha Cakravartī also mentions it in his commentary. The desire to serve first comes in the heart of the heroine, but she does not openly express herself. Kṛṣṇa, the hero, knows her desire by her behavior, by her mood, or by an indication or sign. He can then speak openly, which arouses more longing in the heroine.

In this verse of *Gopī-gīta* the *gopīs* appear to speak openly, but in fact their deep moods are hidden. Śrīmatī Rādhikā is the full feature of *hlādinī-śakti* and the *gopīs* are the bodily manifestations of *hlādinī-śakti*. Thus they are extremely clever in loving matters. Kṛṣṇa is also highly proficient in loving matters, but the *gopīs*, and especially Śrīmatī Rādhikā, are much more expert than He is.

---

dvarād ayaṁ vadanatas tu bahiṣkṛtaś cen
nirvāti śīghram athavā laghutām upaiti

"Pure *prema* is like a lamp that burns steadily within the house of two lovers who know how to relish confidential mellows. If that lamp is taken outside through the door of the mouth – in other words, if the lovers speak about it – the flame of the lamp will be soon reduced and may even be extinguished."

In *Śrī Caitanya-caritāmṛta* (*Ādi-līlā* 4.124), Kṛṣṇa has admitted that Rādhikā is His *prema-guru*:

rādhikāra prema-guru, āmi śiṣya naṭa
sadā āmā nānā nṛtye nācāya udbhaṭa

The love of Rādhikā is My teacher, and I am Her dancing pupil. Her *prema* makes Me dance various novel dances.

In this connection, *Śrī Caitanya-caritāmṛta* (*Ādi-līlā* 4.125) and *Govinda-līlāmṛta* (8.77) record the following conversation that took place between Śrīmatī Rādhikā and Her friend Vṛndā:

kasmād vṛnde priya-sakhi hareḥ pāda-mūlāt kuto 'sau
kuṇḍāraṇye kim iha kurute nṛtya-śikṣāṁ guruḥ kaḥ
tvaṁ tvan-mūrtiḥ prati-taru-latāṁ dig-vidikṣu sphurantī
śailūṣīva bhramati parito nartayantī sva-paścāt

"O My beloved friend Vṛndā, where are you coming from?"
"I am coming from the feet of Śrī Hari."
"Where is He?"
"In the forest on the bank of Rādhā-kuṇḍa."
"What is He doing there?"
"He is learning dancing."
"Who is His master?"
"Your image, Rādhā, revealing itself in every tree and creeper in every direction, is roaming like a skillful dancer, making Him dance behind."

Śrīmatī Rādhikā and the *gopīs* are more accomplished and clever in expressing their *prema* than Śrī Kṛṣṇa is, and they employ many tricks and skills to satisfy His appetite for loving exchanges. Thus, when they tell Him, "Please place Your lotus feet on our breasts," their *prema* does not lessen.

We previously explained Śrī Cakravartī Ṭhākura's statement that someone who directly expresses his feelings by saying, "I love you," for example, exposes that his love is of an inferior quality. Worldly people may express themselves openly like this, but those who are immersed in transcendental love never speak in this way. The lover should inherently know that His beloved is full of love for Him.

Kṛṣṇa knows that the *gopīs* love Him. This is revealed at the end of *Gopī-gīta*, when He will again appear to them, and say:

na pāraye 'haṁ niravadya-saṁyujāṁ
sva-sādhu-kṛtyaṁ vibudhāyuṣāpi vaḥ
yā mābhajan durjara-geha-śṛṅkhalāḥ
saṁvṛścya tad vaḥ pratiyātu sādhunā
Śrīmad-Bhāgavatam (10.32.22)

> I am not able to repay My debt for your spotless service, even within a lifetime of Brahmā. Your connection with Me is beyond reproach. You have worshiped Me, cutting off all domestic ties, which are difficult to break. Therefore please let your own glorious deeds be your compensation.

When the *gopīs* hear this from Kṛṣṇa, they will ask Him, "Why do You remain indebted to us? Just give us what we want and Your debt will be cleared. When Pūtanā tried to kill You by putting poison on her breast, You gave her liberation and a position like that of Your mother. In the same way, You should also reward us accordingly." However, Kṛṣṇa will reply that this is impossible.

Why is it not possible for Him to repay the *gopīs*? In some instances, *prema* is split among many and in other instances it is fixed on one object only. Here, Kṛṣṇa means to say, "My *prema* is divided, not just into millions of parts but into uncountable parts. I have many types of devotees: *jñāni-bhaktas*, *śuddha-bhaktas*, *rasika-bhaktas*, *premi-bhaktas*, fathers, mothers, *sakhās*, and *sakhīs*. I cannot neglect any of them, even for Śrīmatī Rādhikā, who is superior to them all. I must drive the chariot of Arjuna and give My association to Bhīṣma-pitāmaha and Prahlāda. My love is divided into many fractions, but your love for Me is one-pointed. You give all of your love to Me, and there is none left for your children or husbands, what to speak of others. Because You do not love anyone but Me, I will always be indebted to you. Even if I were to offer you a boon, I know that you would only ask to be able to render more service to Me, and this would only increase My debt to you. For this reason, I will not be able to repay you in millions of births." One should try to love Kṛṣṇa as the *gopīs* do, desiring nothing for oneself.

We have just explained a confidential discussion that will take place between the *gopīs* and Kṛṣṇa in the next chapter of *Śrīmad-Bhāgavatam*, when Kṛṣṇa will again appear to them, and now we are returning to this chapter. Having left the *gopīs* so that He would be able to hear their expressions of pure love in separation from Him, Kṛṣṇa is now conversing with them in their hearts. There are many hidden meanings to their loving words, and they will be explained gradually.

The clever *gopīs* say, "Please place Your lotus feet on our breasts."

Kṛṣṇa replies, "This would be sinful. No one should act in this way. The very principle of religion (*dharma*) emanates from Me and follows Me. *Satyasya yonim̐ nihitam̐ ca satye* – all truth comes directly from Me and lives in Me. Moreover, I am the presiding Deity and personification of truth, so I cannot possibly perform any sinful act. If I act in an irreligious manner, others will do the same."

yad yad ācarati śreṣṭhas
tat tad evetaro janaḥ
sa yat pramāṇam̐ kurute
lokas tad anuvartate
Bhagavad-gītā (3.21)

> Whatever action a great man performs, common men follow. And whatever standards he sets by exemplary acts, all the world pursues.

Anticipating Kṛṣṇa's statement, the *gopīs* reply with the words *praṇata-dehinām̐ pāpa-karṣaṇam̐*. They say, "Anyone who remembers You, by taking shelter of Your name and pastimes, very easily becomes free from all sins."

It has been stated several times in *Śrīmad-Bhāgavatam* that one becomes free from the reaction to every kind of transgression just by chanting Kṛṣṇa's name, and we see this in the histories of Ajāmila and of Jagāi and Mādhāi. The *gopīs* continue, "One becomes free from sin simply by chanting Your name, so what benefit awaits one who takes shelter of Your lotus feet? If a person touches Your lotus feet, not a trace of vice can remain in him. Therefore, because we have surrendered to those lotus feet, we are without a trace of sin."

"That sin will come upon Me," Kṛṣṇa says.

The *gopīs* reply, "If You touch with Your lotus feet any corrupt person, he becomes completely free from all sin; so how is it possible that our sin will enter You?"

It is sometimes said that a bona fide *guru* has to suffer the reactions of his disciples' sins. What, then, would happen if he has hundreds and thousands of disciples? Will he then drown in an ocean of sin? Actually, if that *guru* possesses the qualifications of a genuine *guru*, this could not happen. Not even a trace of sin can come within the proximity of a pure, self-realized *guru*. On the contrary, if a disciple simply remembers his *gurudeva's* lotus feet, all of that disciple's sins and the reactions to those sins are burned. No trace of sin remains in him and all good qualities manifest in him. Even if the disciple does not remember and follow his *gurudeva* perfectly, his sins dissolve if his *gurudeva* simply wishes them to be eradicated. But for this to be possible, his *guru* must be fully qualified.

Just as no sin can touch Kṛṣṇa's pure representative, no sin can touch Kṛṣṇa. Now, hearing the *gopīs'* reply – that it is not possible for any sin or impurity to touch Him – He puts forward another playful argument: "Your breasts are so hard," He says. "I hesitate to place My soft lotus feet there."

The *gopīs* respond with the words *tṛṇa-carānugam*. *Tṛṇa-cara* refers to those who graze on grass. In this context, it refers specifically to cows that graze on mountain-grass, and where the earth is hard and full of stones and other sharp objects. "You are correct," the *gopīs* reply. "In comparison to Your lotus feet, our breasts are certainly hard. But we see that Your lotus feet follow the cows as they run over the mountains to graze. They wander where there are grass shoots, edges of dry grains, and small sharp stones, yet Your lotus feet feel very happy there. Why, then, are You not able to place Your lotus feet on our breasts, which are not nearly as rough and hard as those stones? We think You are only pretending."

Kṛṣṇa may then offer another argument: "Your hearts contain many sinful qualities, such as malice, the desire for sensual enjoyment, and so on. By My touching your bodies, these faults will be immediately transferred to Me."

Kṛṣṇa's arguments are only a pretense so as to hear more charming words of affection from the lotus lips of the *gopīs*. But it is certainly true of this world that by one's physical proximity to sinful persons, one may become contaminated by their qualities. Just as virtues come by good association (*sat-saṅga*), immorality and corruption are transmitted by bad association (*ku-saṅga*). Disease, for example, is carried by air and water. If we sit with someone who has a contagious disease like cholera, we may catch that disease from his breath. One may also contract some diseases simply by bathing in the same place in which a contagious person bathed.

Similarly, all qualities favorable for the development of *bhakti* increase automatically in one who takes the association of saintly devotees (*sādhu-saṅga*), and everything detrimental to *bhakti* comes automatically by unfavorable association.

In this world, if someone touches another person's feet, his vices are transferred to the person he touches. A second or third class Vaiṣṇava, whose *bhakti* is not so advanced, will receive the faults and sinful reactions of the person who puts his head at his feet or touches his feet. On the other hand, as we mentioned earlier, if the Vaiṣṇava is an *uttama-bhakta*, this will not happen. Rather, that perfect Vaiṣṇava will reform the person who touches his feet. If an ordinary person takes the *prasādam* remnants of a neophyte Vaiṣṇava, that person will imbibe the Vaiṣṇava's qualities and the neophyte Vaiṣṇava will imbibe that person's bad qualities. Again, in relation to the pure Vaiṣṇava, that does not apply.

In this regard, Śrīla Bhaktisiddhānta Sarasvatī Ṭhākura Prabhupāda tells a story of a man drowning in a deep river. The man was crying out, "Save me! Save me!" but no boat was in sight. Another man, standing on the river bank, was watching him and thinking, "I cannot swim. If I try to rescue him, he will catch hold of me and I will drown before he does." The import is that the neophyte devotee who is in the role of *guru* should be merciful to sense enjoyers and try to attract them to the path of *bhakti*, but very skillfully. If he is not careful, both *guru* and disciple will drown. First the *guru* will drown, and then the disciple. One may argue that a disciple is already a recipient of his *guru's* mercy, so why must the *guru* be affected if the disciple takes his remnants? Yet, Śrīla Rūpa Gosvāmī, Śrīla Sanātana Gosvāmī, and all of our *ācāryas* have said that to give *dīkṣā* initiation to unqualified persons is *nāma-aparādha*. The scriptures state, "Do not accept unqualified disciples."[3]

Now, in Śrī Kṛṣṇa's loving conversation with the *gopīs*, He may argue, "You have no wisdom, intelligence, or discrimination, so I cannot place My feet on your breasts. It is inappropriate for Me to even associate with you ignorant girls."

In this regard, Śrīla Jīva Gosvāmī gives an additional meaning to the words *tṛṇa-carānugam*. *Tṛṇa-cara* refers to cows and other animals that have little or no wisdom. If cows are offered high quality sweets like *rasagullā* and *rabrī*, they will smell them and then leave them alone. But they always like to eat grass, even if it is dry. If cows or other animals are given a little grass on the way to the slaughter house, they quarrel among themselves for it. Unaware of their imminent slaughter, they squabble with each other over some insignificant grass, while doing nothing to save themselves.

Thus, when the *gopīs* utter the words *tṛṇa-carānugam*, their retort also has this meaning: "We know that we are foolish," they say, "but we are not as foolish as the cows, who do not know the difference between grass and tasty edibles. We may be ignorant to some extent, but we are more qualified than they are. You follow the cows, so what is the harm in Your following us and placing Your lotus feet on our breasts?"

The *gopīs*' mood is so deep that they weep as they speak, whereas we simply hear their words and smile. We are unable to perceive their pain in separation from Kṛṣṇa. We can intellectually understand

---

3 "To make many disciples in order to accumulate wealth and increase one's pride and prestige is one of the principal obstacles on the path of *bhakti*. In his commentary on *Śrī Bhakti-rasāmṛta-sindhu* (1.2.113) Śrīla Jīva Gosvāmī has written that one should not accept many unqualified persons as disciples, even for the purpose of expanding the *sampradāya*: *sva-sva-sampradāya vṛddhy-artham anadhikāriṇo 'pi na saṅgṛhnīyāt*. To make many disciples one will have to accept many unqualified persons whose hearts are devoid of *śraddhā*. To make disciples of faithless persons is an offence, which presents obstacles in the practice of one's *bhajana*, and ultimately one will have to fall down into hell" (*Śrī Bhakti-rasāmṛta-sindhu-bindu*, Verse Four, *Śrī Bindu-vikāśinī-vṛtti*).

their logic and arguments to a small degree, but we lack the spiritual sensitivity to perceive the depth of their emotions. We cannot actually comprehend the exchange of moods between the *gopīs* and Kṛṣṇa as they converse. Still, even though we lack realization, if we continue to do *anuśīlana* (reading and hearing under the guidance of a qualified *tattva-jña-rasika-guru*[4]), one day we will certainly acquire taste and transcendental greed. At that time we will be able to really hear the depth of their words, and we will be able to experience their mood of separation from Kṛṣṇa.

Absorbed in the *gopīs*' repeated entreaty to place His lotus feet on their breasts, Kṛṣṇa next argues, "I cannot place My lotus feet on your breasts, because your breasts are decorated with so many valuable, golden ornaments."

To this the *gopīs* reply with the words *śrī-niketanam*, which have two meanings. When the emphasis is placed on *niketanam*, the phrase *śrī-niketanam* refers to Śrī Kṛṣṇa's feet being the abode (*niketanam*), of beauty (*śrī*). In that regard the *gopīs* say, "Yes, we admit that our breasts are decorated with many lovely ornaments, but we know that Your lotus feet are the very abode of all kinds of beauty, softness, and other pleasing attributes; they are the abode of all six auspicious qualities. We believe that our beauty has also come from Your lotus feet, so we want Your feet to become the greatest ornament of our breasts."

When the emphasis is placed on *śrī*, the phrase *śrī-niketanam* signifies that Śrī, or Lakṣmī, is the abode (*niketana*) of Kṛṣṇa's lotus feet. In this regard the *gopīs* imply, "If You are not willing to place Your lotus feet on our bodies, why do You place them on the heart of Śrī Lakṣmī? She always keeps them on Her heart in a spirit of service to You. If You can keep them on her heart, then why not on ours?"

Kṛṣṇa responds, "Why should I keep them on yours?"

"Because we are *gopīs* and You are a *gopa*. Lakṣmī is not a *gopī*, yet You keep Your feet there. Having taken birth in the *gopa* dynasty, we have that birthright."

---

4 *Tattva-jña* means one who has full knowledge of *tattva* or the essential philosophical principles, reality, and truth. *Rasika* means one who is expert in relishing *rasa*.

It is a fact that Śrīmatī Lakṣmī-devī does not leave Lord Nārāyaṇa's lotus feet, not even for a moment, and there is a reason for this. Once, in the form Vāmanadeva, Lord Nārāyaṇa visited the palace of Bali Mahārāja in order to trick him into giving up his kingdom. Bali Mahārāja's kingdom consisted of the entire universe of fourteen worlds: the upper planetary systems of Bhūr, Bhuvar, Svar, Mahar, Janas, Tapas, and Satya, as well as the seven lower planetary systems. Lord Nārāyaṇa retrieved that entire kingdom.

In the presence of Lord Brahmā and Prahlāda Mahārāja, Lord Nārāyaṇa gave the planet of Sutala to Bali Mahārāja and invited Śrī Prahlāda to stay for some time in Bali Mahārāja's palace. Upon hearing this, Prahlāda whispered something in Bali Mahārāja's ear that obviously pleased him. Bali Mahārāja then turned to Lord Nārāyaṇa and said, "You have given me Sutala as my residence, and I will obey Your order, but I beg something else from You. Please stay with me there. The palace there has fifty doors, and I humbly request You to be at whatever door I pass through, whether I am entering or leaving. In this way, I will always be able to see You." Lord Nārāyaṇa agreed to this, and thus He remained in Bali Mahārāja's palace.

Time passed, and Lakṣmī began to wonder why her husband had not returned. "My Prabhu left quite some time ago to trick Bali," she thought, "but still He has not returned home. Where can He be?" Suddenly, Śrī Nārada Muni appeared before her, and she inquired about her husband's whereabouts from him.

Nārada related what had taken place. He explained how Lord Nārāyaṇa had tricked Bali Mahārāja, and how Bali had in turn 'tricked' Lord Nārāyaṇa so that He was unable to leave Bali's palace.

"Please tell me what I should do," Lakṣmī said. Then, under Nārada's instruction, Lakṣmī assumed the form of an old and poor, but very beautiful, *brāhmaṇa* lady, and went to Bali Mahārāja's palace when he was giving charity. Amid the clamor of the occasion, Bali Mahārāja saw that an elderly lady had entered the palace and was sitting quietly and patiently on a bench at the back of the assembly.

While everyone else was pushing forward and jostling each other to take as much charity as they could from him, that *brāhmaṇa* lady simply sat silently. Bali Mahārāja thought, "That *brāhmaṇī* cannot be an ordinary lady, because she is sitting and waiting so patiently. No common person can do this; she must be someone extraordinary."

Descending from his throne, he approached the lady and offered his obeisances. "O Mother," he said. "Who are you and what do you want? It appears that you have a desire for something, but for some reason you are not expressing it. It seems to me that You are seeking an opportunity to see me after everyone else has left. Please tell me what You want."

"Yes," she said. "I have come to ask for something, but I am afraid you will not give it to me."

"I will give you anything you ask for."

"Is that for certain?"

"Yes, I will definitely give you whatever you ask for."

"Do you give your word that you will do that?"

"Yes, I give my word."

When Bali Mahārāja had promised three times that he will give her what she would ask for, Lakṣmī sought further, "You must vow to give me whatever I ask for. Will you do this?" Upon hearing these words, Bali Mahārāja remembered how Lord Nārāyaṇa in the form of Vāmanadeva had made the same request to him.

"Who are you?" he asked.

She remained silent and did not reply. Finally he said, "Very well, please tell me what you want."

Without saying a word, that *brāhmaṇī* simply pointed toward Śrī Vāmanadeva, at which moment Bali Mahārāja recognized her as Lakṣmī. He became simultaneously overjoyed and sorrowful, fearing that he would now lose his Lord.

Bali prayed, "O Śrī Nārāyaṇa, Lakṣmī-devī has come to take You away," he said. "But I cannot bear the thought of You leaving. Please make some type of arrangement so that You can simultaneously live here and with Lakṣmī."

Lord Nārāyaṇa manifested a second form that would remain with Bali Mahārāja, and then, in His original form, He returned to Vaikuṇṭha. From that time on, Lakṣmī has been afraid that He might leave her again, and she therefore always holds His feet on her lap and heart.

Now, with the words *śrī-niketanam*, the *gopīs* emphasize the word *śrī*, which refers to Lakṣmī. In this instance *śrī-niketanam* means "Lakṣmī's lap is the abode of Your lotus feet." They question Kṛṣṇa, "Since Your lotus feet are the ornaments of Lakṣmī's breasts, why can they not ornament ours? They should become the ornament of our hearts."

Kṛṣṇa replies, "You are begging Me to do this, but I cannot. Your hearts are burning with too much heat, and if I place My feet on them, that heat will enter My feet and they will be burnt."

The *gopīs* respond with the words *phaṇi-phaṇārpitam*. They say, "But You placed Your soft, sweet lotus feet on the hoods of the Kāliya serpent, even though He was biting Your chest, feet, and other tender parts of Your body. You did not feel any burning sensation then. You even boldly placed Your feet on his hoods and performed a wondrous dance there, so why not place Your feet on our breasts?"

Now, although the *gopīs* have defeated all of Kṛṣṇa's arguments, He continues presenting His own reasoning, and tells them, "I cannot do that; I am afraid of your husbands."

"You were not afraid of Kāliya, so we know You cannot possibly be afraid of our husbands. And even if they do disturb You, You will punish them, just as You punished Kāliya."

Te padāmbujam means 'Your lotus feet.' The *gopīs* continue, "Your lotus feet have so many beautiful qualities." "*Kṛṇu kuceṣu naḥ kṛndhi hṛc-chayam* – please, place them on our breasts and remove the fire of *kāma* in our hearts. The fire of separation and the longing in our hearts will only subside if we meet with You and You perform cherishable pastimes with us." Sometimes a sick person will apply a medicinal balm or ointment externally to cure a disease inside the body. Similarly, in this verse the *gopīs* beg Kṛṣṇa to soothe the fire of separation in their hearts by the ointment of the touch of His lotus feet.

The deep meaning here is that the intense heat of *kāma* actually lies in Śrī Kṛṣṇa's heart, and the *gopīs* long for it to be relieved. But this will not happen unless they meet with Him directly, and this is the real motivation for their proposal. When Kṛṣṇa finally meets with them, the heat of *kāma* will leave His heart and the *gopīs*' state of mind, expressed here, will automatically subside.

Verse Eight

Our complete bewilderment is a serious malady which only You can treat. You are the only doctor to cure us of our critical condition, and the ambrosia of Your lotus lips is the only medicine.

Verse 8

मधुरया गिरा वल्गुवाक्यया
बुधमनोज्ञया पुष्करेक्षण।
विधिकरीरिमा वीर मुह्यतीर्
अधरसीधुनाप्याययस्व नः ॥८॥

madhurayā girā valgu-vākyayā
budha-manojñayā puṣkarekṣana
vidhi-karīr imā vīra muhyatīr
adhara-sīdhunāpyāyayasva naḥ

madhurayā – sweet; *girā* – by Your voice; *valgu* – charming; *vākyayā* – by Your words; *budha* – to the intelligent; *mano-jñayā* – attractive; *puṣkara* – lotus; *īkṣaṇa* – You whose eyes; *vidhi-karīḥ* – maidservants; *imāḥ* – these; *vīra* – O hero; *muhyatīḥ* – becoming bewildered; *adhara* – of Your lips; *sīdhunā* – with the nectar; *āpyāyayasva* – please restore to life; *naḥ* – us.

Translation

O lotus-eyed one, we are bewildered by Your sweet voice, replete with enchanting words that capture even the minds of scholars who are clever and expert in *rasa*. O hero, we *gopīs* are Your maidservants who carry out Your every order. Please restore our lives with the divine ambrosia of Your lips.

Bhāva-prakāśika Vṛtti

With the words *madhurayā girā*, the *gopīs* tell Kṛṣṇa, "Whatever You utter is exceedingly sweet." By speaking the words *valgu-vākyayā*, they tell Him, "Your words are enchanting." *Vidhi* means 'order,' and *vidhi-karīḥ* means 'obedient maidservant.' By these words the *gopīs* say, "We will do everything You tell us to do."

Muhyatīḥ has the same root as the word *moha*, meaning 'illusion.' As soon as a person is in illusion, he cannot distinguish between good and bad, and at times he cannot even function properly. For example, Arjuna became bewildered on the battlefield of Kurukṣetra when his chariot was situated between the two armies. "What should I do?" he wondered, "and what should I not do?" *Muhyatīḥ* implies transcendental bewilderment, which, in its tenth stage (*daśama-daśā*)[1], is like death. *Muhyatīḥ* may also mean 'senseless, as in a faint.'

When we contemplate the two phrases, *madhurayā girā*, 'Your sweet words,' and *adhara-sīdhunā*, 'the nectar of Your lips,' we may ask, "Do they share the same meaning, or is there a difference between them?" The *gopīs*, spellbound by Kṛṣṇa's sweet words, now thirst for the nectar of His lips. But Kṛṣṇa's words are also like nectar. What do the *gopīs* really want? Are they begging Kṛṣṇa to speak further?

Śrīla Viśvanātha Cakravartī Ṭhākura says that only one who receives the mercy of the *gopīs* can understand their thoughts and words. Thus, one can enter deeply into these topics if one has the association of a *rasika* Vaiṣṇava, who has realized the *gopīs'* hearts.

---

1 "*Pūrva-rāga* is fully matured when it occurs in those possessed of *samarthā-rati*. On this level of *pūrva-rāga*, the ten *daśās* (states) beginning from intense longing up to the desire for death can manifest. Since this *pūrva-rāga* is fully matured, the states that manifest in it are also fully matured" (*Jaiva-dharma*, Chapter 37).

"The ten states are intense longing, anxiety, sleeplessness, emaciation, inertia, impatience, illness, madness, delusion, and longing for death" (*Ujjvala-nīlamaṇi*, *Pūrva-rāga* division, 9).

Śrīla Jīva Gosvāmī explains that the *gopīs* have drunk the nectar of Kṛṣṇa's words, which are sweet, melodic, and brimming with literary ornaments (*alaṅkāra*) and exquisite imports. They tell Kṛṣṇa, "Our complete bewilderment is a serious malady, which only You can treat. You are the only doctor to cure us of our critical condition, and the ambrosia of Your lotus lips is the only medicine." With these words they imply that their bewilderment is so sweet that they want to experience it further.

In the previous verse the *gopīs* prayed to Kṛṣṇa to place His lotus feet on their breasts, as an ointment. They wanted this ointment to treat the bewitched and feverish condition that had resulted from their tasting the nectar of Kṛṣṇa's words, but then their mere remembrance of the treatment rapidly increased their disease. Now they pray, "Ointment, which is applied externally, will not do. We need to drink the remedy that will cure us. If You do not give us the nectar of Your lips, we will surely die."

They anticipate that Kṛṣṇa would then ask, "Why will you die?" and thus they begin their reply:

"We recall Your gentle words full of sweetness and various intentions," they say.

The speaker's tone of voice reveals his intended meaning. For example, the words 'You are not a thief' carries quite a clear meaning, but those same words spoken with a tone of sarcasm can actually mean 'You are certainly a thief.' In this way the spoken word may have several different meanings.

Śrīmad-Bhāgavatam and other transcendental literatures were written in a particular tone and with the intention of conveying a particular meaning. That meaning can be known only if the author himself explains it or reveals it to us. For example, when Kṛṣṇa left Vṛndāvana to reside in Mathurā, He sent Uddhava to Vṛndāvana with a message for the *gopīs*. The words in that message carried so many meanings that it was not possible for Uddhava to discern Kṛṣṇa's intended meaning. He may have been able to understand it to a certain extent and in a certain way, but there is a vast gulf of difference between his understanding and that of the *gopīs*.

Another example of this is the way in which Śrī Caitanya Mahāprabhu explained the sixty-four diverse meanings of the *Śrīmad-Bhāgavatam verse:*

ātmārāmāś ca munayo
nirgranthā apy urukrame
kurvanty ahaitukīṁ bhaktim
ittham-bhūta-guṇo hariḥ
Śrīmad-Bhāgavatam (1.7.10)

All different varieties of *ātmārāmas* (those who take pleasure in *ātmā*, or spirit self), especially those established on the path of self-realization, though freed from all kinds of material bondage, desire to render unalloyed devotional service unto the Personality of Godhead. This means that the Lord possesses transcendental qualities and therefore can attract everyone, including liberated souls.

Śrī Caitanya Mahāprabhu explained this verse to Sārvabhauma Bhaṭṭācārya who, although one of the best scholars in the world at that time, could only explain it in nine different ways. Speaking in a variety of moods and tones, Mahāprabhu enlightened him with numerous other meanings of the verse.

It is because of Kṛṣṇa's expertise in speaking that the *gopīs* now address Him with the words *madhurayā-girā valgu-vakhyayā*, which mean that His sweet words are filled with various charming and profound meanings.

Another instance of His sweet and enchanting speech occurred earlier that same evening, when He had called the *gopīs* by the melody of His flute. Upon hearing His alluring flute-song, the *gopīs* immediately abandoned all their household tasks and duties and ran into the forest – in whatever state they were in at that time.

When they first arrived, Kṛṣṇa told them:

svāgataṁ vo mahā-bhāgāḥ
priyaṁ kiṁ karavāṇi vaḥ
vrajasyānāmayaṁ kaccid
brūtāgamana-kāraṇam
Śrīmad-Bhāgavatam (10.29.18)

> O most fortunate ladies, welcome. What may I do to please you? Is everything well in Vraja? Please tell Me the reason for your coming here.

The words *mahā-bhāgāḥ* mean 'greatly fortunate.' Why did Kṛṣṇa use these words to describe the *gopīs*? Let us consider what had taken place prior to this, namely Śri Kṛṣṇa calling the *gopīs* from their homes by His flute-song, and what was about to happen, namely *rāsa-līlā*. After Kṛṣṇa addressed them as greatly fortunate, He told them, "Do not delay, O chaste ladies; return to your husbands at once. The duty of a virtuous woman is to serve her husband under all circumstances, regardless of whether his character is good or bad. He may be rich or poor, beautiful and highly qualified, or lame and ugly, but still she must serve him. It is her religious duty (*dharma*) to do so."

Why did Kṛṣṇa first welcome the *gopīs* and then tell them to go? What was the hidden intention behind His words? Our understanding of the words *mahā-bhāgāḥ* (greatly fortunate), spoken by Kṛṣṇa to the *gopīs* depends on our level of realization, and it follows that our explanation will be in accordance with this.

Śrīmad-Bhāgavatam (10.8.46) also refers to Śrīmatī Yaśodā-devī and Nanda Bābā as *mahā-bhāgā*:

> *nandaḥ kim akarod brahman*
> *śreya evaṁ mahodayam*
> *yaśodā ca mahā-bhāgā*
> *papau yasyāḥ stanaṁ hariḥ*

> Having heard of the great fortune of mother Yaśodā, Parīkṣit Mahārāja inquired from Śukadeva Gosvāmī: O learned *brāhmaṇa*, mother Yaśodā's breast milk was sucked by the Supreme Personality of Godhead. What past auspicious activities did she and Nanda Mahārāja perform to achieve such perfection in ecstatic love?

Although Kṛṣṇa is the Supreme Personality of Godhead, Yaśodā-devī regularly gave Him her breast milk, which He would drink without satiation. "Kṛṣṇa is a helpless baby," Mother Yaśodā considered, "and quite ignorant in all respects. If I do not support and nourish

Him, He may die." Because of this sentiment, Mother Yaśodā, has been called *mahā-bhāgā*.

Why does Kṛṣṇa address the *gopīs* as *mahā-bhāgā*? The *gopīs* are the crest-jewel among all the residents of Vraja. They satisfy Him eternally, in every way. No one else can serve Him as they do, and He realizes this. As a professor examines his students, Śrī Kṛṣṇa was examining the *gopīs*. However, when this 'professor' heard the responses of His 'students,' He became astonished. He realized that they were more elevated than He was, and that He could never reach their level. His intention was to test their love, but instead He became dumbfounded and bewildered. The *gopīs* had left their homes and all material considerations for His sake; no one else could do such a thing. He was astounded by this, and therefore He called them *mahā-bhāgāḥ*.

Svāgatam (*su-āgatam*) means 'your arrival is auspicious,' so it is generally translated as 'welcome.' In this instance, however, it does not mean 'welcome.' Kṛṣṇa was questioning the *gopīs*: "Is your arrival here due to some auspicious or inauspicious occurrence? Have you come here because of a terrible incident in your house? Or maybe there has been an accident? Has there been a disastrous storm, flood, or fire? Or, has Bakāsura, Aghāsura, or any other demon attacked your fathers, mothers, or other relatives? Is this why you have come here, weeping and upset?"

The word *svāgatam* indirectly refers to Kṛṣṇa's longing. He and the *gopīs* both longed to perform amorous pastimes (*vilāsa*) with each other, and both desired the other to be the first to speak about it. This was the reason for His ambiguity here. As is the case with worldly lovers, He wanted the *gopīs* to be the first to say, "This is what we want." He was waiting for their hearts to be expressed with their words, but the *gopīs* had the same wish. They felt, "Kṛṣṇa called us here, so He should be the first to speak frankly."

Both sides watched and waited, but the nature of *prema* is so deep that it cannot be stated openly. If *prema* is expressed openly, by saying, "I love you, I cannot live without you," it is extinguished, for it burns in the hearts of both the hero and the heroine like a lamp. If that lamp remains within the home of their heart, it burns without flickering and emits an excellent light. On the other hand, if it is kept in an open doorway, a breeze is likely to extinguish it.

This is also true for a devotee, even one in the stage of practice. In *Prema-bhakti-candrikā* (Song 9, Verse 19[2]), Śrīla Narottama dāsa Ṭhākura warns *sādhakas* on all levels that one should not disclose one's *bhajana*. *Bhakti* is like camphor in the sense that it evaporates if left in an open place. If a devotee openly tells others, "I am chanting so many rounds. I love Kṛṣṇa. I have so much *bhakti*," his *bhakti* will at once disappear. If anyone asks a truly advanced *sādhaka* about his realizations, he will say, "Oh, I do not have even a trace of *prema*."

Śrī Caitanya Mahāprabhu set the example of this by uttering:

na prema-gandho 'sti darāpi me harau
Caitanya-caritāmṛta (*Madhya-līlā* 2.45)

> My dear friends, I have not the slightest tinge of love of Godhead within My heart.

A true devotee will say, "Looking in my own heart, I find not a scent of *bhakti*, not even a scent of *sādhana-bhakti*. Not a single holy name I chant is actually the pure name (*śuddha-nāma*)." In *Śrī Caitanya-caritāmṛta* it is said that if a devotee is chanting the holy name, but no tears are coming to his eyes and his heart is not melting, this is due to offenses:

'kṛṣṇa-nāma' kare aparādhera vicāra
kṛṣṇa balile aparādhīra nā haya vikāra
Caitanya-caritāmṛta (*Ādi-līlā* 8.24)

> There are offenses to be considered while chanting the Hare Kṛṣṇa *mantra*. Therefore simply by chanting Hare Kṛṣṇa one does not become ecstatic.

We may contemplate this verse and consider whether or not we are chanting *śuddha-nāma*. When *nāma* (the holy name) is pure, it is

---

2 "I will not speak about topics of my internal service here and there without discrimination. Be extremely careful in this regard. Don't become angry. Don't find fault with others. Offer obeisances to the devotees' feet."

one in quality with *nāmī* (the possessor of the name). Śrī Caitanya Mahāprabhu once said, "My Gurudeva told Me, 'You are ignorant, and therefore You are not qualified to read Vedānta. You should just chant *hari-nāma.*' He then told Me this verse:

harer nāma harer nāma
harer nāmaiva kevalam
kalau nāsty eva nāsty eva
nāsty eva gatir anyathā
Caitanya-caritāmṛta (*Ādi-līlā* 17.21)

> In this Age of Kali there is no other means, no other means, no other means for self-realization than chanting the holy name, chanting the holy name, chanting the holy name of Lord Hari.

"Then he gave Me a *mantra*, the *gopāla-mantra*," Mahāprabhu continued, "and he told Me, 'Accept this *mantra* as non-different from Kṛṣṇa. It is Kṛṣṇa Himself; have no doubt about this.' I began to do as My Gurudeva told Me, and soon a beautiful young cowherd boy came within My vision. I ran to catch hold of Him, but He hid Himself. I ran towards Him again, and I was just about to catch Him when, all of a sudden, He vanished. I fell down and wept bitterly, and when He appeared to Me again, I began to laugh. Whenever I chant this *mantra*, various incidents like this take place, and many transformations appear in My body and heart."

This is the standard of chanting real *hari-nāma.*

A true *sādhaka* thinks in this way: "Although I have been chanting for many years, no spiritual symptoms appear within my heart. I tell myself and others that I am a Vaiṣṇava, but actually I am not. I do everything for my own interest so that others will praise me. Although I have many bad qualities, I do not want anyone to talk about them, and I become furious if anyone points them out and discusses them. When I consider all these facts, I can understand what kind of devotee I am." This is the mood taught to us by Śrīla Bhaktivinoda Ṭhākura and Śrīla Narottama dāsa Ṭhākura, whose humility is revealed in their writings. They were perfect in self-realization, and yet they judged the level of their *bhakti* in this way.

Śrīla Narottama dāsa Ṭhākura has written a beautiful song which aptly describes this mood, the first and last verses of which are as follows:

gorā pahuṅ nā bhajiyā mainu
prema-ratana-dhana helāya hārāinu
Prārthanā, Ākṣepa (Song 42, Verse 1)

Alas! Failing to worship Śrī Gaurasundara, I have neglected that most precious treasure of *prema* and lost it.

kena vā āchaye prāṇa ki sukha pāiyā
narottama dāsa kena nā gela mariyā
Prārthanā, Ākṣepa (Song 42, Verse 5)

Why am I living? What is the standard of my happiness? Narottama dāsa says, "Why did I not die long ago?"

In this *kīrtana*, Śrīla Narottama dāsa Ṭhākura expresses, in a very soulful mood, a heartbreaking scene. When we sing this *kīrtana*, however, we do not weep, and repentance does not appear in our hearts. This is our problem.

In his humility, Śrīla Bhaktivinoda Ṭhākura has written: "*He gopīnātha, āmi to' kāmera dāsa* – O Gopīnātha, beloved of the *gopīs*, I am the most faithful servant of lust." Has he told an untruth, or has spoken honestly about his feelings? The answer is that when *bhakti* comes, these genuine feelings of humility also come. Although immersed in pure devotion, Śrīla Bhaktivinoda Ṭhākura really feels that there is no *bhakti* in his heart. Such great devotees compare their own *bhakti* with the *mahā-bhāva* of Śrīmatī Rādhikā and the *gopīs*, and think, "Where is my *prema*? I have no *prema*, nothing at all." They feel and act as if they are on the level of needing to practice *sādhana-bhakti*, but in fact they are spiritually perfect.

Śrī Caitanya Mahāprabhu once wrote a commentary on *nyāya* (the theory of logic). At that time, Raghunandana had also written a commentary, which he deemed superior to all others. One day, as he and Caitanya Mahāprabhu were traveling together in a boat, they discussed the commentaries they had each written.

Raghunandana was very curious to see Caitanya Mahāprabhu's commentary and asked to look at it. Śrī Caitanya Mahāprabhu gave it to him to read and, as he read, Raghunandana began to weep. Mahāprabhu asked why he was weeping, and Raghunandana replied that no one would appreciate his own commentary after reading the commentary of Mahāprabhu. Raghunandana was disheartened because he had considered himself to be a great logician.

Mahāprabhu had not come to this world to show everyone His erudition as a great logician. Furthermore, He did not want to disturb Raghunandana. For these reasons, He threw His own commentary into the Gaṅgā. He did not consider His own commentary to be so important, yet Raghunandana understood, "His commentary is far better than mine."

Similarly, if we compare ourselves with any pure devotee, we will understand our lowly position. Although we may be chanting and performing many aspects of *kṛṣṇa-bhajana*, when we can truthfully compare ourselves with Śrīla Bhaktivinoda Ṭhākura, Śrīla Kṛṣṇadāsa Kavirāja Gosvāmī, Śrīla Raghunātha dāsa Gosvāmī, Śrīla Rūpa Gosvāmī, and with our own Gurudeva, we will see that we do not have even a particle of *bhakti*. When we honestly compare ourselves with elevated devotees, we will be humbled. As long as we do not do so, we will think, "I am such a good devotee. I am preaching so well; in fact, I am preaching more than my Gurudeva."

Actually, only a *madhyama-adhikārī* can think, "I am worthless in comparison to these elevated devotees." The *kaniṣṭha-adhikārī* (third-class devotee) cannot think in this way, nor can he even imagine such contemplation. The *uttama-adhikārī* considers, "Everyone in this world is a greater devotee than I. Everyone is my *guru*." If the *uttama-adhikārī* gives initiation and makes disciples, it is understood that he is playing the role of a *madhyama-adhikārī* and is seeing everyone from the *madhyama* perspective.

In conclusion, a genuine devotee will not reveal his *bhajana* to others. The pure devotee will naturally not do this, and it is essential for the *sādhaka* not to do it as well. If someone tells others, "I love Kṛṣṇa; my *bhajana* is so strong," his *bhakti* will evaporate, just as camphor evaporates in an open doorway.

We have been discussing this topic because of its relevance to the theme of Śrī Kṛṣṇa's exchanges with the *gopīs* – the indirect imports in their loving words. If the words "I love you; I cannot live without you" are spoken, the beauty of that sentiment vanishes. Such love is third-class.

Even so, Śrī Kṛṣṇa, the *nāyaka* (hero), wants to be the first to hear the *gopīs*, the *nāyikās* (heroines), speak these charming words, which are like an elixir. And the *gopīs* also want to be the first to drink that nectar. The moods of both the *nāyaka* and *nāyikā* are very profound.

After welcoming the *gopīs* to Vaṁśī-vaṭa and addressing them as greatly fortunate, Śrī Kṛṣṇa asked them, "*Priyaṁ kiṁ karavāṇi vaḥ* – what may I do to please you?" His mood here seemed in contrast to the words He spoke next:

rajany eṣā ghora-rūpā
ghora-sattva-niṣevitā
pratiyāta vrajaṁ neha
stheyaṁ strībhiḥ su-madhyamāḥ
Śrīmad-Bhāgavatam (10.29.19)

This night is quite frightening, and frightening creatures are lurking about. Return to Vraja, slender-waisted girls. This is not a proper place for women.

The external meaning of His words is this: "You should go. The night is fearsome (*ghora*), and there are many ferocious creatures (*ghora-sattva*) roaming about." According to the rules for the conjunction of letters in Sanskrit grammar, this can also have the opposite meaning: "The night is not at all fearsome (*aghora*), and the animals are not even slightly ferocious (*aghora-sattva*)." The learned *gopīs* understood that Kṛṣṇa's words had two meanings: "You must go" and "You must not go."

It is the mood of the person speaking that determines the meaning of his words, and for this reason Kṛṣṇa assumed a mood of gravity in an attempt to show His seriousness. Even so, the *gopīs* understood that He wanted them to stay. They felt, "He is indirectly begging something from us; He is speaking something in our favor." They waited there, thinking, "He should tell us directly what He wants."

In *Śrī Vidagdha-Mādhava* (5.31) Śrīla Rūpa Gosvāmī cites an example of Śrī Kṛṣṇa openly revealing His desire. Kṛṣṇa told Śrīmatī Rādhikā, "*Kaṭhorā bhava mṛdvī vā prāṇās tvam asi rādhike asti nānyā cakorasya candra-lekhāṁ vinā gatiḥ* – O Rādhikā, You may be harsh or gentle. Your face may express a sweet mood or it may express a mood of sulky anger. In Your sulky anger, You may not listen to Me even if I offer My head at Your lotus feet and beg You to stay here. Instead, You will ready Yourself to leave. Whatever You may do, O Rādhikā, You will always be My life and soul."

There is a bird known as *cakora*, who only drinks the rays of the moon. If it could not drink the moon-rays, this bird would die, for the moon is its life and soul. In His prayer to Śrīmatī Rādhikā, Kṛṣṇa was comparing Himself to that bird.

In his *Stava-mālā*, Śrīla Rūpa Gosvāmī expresses a similar mood:

viracaya mayi daṇḍaṁ dīna-bandho dayāṁ vā
gatir iha na bhavattaḥ kācid anyā mamāsti
nipatatu śata-koṭir nirmalaṁ vā navāmbhas
tad api kila payodaḥ stūyate cātakena

O Lord of the poor, You may do what You like with me. You may give me mercy or You may punish me. In any case, I have no one to look to in this world besides Your Lordship. I am just like the *cātaka* bird, who always prays for the cloud, regardless of whether that cloud showers rain or throws a thunderbolt.

The meaning expressed herein is this: "Although I am dishonest and my behavior is nefarious, I have no goal but to attain You. I am like the *cātaka* bird who watches longingly the clouds in the sky, equally regardless of the threat of a very dangerous thunderbolt or the promise of sweet, thirst-quenching drops of *rohiṇī-nakṣatra*[3] rain."

In this same mood, Kṛṣṇa would tell Śrīmatī Rādhikā, "Whether You are in a contrary mood or a submissive mood, You are My very life and soul." He would utter enchanting words like these to the *gopīs*, and now, as they search everywhere for Him, they recall, "How gently, softly, and sweetly He spoke to us."

---

[3] The stellar constellation named Rohiṇī in Vedic astronomy.

It is stated in the previous chapter of *Śrīmad-Bhāgavatam*:

gatyānurāga-smita-vibhramekṣitair
mano-ramālāpa-vihāra-vibhramaiḥ
Śrīmad-Bhāgavatam (10.30.2)

As the cowherd women remembered Lord Kṛṣṇa, their hearts were overwhelmed by His movements and loving smiles, His playful glances and enchanting talks, and by the many other pastimes He would enjoy with them.

gati-smita-prekṣaṇa-bhāṣaṇādiṣu
priyāḥ priyasya pratirūḍha-mūrtayaḥ
asāv ahaṁ tv ity abalās tad-ātmikā
nyavediṣuḥ kṛṣṇa-vihāra-vibhramāḥ
Śrīmad-Bhāgavatam (10.30.3)

Because the beloved *gopīs* were absorbed in thoughts of their beloved Kṛṣṇa, their bodies imitated His way of moving and smiling, His way of beholding them, His speech and His other distinctive features. Deeply immersed in thinking of Him and maddened by remembering His pastimes, they declared to one another, "I am Kṛṣṇa!"

These verses describe some of the symptoms of the *gopīs*. The true *sādhaka* does *anusaraṇa* of their moods, which means that he serves Śrī Kṛṣṇa under their guidance. There are two words in this connection: *anusaraṇa*, which means 'to follow,' and *anukaraṇa*, which means 'to imitate.' We want to follow, not to imitate. According to our ability and our level of spiritual qualification, we want to be able to follow those who are superior to us in *bhakti*; we do not wish to merely imitate them.

For example, we should not imitate the way our *gurudeva* wears a turban, the way he walks, or the way he carries a stick. We need not have the type of car he has, or the fact that he has a motor-car in Vṛndāvana, another one in Māyāpura, and others in the West. There is no benefit in imitating him by wearing eye-glasses with the same golden frames as his. Rather, we aspire to follow our *guru*'s teachings according to our qualification.

The two verses above describe the *gopīs'* remembrance of their beloved Kṛṣṇa. The word *gati* indicates their reminiscence of His attractive way of walking. The *gopīs* had seen His charming threefold bending form when He stood under the shade of a *kadamba* tree, His back leaning against it, and they now remember how He smiled as He called them by playing an ambrosial melody on His flute. With His eyes, He revealed everything He wanted from them at that time.

"We saw You," the *gopīs* say, "and we became bewildered. Now we do not know what to do and what not to do."

As conditioned souls, we can speak about Kṛṣṇa's smile, but a *gopī*, who has actually seen that smile, especially as Kṛṣṇa glances toward her, can realize the nectar hidden there. The *gopīs* saw with their own eyes how He walked and how beautiful He looked, and at that time they considered, "Kṛṣṇa certainly wants us to give Him our entire body, mind and heart, and all that we possess."

They were ready to give Him whatever He wanted, and that is why, in the second verse of *Gopī-gīta*, they referred to themselves, not only as maidservants but unpaid maidservants (*aśulka-dāsikā*). Kṛṣṇa had acquired them without any payment.

As mentioned above, in the *Śrīmad-Bhāgavatam* (10.30.2) the *gopīs* referred to Kṛṣṇa's conversations with them as *mano-ramālāpa*, meaning 'conversations that charm the mind.' Now, in their *Gopī-gīta*, they remember how they had replied to Him when they first arrived at Vaṁśī-vaṭa some hours earlier. At that time Kṛṣṇa had urged them, "Leave this place. Go back to your homes and serve your husbands." They had replied, "We consider You our *guru*, and a most excellent one. There is no *guru* in this world who can give us the instructions You gave. You have told us that we should serve our husbands, and You have given a profound explanation as to why a chaste wife should serve her husband even if he is lame, blind, poor, or bereft of good qualities. These teachings are so beautiful and so marvellous that in our hearts we have determined to make You our *guru*; so we should worship You first."

"They have defeated Me," Kṛṣṇa concluded. "I must think of something else to say."

The *gopīs* now remember such captivating conversations. At that time they could not appreciate just how delightful these exchanges were, but after Kṛṣṇa disappeared from their sight, they began to remember them in various ever-fresh ways. They now remember His pastimes with them, and everything else about Him. Those conversations come to the minds of the *gopīs* in the same way that a scene appears in the inner vision of an artist, who then creates an image of what he has seen.

The previous chapter describes how the *gopīs* became so absorbed in Śrī Kṛṣṇa that they began to think that they were actually Him. While imitating Him, they exclaimed, "Oh, look, I am Kṛṣṇa! See how I am walking in such a charming way, and see how I express My love for you. See how I smile and play My flute. Just watch; see how I kill Pūtanā." They were completely absorbed in these moods, and after some time they fainted.

Now, in this eighth verse of *Gopī-gīta*, they continue to recall Kṛṣṇa's enchanting words. As they speak, they are so overwhelmed with bliss that they become disoriented for a while and can say no more. When they return to external awareness, they continue, "Oh, how beautiful it was when we became bewildered by Kṛṣṇa's words.

"Where have these words come from? Water comes from the ocean through the clouds. Because the ocean has the power to generate all the nectarean waters that give refreshment and sustain life, it is certain to contain special nectarean potency. Similarly, all the words coming from Kṛṣṇa's lotus mouth are exquisite, fascinating, and fully imbued with nectar. We have already become enthralled and enchanted by hearing the words emanating from His lips, so what would happen if we directly drink the nectar from the very reservoir of those words – His lips? We would be bewildered to the point of fainting. We hanker for this."

Why does a drunkard not give up the habit of consuming alcohol, but continues to drink more and more? In his inebriated condition he falls into the gutters and sewers by the side of the road and imagines, "I am the emperor of the entire world," or, "I am blissfully submerged in the waters of the heavenly Gaṅgā." Although dogs come and lick his face, he remains absorbed in his

illusory world. He drinks because he again wants to experience a condition of bewilderment. In a similar way, the *gopīs* again yearn to be bewildered.

According to the *gopīs*, Kṛṣṇa's words are so thoroughly imbued with elixir that all living creatures of the world are mesmerized by them. Serpents, deer, birds, and all other species listen to His words and become entranced. When He plays His flute or utters any words, the cuckoos stop their singing to listen, and all the male and female parrots become spellbound. Just like sages in meditation, they close their eyes and listen, as do the cows and everyone else.

As far as Kṛṣṇa is concerned, He is pleased to hear the words of His beloveds, especially the words of Śrīmatī Rādhikā. Her singing is ambrosial, and Her speech even more so. With Her every utterance, Kṛṣṇa becomes overwhelmed and bewildered and can no longer play His flute. How sweet are Rādhikā and Her associates!

Kṛṣṇa longs to hear them say, "We yearn to drink the nectar of Your lips. The words coming from Your lips are captivating, so how beautiful will be the nectar coming directly from Your lips."

In the praises and prayers glorifying Rādhā and Kṛṣṇa, especially those found in Śrīla Jayadeva Gosvāmī's *Gīta-Govinda*, we find examples of alliteration[4] (*anuprāsa-alaṅkāra*). For example, in the line "*dhīra-samīre yamunā-tīre vasati vane vana-mālī*," the words *vasati*, *vane*, and *vana-mālī* all start with the syllable '*va*.' There are also many examples of alliteration in *Śrīmad-Bhāgavatam*. One such example is in the first verse of *Gopī-gītā*, wherein the first and seventh syllables in each line are the same, thus further refining the cadence of the song and making it more melodic. This sounds so beautiful:

jayati te 'dhikaṁ janmanā vrajaḥ
śrayata indirā śaśvad atra hi
dayita dṛśyatāṁ dikṣu tāvakās
tvayi dhṛtāsavas tvāṁ vicinvate

---

[4] An alliteration is the repetition of an initial sound, usually of a consonant or a cluster of letters, in two or more words or a phrase, line of poetry, etc. It is also called initial rhyme.

Lord Śiva has sung marvellously to Śrīmatī Rādhikā in his *Śrī Rādhā-kṛpa-katākṣa-stava-rāja* (Verse 12), which is recorded in the *Ūrdhvāmnaya-tantra*:

makheśvari kriyeśvari svadheśvari sureśvari
tri-veda-bhāratīśvari pramāṇa-śāsaneśvari
rameśvari kṣameśvari pramoda-kānaneśvari
vrajeśvari vrajādhipe śrī-rādhike namo 'stu te

You are the mistress of all kinds of sacrifices (especially of the topmost *yugala-milana-yajña*), of all actions (since You are the root of all potencies – *mūla-śakti-tattva*), and of the *mantras* uttered at *yajñas*. You are the mistress not only of the sacrificial offerings presented to the demigods, but, indeed, of all the demigods, of the words of the three Vedas, and of the enforcement of all scriptural principles. You are mistress of Śrī Ramā-devī (the goddess of fortune), of Śrī Kṣamā-devī (the goddess of forgiveness), and especially of the delightful *kuñjas* in Vṛndāvana. When will You mercifully make me Your *dāsī* and grant me the qualification to render service in Your amorous pastimes with the Prince of Vraja? O Śrīmatī Rādhikā, owner and maintainer of Vraja, I offer my obeisances to You time and again.

This beautiful prayer contains all literary ornaments, including alliteration. If Śrīmatī Rādhikā hears someone soulfully sing this prayer, She is so pleased that She bestows Her mercy upon that person.

Another example of beautiful ornamentation is found in Śrī Śaṅkarācārya's glorification of the Gaṅgā:

devi sureśvari bhagavati gāṅge
tri-bhuvana-tāriṇi tarala-taraṅge
śaṅkara-mauli-vihāriṇi vimale
mama matir āstām tava pāda-kamale

The poetry of Śrīla Rūpa Gosvāmī is still more charming than that of Śrī Śaṅkarācārya. How beautiful, then, is the poetry of *Śrīmad-Bhāgavatam*, in which Śrī Kṛṣṇa's own words have come from the lotus mouth of Śrī Śukadeva Gosvāmī.

In this eighth verse of *Gopī-gīta*, the *gopīs* say, "Your words attract those who are intelligent and learned (*budha-manojñayā*)." Many

Sanskrit scholars know the complexities of Sanskrit grammar, the numerous and diverse dictionary meanings of all letters, words, phrases, and various intricate meters, and can chant all the Vedic hymns and verses; but they cannot understand Śrī Kṛṣṇa's sublime pastimes. When the *gopīs* utter the word *budha*, which means 'intelligent,' they refer to those who are *rasika* and *bhāvuka*, those who relish the humors of *rasa*. One who can understand the inner feelings of Śrī Kṛṣṇa and the *gopīs* is actually intelligent.

Thus, it is the *gopīs* themselves who are intelligent. They are the most comprehending and learned among all living beings in all the universes. No one is equal to them.

The *gopīs* say that along with the literary ornamentation, Kṛṣṇa's speech contains many direct and indirect meanings. The word *abhidhā* denotes the direct meaning of an utterance, whereas the word *vyañjanā* denotes the indirect meaning. The statement "Benares is on the Gaṅgā" is an example of *vyañjanā*. Benares is not actually on the water of the river; it is by the side of the river. On the other hand, to say, "They were bathing in the Gaṅgā" is *abhidhā*, the direct meaning, because in order to bathe, people actually enter the water.

Similarly, Kṛṣṇa's every word contains many lovely meanings. His words are sweet, the meanings of His words are sweet, and hearing His words is sweet. Everything about Him is so sweet.

The *gopīs* address Him as *vīra*, hero. *Vīra* is generally interpreted to mean 'one with bodily strength,' but this is not what the *gopīs* mean. They say, "You are *vīra* because You are fully conversant with *rasa*,[5] and You can thus satisfy our every desire for *rasa*. By hearing Your delightful, melodious words, we have become Your obedient maidservants. We yearn to hear them again, but our more intense desire is to taste the nectar of Your lips, from where Your sweet words have come."

---

5 "*Raso vai saḥ, rasaṁ hy evāyaṁ labdhvānandī bhavati* – He (Śrī Kṛṣṇa) Himself is *rasa*, the integrated form of all mellow-filled relationships. And certainly one who achieves this *rasa* becomes filled with bliss" (*Taittirīya Upaniṣad* 2.7.1).

Verse Nine

If You speak these delightful words directly to us, they are sweeter than celestial nectar. But if, in Your absence, we hear anyone else repeat the same words, then it is like death for us.

Verse 9

तव कथामृतं तप्तजीवनं
कविभिरीडितं कल्मषापहम्।
श्रवणमङ्गलं श्रीमदाततं
भुवि गृणन्ति ते भूरिदा जनाः ॥९॥

tava kathāmṛtaṁ tapta-jīvanaṁ
kavibhir īḍitaṁ kalmaṣāpaham
śravaṇa-maṅgalaṁ śrīmad ātataṁ
bhuvi gṛṇanti ye bhūri-dā janāḥ

tava – Your; *kathā-amṛtam* – the nectar of pastime topics; *tapta-jīvanam* – enlivening the hearts of those afflicted by the threefold material miseries; *kavibhiḥ* – by enlightened sages; *īḍitam* – praised; *kalmaṣa-apaham* – dispells the ignorance of sinful life; *śravaṇa-maṅgalam* – creates auspiciousness simply by hearing; *śrīmat* – embued with spiritual potencies; *ātatam* – broadcast all over the world; *bhuvi* – on the Earth; *gṛṇanti* – chant and proclaim; *ye* – those who; *bhūri-dāḥ* – most magnanimous; *janāḥ* – persons.

Translation

Nectarean discussions about You are the life and soul of those who are tormented by separation from You, and greatly learned personalities, such as Brahmā, Siva, and the four Kumāras, sing of them. Those narrations vanquish the distress of past sins (*prārabdha* and *aprārabdha*[1]). Immediately upon being heard, they bestow the highest auspiciousness, and especially the wealth of *prema*. The nectar of Your narrations is expanded by those who glorify Your pastimes, and therefore such narrators are truly the most generous benefactors in the world.

Bhāva-prakāśika Vṛtti

In the previous verse the *gopīs* told Kṛṣṇa, "We always remember Your conversations with Śrīmatī Rādhikā and us in the *kuñjas* and other solitary places. When You called us with the melody of Your flute, we came to You from our homes, leaving everything behind. At that time You told us, '*Svāgataṁ vo mahā-bhāgāḥ, priyaṁ kiṁ karavāṇi vaḥ* – O most fortunate ladies, welcome. How can I please you?' "

When Śrī Kṛṣṇa spoke these words, His face was grave; it seemed as though He were speaking the complete truth, revealing what was really on His mind, without concealing anything. "Why have you come here?" He asked. "Have you come because of any mishap in your home? You are not even dressed properly. Is everything in order in your homes and in your hearts?"

The *gopīs* also remember Kṛṣṇa telling Rādhikā, "Whether You act in a contrary manner or submissively, You are the life of My life. Sometimes You come to Me, but upon seeing Me, You turn and leave. Sometimes You become angry for no reason. At such times, I request You again and again to be pleased with Me, but You do not listen and You disagree with whatever I say. At other times, You eagerly meet and perform loving pastimes with Me. Still, whether You are contrary or submissive, You are My life and soul. Without You, I would die. You stand in a certain way and cast glances at Me from the corner of Your eyes, and those glances directly enter My heart like flower-arrows."

The *gopīs* described these conversations as charming to the mind. Everything about Kṛṣṇa – His way of glancing, His every action, His flute playing and so forth – is exceptionally sweet and attractive.

---

1 *Aprārabdha-karma* is the accumulated stock of reactions to activities which are lying in a dormant condition and are waiting to bear fruit at some time. *Prārabdha-karma* is the result of previous activities which has already begun to bear fruit.

Now, in this verse, the *gopīs* say, "*Tava kathā amṛtam* – If You speak these delightful words directly to us, they are sweeter than *amṛta*, celestial nectar. But if, in Your absence, we hear anyone else repeat the same words, then it is like *mṛtyu*, death, for us; *tava kathā mṛtam*."

First we will explain the meaning of this verse according to the *gopīs* with a submissive mood (*dakṣiṇa-bhāva*), who express themselves directly. They may speak the same words as the *gopīs* with a contrary mood (*vāmya-bhāva*), who express themselves indirectly, but the meaning of their words is completely different.

When Śrī Kṛṣṇa asks the *gopīs* why they compare His *kathā* to nectar (*amṛta*), they reply, "Because when we look at the two other types of nectar, Your *kathā* is superior."

There are three types of *amṛta*. Although these three differ vastly in the results attained by drinking them, they are all referred to as *amṛta*. One kind of *amṛta* is found in Svarga, the heavenly planets. It is said that the demigods become free from death by drinking that ambrosia, but that is not true. They live for the period of only one *manvantara*[2] (306,720,000 years), and after that they must die. Still, that drink is called *amṛta*.

The *amṛta* of Svarga can act as a medicine to cure a disease, but it cannot console one who is unhappy. When Bali Mahārāja captured the Nandana-kānana gardens of the heavenly planets, he drank *amṛta*, but still he was grief-stricken, because he had left his wife, children, and kingdom for such a long time.

Moreover, if a person drinks this *amṛta* of heaven, he becomes extremely lusty. After Indra and Candra drank it, they went to Gautama Ṛṣi's wife to satisfy their lusty desires, and were then cursed by Gautama Ṛṣi. Because that *amṛta* increases the desire to taste sense enjoyment in this material world, it is actually a very lowly thing.

The second type of *amṛta* is the nectar of liberation (*mokṣāmṛta*)[3]. In *Śrīmad-Bhāgavatam* (6.11.25), Vṛtrāsura prayed:

---

2 The duration of one *manvāntara* is seventy-one *yugas*, and each *yuga* lasts for 4,320,000 years.

3 *Mokṣa* means liberation from material existence.

na nāka-pṛeṣṭhaṁ na ca pārameṣṭhyaṁ
na sārva-bhaumaṁ na rasādhipatyam
na yoga-siddhīr apunar-bhavaṁ vā
samañjasa tvā virahayya kāṅkṣe

O my Lord, source of all opportunities, I do not desire to enjoy in Dhruvaloka, the heavenly planets or the planet where Lord Brahmā resides, nor do I want to be the supreme ruler of all the earthly planets or the lower planetary systems. I do not desire to be master of the powers of mystic *yoga*, nor do I want liberation if I have to give up Your lotus feet.

The words *na punar bhavaṁ* in the above-mentioned verse mean 'cessation of repeated birth and death.' In this connection, the revealed scriptures state that if someone attains *mokṣāmṛta*, the nectar of liberation, then all the unfructified reactions to his material activities (*aprārabdha-karma*) are finished, but he still has to suffer the reactions that are fructifying (*prārabdha-karma*). On the other hand, even the fructified reactions of one who hears *hari-kathā*, the third type of nectar, are destroyed. One who deeply hears *hari-kathā* does not have to do anything else to attain perfection. He does not even have to practice the other eight limbs of *bhakti*.

The nine limbs of *bhakti* are:

śravaṇaṁ kīrtanaṁ viṣṇoḥ
smaraṇaṁ pāda-sevanam
arcanaṁ vandanaṁ dāsyaṁ
sakhyam ātma-nivedanam
Śrīmad-Bhāgavatam (7.5.23)

Hearing and chanting about the transcendental holy name, form, qualities, paraphernalia, and pastimes of Lord Viṣṇu; remembering them; serving the lotus feet of the Lord; offering the Lord respectful worship with sixteen types of paraphernalia; offering prayers to the Lord; becoming His servant; considering the Lord one's best friend; and surrendering everything unto Him (in other words, serving Him with one's body, mind and words).

Śrī Kṛṣṇa's devotee becomes eligible for Kṛṣṇa to immediately enter his heart, simply by hearing about Him. The devotee becomes liberated from Kṛṣṇa's deluding material potency known as *māyā*, and he is able to see Kṛṣṇa personally. Drinking heavenly nectar does not decrease ignorance, rather it increases it; and the nectar of liberation gives no taste of service to Kṛṣṇa. Consequently, in every respect *hari-kathā* is superior to the nectar of heaven and the nectar of liberation.

The nectar of *hari-kathā* is *tapta-jīvanam*, which means that it gives life to those who are suffering in any painful condition. It gives life to those who are diseased and to those who are unhappy in this world in any way. *Hari-kathā* also gives life to anyone who is feeling separation from Śrī Śrī Rādhā and Kṛṣṇa, and it removes the pain of that separation in every way. The person who hears *hari-kathā* becomes peaceful.

Kavibhir īḍitam: *Kavi* generally means 'a poet or great thinker,' but here it refers to devotees. Because the nectar of *hari-kathā* is far above the two other kinds of nectar, it is glorified (*īḍitam*) by devotees like Lord Brahmā, Lord Śiva, Śrī Nārada Ṛṣi, Śrīla Śukadeva Gosvāmī, Dhruva Mahārāja, and Prahlāda Mahārāja, who are always relishing this superior nectar. They say that it gives life.

It is stated by Dhruva Mahārāja (*Śrīmad-Bhāgavatam* 4.9.10), "*Yā nirvṛttis tanu-bhṛtām* – If embodied souls hear *hari-kathā*, they attain supreme happiness." This spiritual happiness is superior to the pleasure of thinking oneself one in all respects with *brahma*, the impersonal Absolute. The pleasure of impersonalism, what to speak of the temporary happiness derived from the nectar of Svarga, is like a tiny atom of happiness in comparison to the joy resulting from hearing *hari-kathā*. There is actually no comparison.

Śrī Kṛṣṇa states in *Bhagavad-gītā* that those who go to Svarga eventually return to this world. They may go there again and again, but they always return:

te taṁ bhuktvā svarga-lokaṁ viśālaṁ
kṣīṇe puṇye martya-lokaṁ viśanti
evaṁ trayī-dharmam anuprapannā
gatāgataṁ kāma-kāmā labhante

Bhagavad-gītā (9.21)

> When they have thus enjoyed vast heavenly sense pleasure and the results of their pious activities are exhausted, they return to this mortal planet again. Thus those who seek sense enjoyment by adhering to the principles of the three Vedas achieve only repeated birth and death.

Thus, the delight sought in heaven cannot be compared to that of hearing *hari-kathā*, which is able to destroy every type of material desire and ignorance.

When we forget Kṛṣṇa, *māyā* captures us and stimulates our material desires. Actually, *māyā* has two functions by which she accomplishes this; her potency known as *vikṣepātmikā*, which generates a kind of material knowledge and throws the *jīva* into ignorance, and her potency known as *āvaraṇātmikā*, which covers the *jīva's* natural knowledge about his eternal relationship with Śrī Kṛṣṇa. Lust causes us to forget Kṛṣṇa, and that is why it is also called ignorance. Only *hari-kathā* has the potency to uproot this lust.

Māyāvādī *sannyāsīs* sometimes seem to have given up sensual desires, but this is only a show, for the nectar of liberation cannot uproot the desire for material enjoyment. There are two kinds of monists (*advaita-vādīs*) or impersonalists. In one category are the Māyāvādīs, who follow Śaṅkarācārya and who, like Rāvaṇa and similar demons, are offenders to the Supreme Lord. In the second category are personalities like Sanaka, Sanandana, Sanātana, Sanat Kumāra, and Śrīla Śukadeva Gosvāmī, who initially were *brahmavādīs*, or *nirguṇya-vādīs* aspiring for *nirguṇa* Kṛṣṇa. They were not offenders. *Nirguṇa* Kṛṣṇa means Kṛṣṇa without qualities. The *brahmavādīs* accept the existence of God (*brahma*), but they have no information about the sweet qualities of His superior, personal feature, and that is why they worship Him without qualities. This is not offensive, because as soon as they hear about the extraordinary qualities of the Supreme Lord Śrī Kṛṣṇa, they immediately become His devotees and give up their worship of His impersonal feature. It is explained in the Vedas that *brahmavādīs*, or *nirguṇya-vādīs*, want to become one with the Supreme, but they do not try to negate and deny the existence of His personal feature, as do Śaṅkarācārya and his followers. If they meet a devotee, they easily take to the process of *bhakti*.

As stated earlier, when *hari-kathā* actually enters a person's ear, it is not necessary for him to perform any other limb of *bhakti*. He does not even have to chant and remember the holy names of the Lord, engage in worship, or offer Him *stavas* (prayers) and *stutis* (praises). *Hari-kathā* at once takes him to Śrī Kṛṣṇa, as stated in the first chapter of *Śrīmad-Bhāgavatam* (1.1.2):

dharmaḥ projjhita-kaitavo 'tra paramo nirmatsarāṇāṁ satāṁ
vedyaṁ vāstavam atra vastu śivadaṁ tāpa-trayonmūlanam
śrīmad-bhāgavate mahā-muni-kṛte kiṁ vā parair īśvaraḥ
sadyo hṛdy avarudhyate 'tra kṛtibhiḥ śuśrūṣubhis tat-kṣaṇāt

Completely rejecting all religious activities which are materially motivated, this *Bhāgavata Purāṇa* propounds the highest truth, which is understandable by those devotees who are fully pure in heart. The highest truth is reality distinguished from illusion for the welfare of all. Such truth uproots the threefold miseries. This beautiful *Bhāgavatam*, compiled by the great sage Vyāsadeva (in his maturity), is sufficient in itself for God realization. What is the need of any other scripture? As soon as one attentively and submissively hears the message of *Bhāgavatam*, by this culture of knowledge the Supreme Lord is established within his heart.

This verse explains that if a person hears *hari-kathā* with faith, that *hari-kathā* makes such impressions (*saṁskāras*) in his heart that Śrī Kṛṣṇa personally manifests and remains there forever. This takes place at once, without delay (*tat-kṣaṇāt*[4]), as stated in many other places in the scriptures. *Hari-kathā* gives *prema*.

---

[4] "*Tat-kṣaṇāt* means 'immediately.' What is the deeper meaning of this? Suppose a person who is full of *anarthas* begins to hear the *hari-kathā* of *Śrīmad-Bhāgavatam*. He has been in this world for unlimited time, and he is now on the path to perfection. In comparison to unlimited time, if in a year, or two years, or two births, he becomes purified, that may be considered *tat-kṣaṇāt*, immediate.

The example is also given that when a fan is unplugged, it continues to run for a while before it stops. If one stops peddling a cycle, the pedals will continue to move for a short time. The driver of a train puts on the brakes, and yet the train continues to go for two miles, three miles, or four miles. Still, it is considered to have 'stopped.' In this way, there is no fault in using the word *tat-kṣaṇāt*" (Śrīla Nārāyaṇa Gosvāmī Mahārāja. Lecture in Cessnock. Australia, February 2002).

One might argue that a conditioned soul may have a taste for *hari-kathā* at the time of actually hearing it, but then, when he is not hearing, *māyā* attacks him again. In this connection, the above-mentioned *Śrīmad-Bhāgavatam* verse states, *kṛtibhiḥ śuśrūṣubhiḥ*, meaning 'those who have developed intense eagerness to hear.' Regular hearing creates *śraddhā* (faith), followed by *anartha-nivṛtti* (freedom from unwanted habits and thoughts), and then *niṣṭhā* (steadiness), *ruci* (taste), *āsakti* (attachment to Kṛṣṇa), *bhāva* (spiritual emotions), and *prema* (pure love).

Within a seed is the potential for a tree. The seed sprouts and grows two leaves, then four leaves, then twigs and branches, then flowers, and finally fruit. This takes some time. Similarly, a soul may have been wandering in the material world for countless lifetimes, yet *hari-kathā* is so powerful that it may even give the result of *prema* in just one lifetime. This is what is meant by 'immediately.'

After hearing *hari-kathā* for only seven days, Parīkṣit Mahārāja entered Śrī Kṛṣṇa's Vṛndāvana pastimes. He was not killed by the snake-bird that bit him, as some say. Those who were present at the time could not see that his soul had actually left his body before the snake-bird bit him. Parīkṣit Mahārāja was more advanced than Dhruva Mahārāja, Ajāmila, and even Nārada Ṛṣi.

The word *kalmaṣāpaham* in this *Gopi-gita* verse means that *hari-kathā* drives away all sinful reactions. The words *śrīmad-ātatam* mean, "Your *kathā* is distributed throughout the world by those who speak it." And the phrase *bhuvi gṛṇanti ye bhūri-dā janāḥ* implies that those who hear *hari-kathā* will always be indebted to the speaker, no matter how much they give in appreciation. That is why such speakers are called *bhūri-dāḥ*. *Bhūri* means 'in extreme,' and *dāḥ* means 'those who give.' We are indebted to those who give *hari-kathā*, because their gift is so great that whatever we offer in return will not be sufficient.

This is the direct meaning of this ninth verse, as spoken by the *gopīs* whose mood is submissive (*dakṣiṇa-bhāva*). The meaning of the *gopīs* with a contrary mood (*vāmya-bhāva*), who express themselves indirectly, is as follows: "When we directly hear the *kathā* You speak, it is so wonderful that all distress and calamities disappear from our lives. At that time it is far superior to the *amṛta* of heaven and liberation. On the other hand, if You are not present, that *kathā* becomes deadly."

In the sunshine, the lotus in the lake blossoms and spreads its fragrance, whereas a lotus that is out of the water will wither and shrivel. Accordingly, the *gopīs* are telling Kṛṣṇa, "If You are personally telling us *hari-kathā*, it tastes sweeter than nectar. On the other hand, to hear it from someone else simply causes us pain. It reminds us of You, and thus it is *mṛta*, or deadly, because it increases the blazing fire of separation. It is like throwing a few drops of water in a pot of burning oil, which makes the flames soar upward."

Kavibhir īḍitam: Why, then, do the Purāṇas say that *hari-kathā* is like *amṛta*? According to these *gopīs*, the nature of *kavis*, or scholarly poets, is to deliberately embellish in this way. Instead of saying, "The horse is running," a poet will say, "The horse is flying through the air." By his poetic speech he attributes a particular virtue to one who does not have it: "He is such a scholar, he is like Bṛhaspati (the priest of the demigods);" or, "He is as strong as Hanumān."

The *gopīs* argue, "We are always speaking *hari-kathā*, so if it really possesses the qualities of *amṛta*, why we do we feel intense anguish without respite in our separation from You? We have left our homes, our husbands, and all our possessions for You; and now we are roaming like beggars and continually weeping. But there is no one to remove our tears.

"*Kalmaṣāpaham* – the poets have said that *hari-kathā* drives away (*apaham*) all kinds of sinful reactions and inauspiciousness (*kalmaṣa*), including ignorance; but we are evidence to the contrary. We must have performed extremely sinful activities to be so tormented, but that torment is not removed by Your *hari-kathā*. Tonight we are roaming here and there, sobbing bitterly, for You have left us and vanished from our sight. We can thus understand that the nectar of Your *kathā* is not *kalmaṣāpaham*; rather, it gives *kalmaṣa*.

"Everyone says that the nectar of Your *kathā* is *sravaṇa-maṅgalam*, meaning that it is very sweet to hear (*śravaṇa*) and that it brings all auspiciousness (*maṅgala*). But we do not feel like this. We do not have any experience of it giving auspiciousness. We are always discussing Your whereabouts, Your dancing, Your beauty, and Your qualities. We have spoken and heard so much *kṛṣṇa-kathā*, yet our lives are devoid of auspiciousness. If hearing *hari-kathā* is auspicious, You would have come to meet with us."

Bhūri-dāḥ: *Dāḥ* means 'giving,' but it can also mean 'severed.' Hence, *bhūri-dāḥ* means 'giving good fortune,' and also 'severing good fortune.' The anguished *gopīs* say, "We have seen what happens to those who hear Your *kathā* – Your *kṛṣṇa-kathā*. We have considered this deeply and have come to the conclusion that those who speak *hari-kathā* have caused all our good fortune to be severed. They have disturbed and spoiled our lives."

The *gopīs* then explain to Kṛṣṇa how this happens, "*Śrīmad-ātatam* – those who spread *hari-kathā* all over the world are *śrī-mada*." This word is composed of two syllables: *śrī* and *mada*. [The last 'a' in *mada* combines with the first 'ā' in *ātatam*.] *Śrī* means 'wealth and opulence,' and *mada* means 'intoxication.' The *gopīs* say, "The wealthy (*śrī*) become intoxicated (*mada*), as if drunk on alcohol, and then they become rogues and rascals, killing everyone in the world for no reason. They act in this way even though they gain nothing.

"With the aim of whimsically killing everyone for no benefit to themselves, these rogues and rascals summon speakers of *Śrīmad-Bhāgavatam* and promise to give them as much wealth as they want. 'Just propagate the teachings of *Śrīmad-Bhāgavatam*,' they say. 'Go from village to village, door to door. Speak such topics that people will abandon all they possess – their spouses, their fathers and mothers, their children, their wealth, and all material happiness. Let them become street beggars and die miserably.'

"These speakers travel throughout the world. They go everywhere, from town to town, saying, 'We do not want anything from you. Just chant Hare Kṛṣṇa and hear this *hari-kathā*.' In this way they spoil everyone's lives. They are hunters and killers of mankind and are certainly *bhūri-dāḥ*, meaning they cause the death of those who hear them, by destroying their happiness and ruining their lives."

In the future, Kṛṣṇa will leave Vṛndāvana to reside in Dvārakā. At that time, Śrīmatī Rādhikā will again speak like this, saying:

yad-anucarita-līlā-karṇa-pīyūṣa-vipruṭ-
sakṛd-adana-vidhūta-dvandva-dharmā vinaṣṭāḥ
sapadi gṛha-kuṭumbaṁ dīnam utsṛjya dīnā
bahava iha vihaṅgā bhikṣu-caryāṁ caranti
Śrīmad-Bhāgavatam (10.47.18)

To hear about the pastimes that Kṛṣṇa regularly performs is nectar for the ears. For those who relish just a single drop of that nectar, even once, their dedication to material duality is ruined. Many such persons have suddenly given up their wretched homes and families and, themselves becoming wretched, traveled here to Vṛndāvana to wander about like birds, begging for their living.

It is a fact that those who hear *kṛṣṇa-kathā* from the right source will eventually leave their homes, families, and everything they possess. They become like birds, living in the shade of a different tree each day. They roam about in Vṛndāvana with no possessions, like street beggars, weeping. They drink water from the Yamunā River from their cupped hands, because they have no water-pot. They chant, "Hare Kṛṣṇa, Hare Kṛṣṇa" and weep. They do not take food at regular intervals, so they become thin and frail. After hearing *hari-kathā* they are reduced to this condition, no matter what position they previously held in society, be it a prince or anything else.

The *gopīs* conclude, "No one should hear *kṛṣṇa-kathā*. The only reason we are discussing it is that we cannot stop."

They speak like this to beseech Kṛṣṇa to return to them. "Please come here at once," they pray. "If You do not come, we will die, and if we die, everyone will criticize You. They will say, 'Kṛṣṇa is cruel. He is not even slightly kind-hearted. Those poor *gopīs* were weeping, but still He did not go to them.' "

Only the *gopīs* dare to speak, or even think, like this, and only their followers can appreciate their words. It seems that they are blaspheming *hari-kathā* as well as those who preach it, but this is not so. Actually, their speech employs a literary device called *vyāja-stuti*, or praise in disguise, and this literary ornament was also later employed by Śrīla Rūpa Gosvāmī in his writings. In this way, they are not actually being critical; rather, their ironic words carry more ambrosia than ordinary, straightforward praise.

Kṛṣṇa is immeasurably pleased by their words, and thinks, "If I do not bring Myself before them, it will be an insult on My part."

This is the explanation of Śrīla Viśvanātha Cakravartī Ṭhākura, and Śrīla Jīva Gosvāmī has elucidated on this verse in a similar way in his *Vaiṣṇava-toṣaṇī*.

During the Ratha-yātrā festival in Jagannātha Purī, King Pratāparudra recited *Gopī-gīta* to Śrī Caitanya Mahāprabhu. When he uttered this verse, which glorifies *hari-kathā*, Mahāprabhu immediately remembered *rāsa-līlā* and became most ecstatic. Mahāprabhu remembered both the above meanings, as well as every other aspect of this verse.

We can only mentally contemplate these explanations, but Śrī Caitanya Mahāprabhu, whose sentiments are those of Śrīmatī Rādhikā, could actually experience them. He was really seeing Kṛṣṇa in His heart and feeling separation from Him, and Kṛṣṇa also gave Mahāprabhu His *darśana*. Mahāprabhu embraced the king, who then became a recipient of His mercy.

Verse Ten

O cherished beloved, when parted from You, remembrance of You smiling at us, Your tender glance, Your intimate pastimes with us, and Your loving talks with us in solitary places fills our hearts with pain.

Verse 10

प्रहसितं प्रिय प्रेमवीक्षणं
विहरणञ्च ते ध्यानमङ्गलम्।
रहसि संविदो या हृदिस्पृशः
कुहक नो मनः क्षोभयन्ति हि ॥१०॥

prahasitaṁ priya prema-vīkṣaṇaṁ
viharaṇañ ca te dhyāna-maṅgalam
rahasi saṁvido yā hṛdi spṛśaḥ
kuhaka no manaḥ kṣobhayanti hi

prahasitam – the smiling and laughter; *priya* – O beloved master; *prema* – with love; *vīkṣaṇam* – glances; *viharaṇam* – intimate pastimes; *ca* – and; *te* – Your; *dhyāna* – by contemplation; *maṅgalam* – awards auspiciousness; *rahasi* – in solitary places; *saṁvidaḥ* – conversations; *yāḥ* – which; *hṛdi* – the heart; *spṛśaḥ* – touching; *kuhaka* – O cheater; *naḥ* – our; *manaḥ* – minds; *kṣobhayanti* – agitate; *hi* – indeed.

Translation

O beloved master, having seen You as You conversed intimately with us in secret places – Your smiling face, which acts as a stimulus for our amorous desires, Your glancing at us with love, and Your expansive chest, which is the eternal resting place of the goddess of fortune – our hankering to meet with You has increased manifold, and therefore our minds are repeatedly bewildered.

Bhāva-prakāśika Vṛtti

As I have explained previously, Verse Nine has a particular meaning when recited by the *gopīs* whose nature is submissive, and another meaning when spoken by those whose mood is contrary. When spoken in a contrary mood, it means, "We recall that Your loving pastimes with us, especially Your sweet words, were most delightful. But when, in separation from You, we hear someone repeat Your words or recount Your pastimes, it causes us much pain. Our pastimes with You are a source of much joy, but remembrance of them in Your absence is certainly not."

For example, Kṛṣṇa may tell Śrīmatī Rādhikā, "O Rādhikā, You are the very life of My life; I cannot live without You." Although these words fill Rādhikā with happiness, when She is reminded of the same words in Kṛṣṇa's absence, She is overwhelmed with deep sadness. Another example is that Rādhikā's friend may tell Her, "Kṛṣṇa leaves all the other *gopīs* for You." If Rādhikā hears these words when She and Kṛṣṇa are apart, they evoke memories of Their pastimes and cause Her unbearable distress.

Now, in the tenth verse, the *gopīs* continue this line of thought. They utter four phrases, each describing one of Kṛṣṇa's captivating features: "O cherished beloved, when parted from You, remembrance of You smiling at us (*prahasitam*), Your tender glance (*prema-vīkṣaṇam*), Your intimate pastimes with us (*viharaṇam*), and Your loving talks with us in solitary places (*rahasi samvidaḥ*) fills our hearts with pain."

Each *gopī* has met with Kṛṣṇa before, and now relives receiving His side-long glance full of longing, gazing at the beauty of His smile, and being taken in His arms. In her remembrance, she experiences profound separation from Him.

The *gopīs* remember that when Śrī Kṛṣṇa goes out with His countless friends to herd the cows, Baladeva goes ahead while Kṛṣṇa follows a little behind Him. Playing on His flute and smiling, Kṛṣṇa glances at them from the corners of His eyes; and

in response, they worship Him with their eyes. His glance fully expresses the longing in His heart: "Let us meet at Sāṅketa." They read His glance and understand His message.

Śrīla Viśvanātha Cakravartī Ṭhākura explains that in this verse the word *samvidaḥ* means 'friendly, joking conversations' (*narma-saṁlāpa*). As we discussed earlier, *narma* means 'friendly joking' and *saṁlāpa* means 'conversation.' *Narma* may also imply that the conversation has a hidden meaning which is quite opposite to the external meaning.

The *gopīs* remember this example of joking conversation with deep, hidden import: with His flute playing, Śrī Kṛṣṇa called them to the forest, but when they appeared there, He told them to return to their homes. This is called *narma-saṁlāpa*, playful, joking language that implies a completely different meaning from what is spoken. Indirectly Kṛṣṇa was beseeching the *gopīs*, "Do not return to your homes."

rajany eṣā ghora-rupā
ghora-sattva-niṣevitā
pratiyāta vrajaṁ neha
stheyaṁ strībhiḥ su-madhyamāḥ
Śrīmad-Bhāgavatam (10. 29. 19)

> This night is quite frightening, and ferocious creatures are lurking about. Return to Vraja, slender-waisted girls. This is not a proper place for women.

Kṛṣṇa seemed to be saying, "The night is dark and cloudy, and the dense forest is full of wild animals. You should return to your homes and serve your husbands." But later, when He left Vṛndāvana and began residing in Mathurā, He clarified the meaning of these words. He sent Uddhava with a message for the *gopīs*, which read, "That night, after I called you to the forest, you thought I told you to return to your homes. You should know that I did not say that at all. I actually said, 'Do not leave. The moon is full, so the night is not at all dark and frightening. But the sky is cloudy and it may rain; and if it does, where will you take shelter? If You stay here with Me, you will be safe.' "

Kṛṣṇa had uttered the words *rajany eṣā ghora-rūpā*, which apparently mean 'the night (*rajany eṣā*) is dark (*ghora*).' However, there is another 'a' hidden between the words *eṣā* and *ghora*, thus making it *eṣā aghora* – the night is not dark. Similarly, "*rūpā ghora-sattva-niṣevitā* – the forest is inhabited by ferocious beasts," becomes "*rūpā aghora-sattva-niṣevitā* – the animals in the forest are not at all ferocious."

In that verse, the word *na*, meaning 'not,' can be applied to either the first part of the line or to the last part of the line, and thus two optional meanings are derived. In this way, "*pratiyāta vrajam* – go back to Vraja," becomes "*na pratiyāta vrajam* – do not go back to Vraja." And "*na iha stheyam* – do not stay here" becomes "*iha stheyam* – you should stay here."

The *gopīs* on the bank of the Yamunā now refer to their conversation with Kṛṣṇa on that moonlit night. They say, "Within our hearts, we understood what You actually wanted, and that You were too shy to express Your real feelings. We, also, were too shy to openly express ours. Our hearts contain sweet memories of such loving talks and pastimes; but now, in separation from You, these memories are the cause of deep sorrow."

When someone dies, all of his friends and relatives grieve. A woman in mourning will weep for her lover: "He had so much love for me, but now he is no more." In a similar way, the *gopīs* become overwhelmed with the pain of separation from Kṛṣṇa upon remembering His smile, His heart-touching ways, and also His tricky, joking words, full of double meanings that indicated, for example, that they should secretly meet Him in a *sāṅketa-kuñja*[1].

The *gopīs* now say, "We want to be free from these memories, but we cannot. We are absorbed in thinking of Your beautiful smile (*prahasitam*), Your tender glance (*prema-vīkṣaṇam*), Your intimate pastimes with us (*viharaṇam*), and Your amorous talks with us in solitary places (*rahasi saṁvidaḥ*). In this way we are always reminded

---

1 The word *sāṅketa* refers to any assigned place of meeting for the Divine Couple. It is not necessarily a specific place. Although there is also a specific place known as Sāṅketa, which is situated between Nandagrāma and Varṣāṇā, there are many such *sāṅketas* scattered around Vraja.

of You. These four beautiful features bring auspiciousness to the heart (*dhyāna-maṅgalam*), but they also cause the heart to feel agitation (*kṣobhayanti hi*). O cheater, the mere remembrance of these four features causes great disturbance to our hearts.

"You cheat with Your smile, You cheat with Your loving words, and You cheat with Your intimate pastimes. You cheat in everything You do. Your entrance in our hearts gives us some pleasure initially, but later Your presence there becomes like poison and kills us."

Śrīla Jīva Gosvāmī comments on this verse as follows: Kṛṣṇa is saying, "O *gopīs*, You know that I am difficult to attain, so why are you expressing your desires to enjoy intimately with Me? Sometimes you say, 'Please place Your hands on my head'; sometimes you say, 'Please place Your lotus feet on our breasts;' and at other times you say, 'Your smile and everything else about You is so enchanting.' Why do you speak like this? If you feel affection for Me, then just listen to My *hari-kathā* and be satisfied with that. Why do you want to see Me face to face?"

In reply the *gopīs* say, "You, Yourself, are the reason we cannot be satisfied simply by hearing Your pastimes. The fault lies in Your previous loving dealings, in *pūrva-rāga*."

To what are the *gopīs* referring? When Kṛṣṇa goes cowherding, it is with the sole purpose of meeting with them. In fact, wherever He goes in Vraja, it is with the intention to meet with them there. For example, early in the morning He goes to the Yamunā River, saying that He is going there to take bath. But He does not take bath. He simply stands under a *kadamba* tree on Yamunā's bank, waiting for the *gopīs*, whom He knows come there daily to fill their pots with water. On pretexts such as this, He arranges to go wherever they go. If He knows that they are going to Girirāja Govardhana to perform worship, He also finds an excuse to go there. This is the nature of *pūrva-rāga*, anxious anticipation to meet with one's beloved.

The *gopīs* also eagerly want to meet with Kṛṣṇa, and they find endless excuses to do so. They tell their superiors they are going to perform worship of Gaurī (the consort of Lord Śiva) or Sūrya (the Sun-god). But sometimes, just as they are about to meet Kṛṣṇa, one of their superiors comes along, like Jaṭilā or Candrāvalī's husband, Govardhana-malla, and all their plans are foiled.

The *gopīs* know that Kṛṣṇa schemes to make them look at Him. They know that He plays His flute to attract them, and then smiles, even though He has absolutely no reason to smile. "By doing so," they now say, "You increased our ardent longing to be with You and love You.

"But now You have disappeared, and that which You increased now causes us so much pain that we are not able to remain alive any longer. Perhaps we will die."

The prefix *pra* in *prahasitam* means 'in an excellent way, and *prahasitam* means 'the most exquisite smiling or laughter.' At every opportunity, Kṛṣṇa laughs in a charming way and casts His glance toward the *gopīs*, sometimes from behind a tree and sometimes from within a *kuñja*. Somehow or another, He contrives to send them the shafts of His arrow-like glances coming from His loving lotus face, which is adorned with the most graceful and sweet smiles. A glance that carries the deep message of one's heart is known as *prema-vīkṣaṇam*.

The *gopīs* proceed to give an example of the third of Kṛṣṇa's charming features, namely His confidential pastimes (*viharaṇam*): "The way You strolled past us, with one hand on the shoulder of Your friend and the other hand twirling a lotus, can be compared with nothing else."

He rests His hand on the shoulder of a friend to indicate to the *gopīs*, "I want to be with you and place My hand on your shoulder." Similarly, He twirls a lotus to convey to them, "My mind and heart spin with a desire to be with you. If I cannot meet with you, I will die." He sends the *gopīs* signals like this when He is with His cowherd friends, and the *gopīs* perceive them from afar and understand them.

In this verse the word *viharaṇam* means 'a special kind of theft.' The Sanskrit verb *hṛ* means 'to steal.' According to this specific definition, *viharaṇam* does not refer to stealing money, but to stealing the heart. In this connection *viharaṇam* also denotes 'to walk with friends' and 'to walk with a lady.' When the *gopīs* utter *viharaṇam* to refer to their attraction for Kṛṣṇa in *pūrva-rāga*, before their first intimate meeting with Him, it cannot mean 'to walk with a lady.' In this instance, Kṛṣṇa casually walks along with His friends, and

His walking like this is only to show His desire to meet with them. He ambles along, nonchalantly resting one hand on the shoulder of a friend and twirling a lotus in the other. In this way, He intentionally pulls at their hearts. Seeing this, they lose awareness of everything else and thus become mad. This scene is far superior to the scene of their meeting – far, far superior.

Veṇu-gīta is sung in *pūrva-rāga*, but Go*pī-gīta* is sung in the separation that takes place after meeting. Still, even in that separation the *gopīs* may think, "We have never met with Kṛṣṇa." The first meaning of *viharaṇam*, 'to walk with friends,' refers to *pūrva-rāga*. But when the *gopīs* speak of any pastime that took place after they met with Kṛṣṇa, such as His walking along with Rādhikā, Lalitā, Viśākhā, Citrā and so on, then the second meaning, 'walking with a lady' applies.

Sometimes, when Rādhā and Kṛṣṇa are strolling along, side by side, Kṛṣṇa rests His hands on Her shoulders, or the shoulders of another *gopī*. The *gopīs* then espy a creeper entwined around a *tamala* tree. They see the blossoms that laden the creeper and the flowers that adorn the tree delight in each other's company and laugh gaily. And if there are any *mañjarīs* on that creeper, they merrily join in the laughter.

The *gopīs* now remember this incident, as well as a conversation that took place at that time: "Look! How radiant this creeper is!" Kṛṣṇa remarked, indicating that the creeper's happiness is due to being wound about the tree in a tight embrace. With these words, He intimated to the *gopīs* His desire to meet with them like this, upon which they became blissfully intoxicated, their deep moods of love for Him further intensifying.

But now Kṛṣṇa is no longer within their sight, and they are recalling their confidential pastimes with Him: the way He smiled, His loving glance, His amorous pastimes with them, and His intimate conversations with them.

The *gopīs* say, "Again and again, You playfully expressed Your heart's eagerness to be with us. When we remember this, we are filled with hope that we will meet with You very soon."

Each of the four – *prahasitam*, *prema-vīkṣanam*, *viharaṇam*, and *rahasi saṁvidaḥ* – is superior to the preceding one, thus making the fourth the best of all. As mentioned, *prahasitam* means 'smiling' or 'laughing.' When, along with that smiling, there is also glancing with increasing love and affection, it is called *prema-vīkṣaṇam*. The *gopīs*' amorous pastimes with Him (*viharaṇam*) are still superior; as the divine lovers gaze into each other's eyes and blissfully smile, they wander throughout the forest, arm in arm. Superior still, and inclusive of all the other three features, are their secret conversations (*rahasi saṁvidaḥ*), in which they touch each other's hearts by expressing the priceless moods contained there. In this way, there are gradations in the realm of perfection – good, better, and best.

The phrase *rahasi saṁvidaḥ* also has its own speciality. Kṛṣṇa's loving talks with the *gopīs* so deeply touch their hearts that they become embedded there. As a result, the *gopīs* cannot remove remembrance of those intimate conversations at any time, even if they desperately want to do so.

They conclude, "We believed that these interactions were based on true love, but now we see that You are nothing but a cheater and a hypocrite. You never spoke to us from the core of Your heart; You spoke only to cheat us. If You had any love and affection for us at all, You would appear before us, but You do not."

Verse Eleven

When You go cowherding with Your friends, You roam the forest which is covered with sprouts of rice, wheat, and grass that are sharper than needles. Yet Your lotus feet are more tender and soft than a delicate lotus flower; surely these sharp sprouts cause You pain. This very thought disturbs our minds and we become restless.

Verse 11

चलसि यद्व्रजाच्चारयन् पशून्
नलिनसुन्दरं नाथ ते पदम्।
शिलतृणाङ्कुरैः सीदतीति नः
कलिलतां मनः कान्त गच्छति॥११॥

calasi yad vrajāc cārayan paśūn
nalina-sundaraṁ nātha te padam
śila-tṛṇāṅkuraiḥ sīdatīti naḥ
kalilatāṁ manaḥ kānta gacchati

calasi – You go; *yat* – when; *vrajāt* – from the cowherd village; *cārayan* – herding; *paśūn* – the animals; *nalina* – than a lotus flower; *sundaram* – more beautiful; *nātha* – O master; *te* – Your; *padam* – feet; *śila* – by sharp edges of grain; *tṛṇa* – grass; *aṅkuraiḥ* – and sprouting plants; *sīdati* – are experiencing pain; *iti* – thus thinking; *naḥ* – us; *kalilatām* – confusion; *manaḥ* – our minds; *kānta* – O lover; *gacchati* – feel.

Translation

O master, O beloved, when You leave Vraja to take the cows and other animals out to graze, the soles of Your feet, which are more tender than a lotus, must suffer great pain from sharp pebbles, grasses, and the edges of dry grains. When we think about this, our minds become very agitated.

The *gopīs* say, "It is not that You give pain only to others. You give pain to Yourself as well, and because of this we become full of sorrow."

Here they imply that Kṛṣṇa has such a strong desire to give them pain that He gives Himself pain, knowing that they will feel it. They say, "When You go cow-herding with Your friends, You roam the forest, which is covered with sprouts of rice, wheat, and grass that are sharper than needles. Yet Your lotus feet are more tender and soft than a delicate lotus flower; surely these sharp sprouts cause You pain. This very thought disturbs our minds and we become restless."

The word *kalila* means 'confusion leading to sorrow,' and Śrīla Viśvanātha Cakravartī Ṭhākura has revealed a special meaning – to quarrel. He explains that the *gopis*' words can be interpreted in another way, in which case they say, "*Kalilatām* – Our mind incites (*la*) arguments (*kali*), and we are thus absorbed in fighting with our own minds." He describes how the *gopīs* quarrel with their mind and their mind retaliates.

The *gopīs* say, "O mind, if Kṛṣṇa's feet truly feel pain when He goes cow-herding, then why does He go out every single day? If this really hurts Him, He would not go out. Why do you uselessly bother worrying about Him?"

Their mind and heart replies, "O foolish cowherd girls, you cannot understand how Kṛṣṇa's feet are softer than lotus flowers, but you should know that they are extremely tender. Surely pebbles, stone chips, and sharp plant shoots pierce His delicate lotus feet and He feels pain. When I contemplate this, I become engulfed in sorrow."

The *gopīs* say, "O mind, O heart, Kṛṣṇa does not step on these things. He has eyes, so He avoids all sharp objects that cause pain; He walks on the very soft sand."

"It is not like that," their mind retorts. "The cows do not have the sense to walk only on soft sand and grass.

"They run here and there," the mind continues, "often treading on those sharp stones, and Kṛṣṇa follows them."

The *gopīs* say, "It is true that those cows have no intelligence, but Kṛṣṇa has eyes, so why would He run on stones and sharp sprouts that would hurt His feet?"

Their mind replies, "You do not have the slightest trace of love. If you did, you would know that when Kṛṣṇa runs after the cows, He has no time to consider where He is going. He simply runs throughout Vṛndāvana, not even noticing the sharp stones. They definitely pierce His feet, and I cannot bear that thought."

Now conceding that their heart and mind are telling the truth, the *gopīs* say, "Perhaps Brahmā has given us this birth as *gopīs* just to suffer all these miseries."

To this, their mind replies, "O unhappy *gopīs*, yes, perhaps he has; and in that case you should suffer. You can remain alive to suffer; you can remain here and tolerate Kṛṣṇa's pain. As far as I am concerned, accompanied by your life-airs I am abandoning your bodies and, when I do, you will die."

The *gopīs* tell Kṛṣṇa, "You perpetually torment us with suffering, both in meeting (*saṁyoga*) and separation (*viyoga*). When You enter the forest to herd Your cows, we feel unending grief due to separation from You. There are many cows running in every direction and, to stop them from straying, You follow them and with great effort try to gather them together. You run along rough, uneven paths without stopping for a moment, and as You do, rough grains and other sharp objects pierce Your lotus feet. When we think of this, we drown in sorrow, unable to maintain our patience."

Śrīla Viśvanātha Cakravartī Ṭhākura reveals a deep import of the *gopīs*' words. They mean to say, "Cows are only animals. They have no wisdom, nor do they have the power to think, 'Kṛṣṇa will follow us, no matter where we go. His feet will get hurt and He will not be able to stop to rest.' If they understood this, they would not run here and there on rough, uneven pathways. They are mere animals, and have neither intelligence nor discrimination."

Now the *gopīs* say, "These stones, sharp grasses, and sprouts may penetrate Your feet, but they do not penetrate Your heart;

they penetrate ours. We feel pain because You are our *nātha* and our *kānta*." *Kānta* means lover – but much more than lover. *Nātha* generally refers to a beloved, but in this case it means 'giver of pain.' So when the *gopīs* say, "O *nātha*," they are actually saying, "O You who always gives us pain."

Kṛṣṇa says, "Do not be anxious about My feet. Just forget about any discomfort you think I may be feeling."

The *gopīs* reply, "But You are our beloved; we cannot stop thinking about it."

If a husband or beloved does not return from a place at the expected time, his dear wife or sweetheart cannot help but worry that some calamity has occurred and she may not see him again. She becomes very distressed, only to find out later that all is well. Similarly, the *gopīs* express their mood: "You are our beloved, so we are bound to feel like this. If our hearts felt no love for You, we would not feel any pain. Our attachment for You is the root of all our sorrow, but at the same time it is our natural tendency."

The *gopīs*' words are perfectly true. It is only because of attachment that one feels sorrow and pain. They continue, "Our attachment for You is the guilty party. We know we should have no love and affection for You, but the fact is that we do have it; so what shall we do? Now, our earnest prayer to You is that you please remove this attachment from our heart."

Kṛṣṇa may retort, "It is your mind and heart; you can cut it out yourselves. I am not responsible for your mind and heart.

To this the *gopīs* reply, "Our attachment to You is not our fault; it is Yours, because You are our beloved and You are so astonishingly attractive. If You were not so affectionate and attractive, we would have no love for You and everything would be all right. You have made Yourself so beautiful and such a charming lover that our minds have left us and gone to You. Why have You done that? You alone can remove our attachment, because You are now in possession of our mind and heart.

"If You want to please us, do not roam the forest. Come and stay with us. That is the remedy." In each of the verses of *Gopī-gīta* the *gopīs* pray, "Please appear before us."

In the previous verse, they uttered the words *dhyāna-maṅgalam*. The word *dhyāna* generally means 'meditation,' but in the case of the *gopīs* it simply means that they are remembering Kṛṣṇa. The *gopīs*' remembrance is not like a *yogī*'s meditation. When they remember Kṛṣṇa, they forget everything else. Whatever they are doing, whether it is walking, talking, or cooking, they are always immersed in *sahaja-samādhi*, a natural, deep absorption in Śrī Kṛṣṇa. The word *sahajāyate* means 'to come naturally, from birth.' Their full absorption in anything related to Kṛṣṇa comes automatically and naturally.

Śrīla Vyāsadeva had to make some effort to practice *bhakti-yoga*, and in this way he achieved *samādhi*. The *gopīs*, on the other hand, do not require to practice *sādhana-bhakti*, because their hearts are steeped in a *prema* that is situated in the highest stages of *mahābhāva*. They never come out of *samādhi*; they simply go deeper and deeper into it. Their *samādhi* deepens when they see Kṛṣṇa, and it further deepens and thickens as they remember Him when He is out of sight.

Some people are puzzled by this; they wonder which is actually higher, meeting with Kṛṣṇa or being separated from Him. We will understand these topics when we have gained some realization of them, and for now we can pray to the *gopīs* as Śrīla Viśvanātha Cakravartī Ṭhākura and Śrīla Jīva Gosvāmī have prayed: "Neither Brahmā nor anyone else can explain these topics without your mercy. One can understand them by your grace alone." If the *gopīs* bestow their mercy upon us, we will become qualified to fully comprehend the true nature of their pastimes, which cannot be understood by intellectual analysis. At present we must hear these topics so that we can develop a greed to perform *rāgānuga-bhakti*. The fruit of hearing these topics will be that eventually we will feel that we cannot live without hearing them. At that time the *gopīs* will bestow their mercy upon us and we will be able to appreciate something of their unlimited glory.

In one's practice of *vaidhī-bhakti*, one performs an *ārati* ceremony to the Deity of Kṛṣṇa on the temple altar. Śrī Kṛṣṇa already has articles that are millions of times superior to any the aspiring devotee can offer; yet, out of duty, the devotee offers Him articles of worship.

He offers a lamp, water in a conch-shell, and cloth, and then he offers foodstuffs; but he has no feeling. The Vedic scriptures state that even if one performs *arcana* for millions of births, it is not certain that he will develop a taste for *rāgānuga-bhakti*. However, if a person hears and discusses topics such as *Gopī-gīta* in the association of a Vaiṣṇava who is superior to him, and he practice *bhakti* under the guidance of that Vaiṣṇava, it is certain that he can develop this taste and greed. This is made even more effective if he associates with a Vaiṣṇava who is *rasika* and *bhāvuka* and who has realized these topics. We cannot imagine the results of such association. In this way, we will understand the topics of meeting and separation.

The following pastime reveals how there can be separation in meeting. Once, at Prema-sarovara, an incident took place that impelled Śrī Kṛṣṇa to leave Vṛndāvana. Śrīmatī Rādhikā was sitting on His lap, embraced by His arms, and listening to His loving words. A bumblebee began to buzz close by Her, and She became fearful. Kṛṣṇa's cowherd friend Madhumaṅgala chased away the bee with his stick and, returning, he boasted, "I have driven *madhusūdana* away, and he will never come back." *Madhusūdana* means 'bumblebee,' but it is also a name for Kṛṣṇa. Śrīmatī Rādhikā heard these words and assumed Madhumaṅgala was saying, "Kṛṣṇa will never return." Even though She was sitting on Kṛṣṇa's lap, She was immediately thrown into an ocean of painful feelings of separation and began to cry out, "Where is Kṛṣṇa? Where is Kṛṣṇa? Where is Kṛṣṇa?" Her agony became so intense that She fainted.

This stage of love for Kṛṣṇa – feelings of separation in meeting – is called *prema-vaicittya*. *Prema-vaicittya* is experienced at the time of meeting, whereas *divyonmāda* and *citra-jalpa*[1] appear at the time of separation. Happiness and sorrow are both felt at the time of meeting, and also at the time of separation. In *prema-vaicittya*, Rādhikā is externally with Kṛṣṇa, but She feels internally that She is separated from Him. On the other hand, in *divyonmāda* and *citra-jalpa*, when She is externally separated from Him, She thinks, "Now I am with

1 Śrīla Viśvanātha Cakravartī Ṭhākura explains in his commentary on *Bhramara-gīta* that there are ten divisions of divine madness (*divyonmāda*), which are expressed by the ten divisions of *citra-jalpa*, or variegated mad emotional speech.

Kṛṣṇa." Internally She is fully meeting with Him, and this gives joy to Her heart.

Śrī Kṛṣṇa noted Śrīmatī Rādhikā's moods in Her separation from and meeting with Him, and thought, "Rādhikā and the *gopīs* feel My presence when we are separated from each other. But sometimes, they feel separation from Me when I am with them. At those times there is nothing I can do to help them. Their feelings of separation while meeting bring them great distress. It would be best if I go far away so that they can meet Me internally. I should leave Vṛndāvana forever, for it is better that I feel pain so that they will have some happiness."

The *gopīs* feel the same way about Kṛṣṇa: "As long as Kṛṣṇa is pleased, it does not matter how much sorrow or pain we feel." They find some consolation after Kṛṣṇa has gone to Mathurā and Dvārakā and they are in Vṛndāvana, thinking, "Kṛṣṇa is happy with His queens, His sons, and all His other associates, and He also feels joy in meeting with Kubjā. Let Him be happy; we do not want to disturb Him."

Similarly, Kṛṣṇa finds some consolation when He is in Mathurā or Dvārakā: "The *gopīs* are somewhat happy in their feelings of separation. I want their happiness, and they achieve it in those moods and sentiments. If I were to remain in Vṛndāvana, it is possible that they would experience such separation from Me that they would die." These sublime sentiments are especially true of Śrīmatī Rādhikā, who tastes the separation moods of *divyonmāda* and *pralāpa*. Her loving moods have been described in our *ācāryas*' commentaries on *Bhramara-gīta*.

The reason the *gopīs* do not die in the anguish of their separation from Kṛṣṇa is that they think, "Kṛṣṇa would be greatly distressed if we were to die. For this reason alone we must remain alive." Likewise, Kṛṣṇa thinks, "If I were to die, the *gopīs* would feel indescribable pain." He and the *gopīs* want nothing but each other's happiness; this is called pure love.

We hear that Kṛṣṇa left Vṛndāvana in order to kill Kaṁsa and to be with Vasudeva and Devakī, but these are only external reasons. The most essential and prime reason was to please the *gopīs*. Moreover, we must consider whether or not He really left

Vṛndāvana. His going to Mathurā and killing Kaṁsa is described in *Śrīmad-Bhāgavatam*, Chapter Forty-four, and Chapter Forty-five describes the subsequent events, as follows:

When Kṛṣṇa and Balarāma left Vṛndāvana and went to Mathurā with Akrūra, Nanda Bābā also went to Mathurā. The day after they arrived, Kṛṣṇa killed Kaṁsa. Kaṁsa's brothers fought with Kṛṣṇa and Balarāma, and Balarāma killed them all. Later that same day, Kṛṣṇa reinstated Ugrasena as the king of Mathurā, in a grand celebration, with offerings of flowers and much opulent paraphernalia. Ugrasena had previously been king, but Kaṁsa had usurped his position. After Kaṁsa's death, Kṛṣṇa performed the *abhiṣeka* ceremony (a bathing with auspicious ingredients) to again establish him as the king.

After Ugrasena was reinstated, all the important members of the Yadu family, such as Vasudeva, Devakī, Ugrasena, and Akrūra had a long meeting in which they decided: "We must take great care of Kṛṣṇa, because now that He has killed Kaṁsa, He will try to return to Vṛndāvana. Nanda Bābā is waiting in a garden on the outskirts of the city. We must do our best to ensure that Kṛṣṇa and Baladeva do not return with him to Vṛndāvana. We will impress upon Them that They are sons of Vasudeva and Devakī, not Yaśodā and Nanda."

Accordingly, the members of the Yadu family were very affectionate to Kṛṣṇa that day. "You are the son of Devakī and Vasudeva," they told Him, "and we are Your relatives and family members. Do not think that Yaśodā and Nanda are Your mother and father, and do not think that Your real home is Vṛndāvana. You actually belong to Mathurā, and we are Your natural relatives."

Meanwhile, Nanda Bābā was waiting for Śrī Kṛṣṇa and Balarāma Prabhu in his camp outside Mathurā. On the evening of the second day, when it had become dark, Kṛṣṇa and Baladeva approached him. They sat on his lap, one on each side. "Why are you weeping?" They asked him, but Nanda Bābā could not utter a word in response. Understanding his mind, Kṛṣṇa said, "Bābā, you are My father, so why are they saying that Devakī and Vasudeva are Our mother and father? All the Mathurāvāsīs are trying to persuade Us to accept this." During that conversation, Kṛṣṇa and Baladeva and Nanda Bābā discussed many related topics.

Śrīla Viśvanātha Cakravartī Ṭhākura explains in his commentary that everyone wants to live in that place where they receive the most love and affection. Kṛṣṇa receives so much love from Nanda and Yaśodā, whose *prema* is certainly far superior to that of Vasudeva, Devakī, and all the other Mathurāvāsīs. Why, then, did He stay in Mathurā and not return with Nanda Bābā to Vraja? According to the rules of *prema*, He should have gone with him, but according to *Śrīmad-Bhāgavatam*, He did not do this. What is the *siddhānta*, or conclusive philosophical truth, in this connection?

Śrīla Viśvanātha Cakravartī Ṭhākura says that *prema* has two chambers (*prakoṣṭhas*): The first is where the manifest pastimes (*prakaṭa-līlā*) are performed, and the second is where the unmanifest pastimes (*aprakaṭa-līlā*) take place. In *prakaṭa-līlā* Kṛṣṇa and Baladeva did not return to Vṛndāvana, whereas in *aprakaṭa-līlā* They returned.

"*Vṛndāvanaṁ parityajya padam ekaṁ na gacchati* – Kṛṣṇa never sets a foot outside of Vṛndāvana; not a single footstep." This statement refers to *aprakaṭa-līlā*, in which He is always in Vṛndāvana. In *prakaṭa-līlā*, however, He sometimes leaves Vṛndāvana, and sometimes He enters. Śrīla Viśvanātha Cakravartī Ṭhākura has explained that it would be opposed to *bhakti-rasa* if, in *aprakaṭa-līlā*, Kṛṣṇa was not always with those who love Him the most.

Verse Twelve

The moon is splendid with its diffusing rays, and Your face has the same exquisite appearance. In fact, Your face is more beautiful when it is partially hidden by the dust rising from the cows' hooves and by Your curly hair.

Verse 12

दिनपरिक्षये नीलकुन्तलैर्
वनरुहाननं बिभ्रदावृतम्।
धनरजस्वलं दर्शयन् मुहुर्
मनसि नः स्मरं वीर यच्छसि ॥१२॥

dina-parikṣaye nīla-kuntalair
vana-ruhānanaṁ bibhrad āvṛtam
dhana-rajasvalaṁ darśayan muhur
manasi naḥ smaraṁ vīra yacchasi

dina – of the day; *parikṣaye* – at the finish; *nīla* – dark blue; *kuntalaiḥ* – with locks of hair; *vana-ruha* – lotus; *ānanam* – face; *bibhrat* – exhibiting; *āvṛtam* – covered; *dhana* – raised by the multitude of Your cows; *rajaḥ-valam* – smeared with dust; *darśayan* – showing; *muhuḥ* – repeatedly; *manasi* – in the minds; *naḥ* – our; *smaram* – Cupid; *vīra* – O hero; *yacchasi* – You are placing.

Translation

O beloved hero, as the day draws to an end, You return from the forest, Your lotus face partly covered by Your bluish-black locks of curling hair and veiled in a very thin layer of dust rising from the host of cows' hooves. At that time, by repeatedly showing us Your beautiful lotus face so exquisitely ornamented, You arouse amorous desire within our minds.

Bhāva-prakāśika Vṛtti

Dina-parikṣaye: *Dina* means 'day' and *kṣaya* means 'end.' *Dina-parikṣaye* means that the end of the day has come. It is evening. The sun is moving towards the horizon but has not yet set. Some time earlier, around three o'clock, all the cows feel satisfaction from grazing, and Kṛṣṇa calls to them, "*Dhiri, dhiri* (come to Me);" "*niri, niri* (come to the water);" "*chu, chu* (drink water);" "*tiri, tiri* (come out of the water and onto the bank);" and "*hio, hio* (let us go)." The cows have eaten and drunk their fill, and they are ready to return home. They remember their calves and call out, "*Hamba*! *Hamba*! *Hamba*! (I am coming)." Śrī Kṛṣṇa then plays on His flute, gathers His friends and all the cows, and prepares to return home.

Nīla-kuntalaiḥ: *Nīla* means 'dark blue or black' and *kuntalaiḥ* means 'by curly hair.' *Vana-ruhānanaṁ bibhrad āvṛtam*: *Ānanam* means 'face' and *āvṛtam* means 'covered.' Śrī Kṛṣṇa's beautiful curly blue-black hair reaches down to His shoulders and partly covers His face, which appears like a lotus flower covered by bees. The word *bibhrad* refers to Kṛṣṇa's exhibiting the exquisite loveliness of His face, which is likened to the beautifully shining moon.

Dhana-rajasvalam: *Raja* refers to the pollen-like dust of the earth. That *raja* is *dhana*, wealth, and here it refers to *go-dhana*, the wealth of cows. The cows are running, returning to their homes and to their calves. Kṛṣṇa has called their names by playing sweetly on His flute, and they all hurry to be with Him, thinking, "Kṛṣṇa is calling me." Then, as they run, the dust rising from their moving hooves sweeps upward towards the sky, sprinkling the leaves of the trees all around. This pollen-like dust also falls on Śrī Kṛṣṇa, creating a very fine covering on His face, body, and garments.

As Kṛṣṇa returns with the cows, He takes them in His arms and embraces them. His inner motive in doing this is solely

to show His beloved *gopīs* His lotus face, which is beautified by this dust, and to convey to them that He desires to embrace them. And the real reason He plays His flute is not to gather the cows, but to call the *gopīs*. Hearing the deep sound of His flute, the *gopīs* stand on the road, in *kuñjas*, and on the palace roofs, only to see Him return.

Kṛṣṇa's behavior may be likened to that of a person posing for a photograph. That person smiles or poses in a certain way, just to ensure a good picture. Similarly, Kṛṣṇa thinks that the *gopīs* should come and see His lotus face. Therefore, not just once, but again and again, He laughs, embraces the cows, and talks to His friends, with the motive of showing Himself to the *gopīs*. If He notices that the *gopīs* are not looking at Him, He thinks, "They must look at My face. Their loving mood will then increase and bring them to Me."

Smaraṁ vīra yacchasi: When the *gopīs* address Kṛṣṇa with the words, "O hero (*vīra*)," they mean 'hero in *madhura-rasa*.' "You are able to give us whatever we want," they tell Him. "You have the power to give *smara*, so You are our hero." In this connection, *smara* refers to the Sanskrit verb *smṛ* with the suffix *ṇi*, meaning 'to remind.' It relates to an experience of something that brings something else to mind. For example, the *gopīs* see Kṛṣṇa again and again showing them His face that is beautified by the dust of the earth rising from the running cows, and that beauty arouses *kāma* in their hearts.

Something that is ordinarily considered a blemish serves to make Kṛṣṇa or Śrīmatī Rādhikā immeasurably more beautiful. If mud splashes onto Kṛṣṇa's face, or if the dust of the earth falls on it, His beauty increases millions of times. The dust rising from the cows running throughout the land of Vraja makes Him appear so beautiful that whenever the *gopīs* remember Him, they become filled with *kāma*. In the pastimes of Kṛṣṇa and the *gopīs*, *kāma* does not mean 'lust,' it means *prema*. The *gopīs* tell Kṛṣṇa, "We do not want to be attracted to You. We want to be aloof, but how can we be aloof when You show us Your face again and again?"

Now let us go to Śrīla Viśvanātha Cakravartī Ṭhākura's *Sārārtha-darśinī* and Śrīla Jīva Gosvāmī's *Vaiṣṇava-toṣaṇī*. In their commentaries to Verse Eleven, both *ācāryas* have discussed the quarrel between the *gopīs* and their mind, with the *gopīs* on one side, and their heart and mind on the other. As mentioned earlier, the *gopīs* told their mind, "Why are you so restless, agitated, and anxious when Kṛṣṇa goes to herd the cows? There is no reason for your restlessness. What is the use of being so disturbed?"

Their mind replied, "You are not at all *rasika*; you do not possess even a drop of *rasa*. O *gopīs*, due to your ignorance, you are devoid of feeling. Kṛṣṇa will go to the forest, and I want Him to go, but I do not want Him to experience any kind of difficulty. He should play in the forest, but He should not suffer."

"Then why are you so anxious?"

"I am anxious because He follows behind the cows. Those cows wander to places that are filled with sharp grass shoots, edges of dry grains, chips of stone, and other things that will hurt Him."

To this the *gopīs* responded, "You are simply blinded by *prema*. This is not true at all. Kṛṣṇa has eyes. He will see where it is safe to walk and will only place His feet where the grass is silken and the sand is soft."

Their mind replied, "O *gopīs*, you think like this because you are neither intelligent nor *rasika*. Cows have no wisdom or discrimination. They will not remain on smooth paths. They will stray, and Kṛṣṇa will follow them in order to bring them back to the path."

The *gopīs* said, "Yes, we agree that Kṛṣṇa will go to those places; but Brahmā has created us to suffer, so we are suffering."

Their mind then told them, "It is all right for you to stay here and suffer, but I will not. I am going to leave your body along with your life-airs. I must leave. You should stay here and suffer alone."

The *gopīs* now tell Kṛṣṇa, "By not being with us, You make us suffer. When You herd the cows, we feel separation from You and become afflicted with sorrow. But it is not only then that we feel this pain; we feel the same grief when we are with You. How is this so? In the evening, along with Your cows and friends, You return to the cowsheds in the village of Vṛndāvana. At that time Your face is finely veiled by the foot-dust of the cows and by Your beautiful, bluish-black curly hair. Why do You let that dust cover Your face? You should not allow this, because then we cannot fully see it."

The *gopīs* want to see Kṛṣṇa's face clearly, but at the same time they become utterly fascinated when it is covered by a thin layer of dust and appears just like the moon rising from the darkness. They say, "The moon is splendid with its diffusing rays, and Your face has the same exquisite appearance. In fact, Your face is more beautiful when it is partially hidden by the dust rising from the cows' hooves and by Your curly hair."

When they say that the foot-dust of the cows is a wealth, they indicate its immense value, as it is utilized by Śrī Kṛṣṇa to increase the beauty of His lotus face. Śrīla Viśvanātha Cakravartī Ṭhākura has also shown this with reference to the *Viśva-prakāśa* Sanskrit dictionary: *dhana* (wealth) refers to *go-dhana* (the wealth of cows).

Śrī Kṛṣṇa becomes gladdened by their words and thinks, "I am most fortunate. Taking these cows out to graze in the forests of Vṛndāvana has given Me an opportunity to meet with you *gopīs*. It is only by the medium of the cows that I can freely be with you." Kṛṣṇa feels indebted to the cows and is happy when their foot-dust settles on His face. This is His inner mood.

He also has an inner reason for wearing a peacock feather. The peacocks' and peahens' beautiful dancing with each other induces Him to dance as well. The peacock feather stimulates His love for the *gopīs*, for it induces Him to dance with them. In fact, *rāsa-līlā* was inspired by the dancing of the peacocks. For this reason Kṛṣṇa has placed their feathers on His head, and for this reason also, they are a wealth.

The *gopīs* are accustomed to watching Kṛṣṇa as He returns from the pasturing grounds with the cows, His arms entwined about the heads of the cows in an embrace. They also observe Him as He appears to search for His cowherd friends. To ordinary people it seems that He is simply seeking the cowherd boys and cows. He does not want to openly reveal His true motive, which is actually to look for the *gopīs*. Moreover, among millions of *gopīs* He is looking for one *gopī* in particular. Now, in their song of separation, the *gopīs* say, "When we see You searching in this way, we become restless and feel that we cannot live a moment longer without You. Seeing

You embrace the cows and cowherd boys, we desire that You do the same with us." This is called *smara*.

"We suffer greatly in separation from You," the *gopīs* continue, "from morning until the time we see You again. But then, when we do see You, we suffer even more than before because our desire to see You has increased. At that time we may be compared to a thirsty person standing on the bank of the River Gaṅgā, thinking, 'Gaṅgā is here. I have come from very far away to drink its water, and I have been through so many difficulties to get here. The water is beautiful and sweet, but there is no place of access (*ghāṭa*) whereby I can reach the water.' It is very difficult. We are thirsty, and 'flowing water' is available in huge quantities, but we cannot drink it. Your face is exceedingly attractive because of the dust that partially hides it; but the cowherd boys and cows are present when You return from herding the cows, and so are our fathers and mothers. The *smara* You give us at that time cannot satisfy us; it only pains us.

"You consider, 'Whoever sees My face will drown in an ocean of happiness,' and this is especially true for us; *smara* certainly appears in our hearts. You know this, and that is why You show us Your face again and again. You want to increase our *smara*, but because You cannot give us what we want, that *smara* only increases our distress."

According to the *gopīs*, Śrī Kṛṣṇa calls them with the promise that He will give them what they want. "Come and take it," He announces. But when they come He deceives them, giving them only distress, calamities, and agony. They want to avoid seeing Him, but He calls them and they cannot stay away. The melody of His flute pulls them forcibly to Him and they are compelled to see Him; but when they arrive, there is no meeting.

They tell Him, "You maddened us with the melody of Your flute, You dragged us here to this secluded forest at night, and now we are weeping and wandering here and there, unable to see You. We have come to the conclusion that You are certainly a hero, for You are expert in giving suffering to others; You are, indeed, most munificent in this. You show Your prowess in killing millions of *gopīs*, but You should understand that all the agony You cause us will come upon Your head. You will be held responsible for this.

"You have taken away our *dharma*, the religious principle of fulfilling one's duties and responsibilities to one's family and dynasty; and You have taken away our shyness, patience, chastity, and other feminine virtues. Although You have taken everything from us, we still cannot do what You want us to do: die. At the same time You do not want us to die because, if we die, You will not be able to find anyone else who can suffer as much as we have without dying. You see that we are suffering, and this makes You so pleased. O Kṛṣṇa, You are certainly a hero."

There is a point to note in *Vaiṣṇava-toṣaṇī*: Although *dina-parikṣaye* generally means 'the end of the day,' in this context the *gopīs* mean to say that they have come to the end of their life. They express their tragic mood thus: "We have lost our tolerance and we are about to die, so please come at once and meet with us." This point is very important. It is easy to understand the ordinary meaning of *dina-parikṣaye*, but it is difficult to grasp the inner meaning of the *gopīs*' pathos.

As stated before, *nīla-kuntalaiḥ* means 'by locks of curly, blackish hair.' Beauty actually lives in blackness. No matter how large one's eyes may be, they will not be beautiful if there is no black dot in the middle. One's face may be beautiful, but it will not look as beautiful if one's hair is white instead of black. What would happen if all the *gopīs*' black hair were cut off? You cannot imagine. Likewise, the *gopīs* loveliness is exquisite, but if blackish Kṛṣṇa were not with them, everything would be different. When Kṛṣṇa's face is decorated and partly shrouded by His black hair, it becomes more beautiful, and then there is *smara*.

In one of his commentaries, Śrīla Viśvanātha Cakravartī Ṭhākura explains a specific point concerning the unique fortune of the family lineage of the cowherd community – the young *gopas* and young *gopīs*, the paternal *gopas* and the maternal *gopīs*. The sight of Kṛṣṇa's beautiful face is meant for the *gopas* and *gopīs* alone. No one but they can fully see and relish it. Neither Vasudeva nor Devakī, nor any of the Dvārakāvāsīs, can see this resplendent sight. Moreover, *smara* would not appear in the *gopīs*' hearts in quite the same way if they were to see Kṛṣṇa wearing His golden crown and opulent royal paraphernalia. The only desire of the *gopas* and *gopīs* is this: "May I always behold Kṛṣṇa's lovely face." They do not want to see Dvārakādhīśa Kṛṣṇa, Mathureśa Kṛṣṇa, or any other form of Kṛṣṇa. They only want to see Him in His form as a cowherd youth.

In their *Veṇu-gīta*, as they discuss Śrī Kṛṣṇa's beauty while He is cowherding, the *gopīs* say that He is naturally decorated in a wonderful way. He carries two types of ropes for binding cows: one on His turban and the other on His shoulder. Rolled up on His turban is a type of rope for binding the back legs of the cows at the time of milking, and on His shoulders He carries a rope for binding a calf nearby a cow in order to start the flow of milk. These are not mere ropes – they link the *gopīs*' minds and hearts with Krsna. The *gopīs* have so much *smara* at that time, not only by seeing the beautiful vision of His face, but also by seeing the way in which He wears the ropes.

Now they say, "You have given us *smara* and also so much pain by showing us Your face. We did not want to see it. We were in our rooms at home, behind closed doors, but someone came and opened those doors. He entered our hearts, stole them, and forcibly dragged us here." *Muhur manasi naḥ smaraṁ vīra yacchasi.* Here, *manasi* refers to Kāmadeva, the presiding deity of the mind, and it is the mind that manifests *smara*. The *gopīs* say, "You drag us towards You, and then You put that *smara* in our mind by showing us Your face. Why do You repeatedly show Your face? We want a remedy for our *smara*, but instead it increases. We know that You are a hero, but Your heroism goes only as far as giving *smara* and killing *gopīs*."

Verse Thirteen

We are experiencing so much anguish, and we are in a calamity that is worse than any other. Please remove this agony.

Verse 13

प्रणतकामदं पद्मजार्चितं
धरणिमण्डनं ध्येयमापदि।
चरणपङ्कजं शन्तमञ्च ते
रमण नः स्तनेष्वर्पयाधिहन् ॥१३॥

praṇata-kāma-daṁ padma-jārcitaṁ
dharaṇi-maṇḍanaṁ dhyeyam āpadi
caraṇa-paṅka-jaṁ śantamaṁ ca te
ramaṇa naḥ staneṣv arpayādhi-han

praṇata – those who are surrendered; *kāma* – the desires; *dam* – fulfilling; *padma-ja* – by Lord Brahmā; *arcitam* – worshiped; *dharaṇi* – of the earth; *maṇḍanam* – the ornament; *dhyeyam* – the proper object of meditation; *āpadi* – in time of distress; *caraṇa-paṅkajam* – the lotus feet; *śantamam* – giving boundless bliss; *ca* – and; *te* – Your; *ramaṇa* – O lover; *naḥ* – our; *staneṣu* – on the breasts; *arpaya* – please place; *adhi-han* – O destroyer of all kinds of sorrows.

Translation

O dear most beloved, O destroyer of all sorrow, Your lotus feet, which fulfill all desires of Your surrendered devotees, are worshiped by Brahmā, who was born from the lotus, and they are the ornament that embellishes the earth. When meditated upon they remove all calamity, and when accepting service, they bestow supreme bliss. Kindly place such lotus feet upon our breasts.

Bhāva-prakāśika Vṛtti

The words *praṇata-kāma-dam* have two meanings here: "You immediately fulfill all the desires of those surrendered (*praṇata*) unto You," and "You bestow nothing less than *kāma* in the hearts of those surrendered unto You."

Kāma is the superlative expression of Kṛṣṇa's mercy. Here, *kāma* means *prema*, transcendental love, the exalted love of the *gopīs*' *kāmātmika-bhakti*[1]. If one approaches Śrī Kṛṣṇa under the guidance of a *kāmātmika-bhakta*, Kṛṣṇa gives him *kāmānuga-bhakti*[1].

Padmajārcitaṁ dharaṇi-maṇḍanam: *Padmajārcitam* means 'worshiped by Brahmā,' and *dharaṇi-maṇḍanam* means 'ornament of the earth.' Both these words are adjectives describing Śrī Kṛṣṇa's lotus feet (*caraṇa-paṅkajam*). "Your lotus feet, which are the ornaments of the earth, are always worshiped by Brahmā." Here, the *gopīs* say, "Just as Your lotus feet are the ornaments of the earth's heart, they are also the ornament of our hearts."

Dhyeyam āpadi: *Āpadi* means 'at times of distress.' If anyone remembers Kṛṣṇa's lotus feet, he or she becomes free from all varieties of obstacles, miseries, and calamities. An instance of this is Kṛṣṇa's appearance before the *gopīs* when they completed their singing of Gopī-*gīta*. At that time, a *gopī* came to Him and placed both of His hands in hers. Another *gopī* placed His arms on her shoulders. Another came to Him with *tāmbūla-beṭīkā* (betel nut) in her hands, and another placed His lotus feet on her breasts. Another *gopī* was in such an angry mood that, from a distance, She stared at Him from the corners of Her eyes.

---

1 "*Kāmātmika-bhakti* and *kāmānuga-bhakti*: "One can attain one's inherent constitutional nature in unalloyed *prema* by developing the moods of either the *gopīs* (*kāmātmika*) or the love of Kṛṣṇa's parents, friends, and servants (*sambandhātmika*). Both these moods are the shelter of Kṛṣṇa's eternally perfect associates. A *kāmānugā-bhakta* is one who has greed to follow in the wake of *kāmātmika-bhakti*" (*Jaiva-dharma*, Chapter 21).

Biting Her lips, that *gopī* wanted to give Him pain by shooting Him with the arrows of Her eyes. Another *gopī* looked towards Him as if she wanted to take Him into her heart. Another *gopī* immediately took Him through her eyes into her heart, where she embraced Him tightly, thinking herself to be alone with Him in a solitary place. Simply by her absorption in Him, that *gopī* became so full of spiritual pleasure that her hair stood on end in ecstasy and all her miseries at once disappeared.

The *gopīs* do not feel material miseries, so what is their misery? The only calamity they face is separation from Kṛṣṇa, and that pain of separation disappears only when they meet with Him. They pray in this verse of *Gopī-gīta*, "O *ramaṇa* (delightful beloved), please place Your lotus feet on our hearts so that our suffering in separation from You, and our disease of *kāma*, will cease."

Śrīla Viśvanātha Cakravartī Ṭhākura has revealed the words of Kṛṣṇa and the *gopīs* in the previous verse: "You always give us miseries and calamities," the *gopīs* said, "whether we are meeting with You or we are apart."

"Why do you need Me, then?" Kṛṣṇa replied. "You should leave Me, and remain far away. Do not come to Me again and do not call Me."

Thrown into anxiety by hearing this, the *gopīs* thought, "Now we have made Kṛṣṇa angry." They now try to appease Him, speaking this thirteenth verse in order to pacify His sulky mood (*māna*).

Śantamaṁ ca te: one meaning is 'always pleasing.' The *gopīs* say, "You are always pleasing to us. It is true that those sharp words came out of our mouths, but we really did not mean what we said. It was a mere slip-of-the-tongue. We need You, only You, and no one else."

Praṇata-kāma-dam: Here they say, "You fulfill every desire of Your surrendered souls. Even if an offender surrenders to You, You do not neglect him; rather, You forgive him. In fact, You not only forgive him, You benedict him."

Kṛṣṇa's pastime of subduing the serpent Kāliya is an example of this. Kāliya was opposed to both the Supreme Lord and His bird carrier, the great devotee Garuḍa. He was also angry with his wives because they had told him, "Do not oppose Kṛṣṇa." When Kṛṣṇa jumped into the Yamunā River to fight with him, he bit Kṛṣṇa on all the tender parts of His body in which the vital organs are located, including His heart. Normally, a person who is bitten in those places would die.

Kāliya was saved only by the intervention of his wives. When they first saw Kṛṣṇa fighting with him, his wives remained silent. They did not pray that Kṛṣṇa bestow His mercy upon him, because they considered him foolish. However, when Kṛṣṇa jumped upon his hoods and began to crush them one by one, they perceived a change in his mind and heart.

As Kāliya began to vomit blood, he thought, "This boy is more powerful than Garuḍa. I managed to escape from Garuḍa and flee, but I cannot do that now and I am about to die. I never imagined that anyone could have such power. Now I realize that the words of my wives were true. He is not an ordinary person. Perhaps He is God Himself; that may be why He is so powerful. Whoever He is, whether He is God or someone else, He is invincible." At this point, Kāliya submitted to Śrī Kṛṣṇa, "Now I surrender unto You."

Kāliya's wives had previously thought, "We do not want to have a husband who is brutal and opposed to Kṛṣṇa. He should die." When he became somewhat submissive, however, they became pleased. Kṛṣṇa had placed His feet on Kāliya's hoods, so a change of heart was inevitable for him. When that change took place, it happened suddenly, and Kāliya's wives immediately began to pray, "Now that he has become Your devotee and is praying for You to be merciful, please bestow Your mercy upon him. We no longer want to be made widows."

Initially Kṛṣṇa did not listen to the serpent's pleas even though Kāliya had surrendered to Him, but when the wives of Kāliya began offering their prayers, Kṛṣṇa listened. "Kāliya has surrendered to Me," He considered, "so I must bestow My mercy upon him." He told Kāliya, "I cannot allow you to stay here, as all the Vrajavāsīs are afraid of you. I know that you will not bite them or cause them any difficulty, because you are now a devotee. Still, it is best that you leave. Go at once to Ramaṇaka-dvīpa."

Kāliya accepted this instruction, and Kṛṣṇa assured him, "My footprints will always remain on your hoods, and because of that, Garuḍa will now be on friendly terms with you." Kāliya then left the

Yamunā and Vraja, carrying Śrī Kṛṣṇa's footprints on his head and meditating upon them. This pastime shows that even if an offender comes to Kṛṣṇa and begs for mercy, Kṛṣṇa will forgive him and bestow His mercy.

Padma-jārcitam: *Padma-ja* refers to Brahmā, who had previously committed many offences against Śrī Kṛṣṇa. He had given boons to Hiraṇyakaśipu, Hiraṇyākṣa, Rāvaṇa, and other demons, and by such boons those demons became powerful and fought with Kṛṣṇa and His incarnations like Śrī Rāmacandra.

When Kṛṣṇa killed the demon Aghāsura, Brahmā saw that a light as brilliant as lightning burst out of Aghāsura's head and remained in the sky. Then, as Kṛṣṇa and His cowherd friends and calves came out of the demon's stomach, that light entered Kṛṣṇa's lotus feet.

Brahmā understood that this cowherd boy was none other than the Supreme Personality of Godhead. He then desired to see more of the Lord's pastimes, but he wanted his own power to be the cause of initiating them. He thought, "I will see what happens when I cover Kṛṣṇa's power with my deluding potency (*māyā*)." He kidnapped the calves and cowherd boys and took them to a cave, where he waited to see what Kṛṣṇa would do. He then left for his planet, Satyaloka, for what was just a moment of time on that planet, but an entire year according to the timescale on earth. When he returned, however, he saw that Kṛṣṇa was playing with the calves and the cowherd boys, just as before.

"Who are these calves and boys?" Brahmā asked himself. "I have just put them in a cave." With the four eyes on two of his heads he looked forward to the cave, and with his other four eyes he looked behind him to Kṛṣṇa. Now he could see both sets of calves and cowherd boys at the same time, and he could not decide which ones were real.

Finally he understood, "This is not the work of my *māyā*. It is Kṛṣṇa's *māyā*." At that point he shut his eyes, fell flat on the earth, and wept. When he opened his eyes, he no longer saw any calves or boys. He saw Kṛṣṇa only, and he saw that each of the calves and boys, with their flutes and other paraphernalia, now appeared as Kṛṣṇa in His four-armed feature of Lord Nārāyaṇa. Why did he see Kṛṣṇa in this form? His worshipful Lord is Garbhodakaśāyī Viṣṇu (an expansion of Nārāyaṇa, who is an expansion of Kṛṣṇa), not the original Supreme Lord Vrajendra-nandana Śyāmasundara of Vraja.

Brahmā now exclaimed, "Oh, He is my worshipful Deity!"

He closed his eyes again, and when he opened them, he saw Kṛṣṇa alone, looking exactly as He looked before, wearing the same garments. Kṛṣṇa was holding some rice and yoghurt in His hand, anxiously searching for His calves and friends. He looked as if He had no idea of what was going on.

In this way, Brahmā had been an offender at Kṛṣṇa's lotus feet. He had given difficulties to the Lord and also to the Lord's cows and calves, and he had committed many other offenses as well. Now realizing this, he fell at Kṛṣṇa's lotus feet and offered many prayers. These prayers are recorded in the fourteenth chapter of Canto Ten, *Śrīmad-Bhāgavatam*:

tad astu me nātha sa bhūri-bhāgo
bhave 'tra vānyatra tu vā tiraścām
yenāham eko 'pi bhavaj-janānāṁ
bhūtvā niṣeve tava pāda-pallavam
Śrīmad-Bhāgavatām (10.14.30)

My dear Lord, I therefore pray to be so fortunate that in this life as Lord Brahmā or in another life, wherever I take my birth, I may be counted as one of Your devotees. I pray that wherever I may be, even among the animal species, I can engage in devotional service to Your lotus feet.

tad bhūri-bhāgyam iha janma kim apy aṭavyāṁ
yad gokule 'pi katamāṅghri-rajo-'bhiṣekam
yaj-jīvitaṁ tu nikhilaṁ bhagavān mukundas
tv adyāpi yat-pada-rajaḥ śruti-mṛgyam eva
Śrīmad-Bhāgavatām (10.14.34)

My greatest possible good fortune would be to take any birth whatsoever in this forest of Gokula and have my head bathed by the dust falling from the lotus feet of any of its residents. Their entire life and soul is the Supreme Personality of Godhead, Mukunda, the dust of whose lotus feet is still being searched for in the Vedic *mantras*.

Brahmā prayed, "You are the Supreme Lord of all those who are supreme. No one can count Your glorious qualities. Someone may be able to count the particles of dust on the earth or the tiny particles of fog, but no one can count Your glorious qualities."

Who can count tiny particles of fog? Baladeva Prabhu can count them, and Nityānanda Prabhu can also count them, but even They cannot count Śrī Kṛṣṇa's glories. Baladeva Himself failed to understand the real significance of this pastime. When Kṛṣṇa expanded Himself to become all the calves and cowherd boys, Baladeva was not aware of what had happened, and He remained unaware for an entire year. Even after He learned what had taken place, He was able to understand it only by Kṛṣṇa's mercy.

Baladeva Prabhu cannot enter the arena of the *rāsa* dance in a male form, and He is not aware of how Śrī Kṛṣṇa sports and dances with the *gopīs*. Because He has a very strong desire to enter the pastimes of *mādhurya-rasa*, He has another form, as Anaṅga Mañjarī, to taste that mellow.

In this way, the *gopīs* say that both Kāliya and Brahmā were offenders at Kṛṣṇa's lotus feet, but Kṛṣṇa bestowed His mercy upon them when they came to Him and surrendered.

Dharaṇi-maṇḍanam: *Maṇḍanam* refers to decorations that enhance one's beauty. For example, our *tilaka* is *maṇḍanam*. We adorn our bodies with ornaments (*ābharaṇa*) and decorations (*maṇḍanam*). Neck beads and rings are ornaments because they are not attached to the body, whereas decorations made with unguents are directly attached to the body.

The *gopīs* decorate their cheeks with pictures of *makarī* (the female *makara*). *Makara* means 'crocodile,' but in this connection it refers to a particular type of sea creature. It cannot refer to a crocodile because crocodiles are very dangerous, and dangerous things cannot enter *kṛṣṇa-līlā*. Kāmadeva is celebrated for riding on a *makara*, and his flag also bears the emblem of a *makara*. The *makara* is always associated with amorous love.

The *gopīs* tell Kṛṣṇa, "Your feet are the ornament of the earth." When they use the word 'earth' here, they do not refer to the earth on which we tread. Rather, they refer to the personification of this earth planet, Dharaṇī-devī, or Bhū-devī, who always keeps Śrī Kṛṣṇa's lotus feet as an ornament on her breast. The *gopīs'* inner meaning is this: "Your lotus feet are an ornament for Bhū-devī's breasts, so why will You not make them an ornament for ours as well?"

Dharani-mandanam has yet another meaning here. The *gopīs* think that their breasts should be the ornaments of Kṛṣṇa's feet. To please Him, they want all the parts of their bodies to be the ornaments of His feet, hands, and entire body. He looks most beautiful when He is with the *gopīs*. When they are not with Him, He cannot manifest His supreme splendor. In this way both meanings are given: They want Him to be the ornament of their breasts, and they want to be the ornament of His lotus feet.

They continue, "If anyone remembers Your lotus feet, all his miseries disappear. What is the evidence of this? When Gargācārya described Your horoscope, he told Your mother and father, 'In order to increase the transcendental bliss of the cowherd men of Gokula, this child will always act auspiciously for you. Only by His grace will you surpass all difficulties.' Gargācārya is renowned as a knower of past, present, and future, and he has said that if someone takes shelter of You and remembers Your lotus feet, all inauspiciousness leaves him at once. But we are experiencing so much anguish, and we are in a calamity that is worse than any other. Please remove this agony. We are not satisfied by simply remembering You. We must keep Your lotus feet on our heads or on our bodies. That means You will have to meet with us."

If we were to place all the miseries of the world, including suffering in hell, on one side of a scale, and the *gopīs'* feelings of separation on the other, we would see that the misery in the *gopīs'* hearts is far greater. They tell Kṛṣṇa, "Our intolerable distress can only be relieved if our hearts are touched by Your lotus feet. That will be the source of all happiness for us. *Santamaṁ ca te* – it will give us unfathomable bliss."

Arpaya ādhi-han: *Ādhi* means 'miseries,' and *han* means 'one who removes.' *Arpaya ādhi-han* refers to one who removes all kinds of miseries, diseases, and everything inauspicious. Because the *gopīs'* misery is their *kāma*, their prayer is this: "The *kāma* that lives in our hearts can be removed by You, like magic. If You place Your lotus feet on our hearts, all our torment will cease.

"You will not feel any inconvenience or discomfort by doing this. On the contrary, it will be very easy and pleasing for You. It will make You happy because You are our beloved (*ramaṇa*). O beloved, please listen to our prayer, and become pleased to perform pastimes with us here."

Generally *śantamam* means 'happiness,' but it also means 'all-auspiciousness.' If a devotee performs *sādhana-bhakti*, he will be relieved of all varieties of inauspiciousness: (1) *aprārabdha*, the accumulated stock of sins that are lying in a dormant condition; (2) *kūṭa*, sins that are tending towards producing seeds, which means that they are beginning to take shape as sinful desires; (3) *bīja*, seeds that are already established as sinful desires (the desires to commit sinful activities, which are situated within the heart of the living entity, are called *pāpa-bīja*, the seeds of sins); (4) *prārabdha*, fructified sins; and (5) *avidyā*[2], ignorance or illusion. Why are all our miseries not leaving us? It is because we have not fully surrendered.

The miseries of sincere devotees surely disappear, but Kṛṣṇa thinks, "In order to have *prema* for Me, they must continue their practice of *bhakti*. The results of their past *karma* have already been nullified, so they are no longer subject to birth and death. But if they do not take birth, how will they be able to practice *bhakti* and achieve *prema*?" It will not be possible for such devotees to go to Vraja, because one cannot go there unless one's heart is imbued with *kṛṣṇa-prema*. Śrī Kṛṣṇa thus creates circumstances by which such devotees take birth and continue their practices of *sādhana-bhakti*.

---

2 *Avidyā* means spiritual ignorance, illusion. Ignorance is of four kinds: to mistake that which is impermanent to be permanent, that which is full of misery to be blissful, that which is impure to be pure, and that which is not the self to be the self. *Avidyā* is one of the five types of miseries destroyed by *bhakti*.

"There are four stages of reactions to sinful activities. Sinful reactions may be experienced in this life, they may be dormant until future lives, the reactions may be in a seed-like state as desires, or the tendency to become seeds of desire. In any case, all types of sinful reactions are vanquished one after another if a person engages in the devotional service of Lord Viṣṇu" (*Pādma Purāṇa*).

When one sincerely chants *hari-nāma* and hears Kṛṣṇa's pastimes, all his *karma* is destroyed. Such devotees have no more *prārabdha-karma* – no material body and no place in the material world – so how will they practice *bhakti*? Bearing this in mind, Kṛṣṇa mercifully makes an arrangement so that they may come to this world, accept a material body, and attain the association of a pure devotee; this is essential. In such association, they can then advance through the stages of *niṣṭhā*, *ruci*, *āsakti*, and *bhāva*, and then attain *prema*.

As mentioned above, in order to have this association one must take birth, but one will certainly not take birth if one's *prārabdha-karma* and *aprārabdha-karma* have all been washed away. Thus, there are some people in this world who have no sinful or pious reactions to taste, whose hearts bear some impressions (*saṁskāras*) as a result of their past association with a pure devotee, and who have chanted a semblance (*ābhāsa*)[3] of the Hare Kṛṣṇa *mantra*. It is by Kṛṣṇa's mercy that such devotees taste the happiness and distress which is similar to that of *prārabdha-karma*.

Why must there be both happiness and distress? If there is no distress, there can be no sentiment of separation from Kṛṣṇa. Without separation, the devotee cannot practice chanting *hari-nāma*, "Hare Kṛṣṇa, Hare Kṛṣṇa," while weeping and shedding tears. Without this mood, the holy name will not be the pure name (*śuddha-nāma*). One should certainly try to chant in this way, but simply trying will not suffice. This is why Kṛṣṇa gives the devotees suffering; so that they will chant *hari-nāma* with tears and a deep feeling in their heart: "O Kṛṣṇa save us, save us!"

---

3 *Nāma-ābhāsa* is a semblance of the holy name. It is the stage of chanting in which one is becoming cleared of sins and offences but has not yet attained pure chanting.

Verse Fourteen

The nectar of Your lips increases the pleasure of amorous meeting, and it eliminates all sorrow due to separation from you.

Verse 14

सुरतवर्धनं शोकनाशनं
स्वरितवेणुना सुष्ठु चुम्बितम्।
इतररागविस्मारणं नृणां
वितर वीर नस्तेऽधरामृतम् ॥१४॥

surata-vardhanaṁ śoka-nāśanaṁ
svarita-veṇunā suṣṭhu cumbitam
itara-rāga-vismāraṇaṁ nṛṇāṁ
vitara vīra nas te 'dharāmṛtam

surata – the pleasure of amorous meeting; *vardhanam* – which increases; *śoka* – all sorrow; *nāśanam* – which eliminates; *svarita* – vibrated; *veṇunā* – by Your flute; *suṣṭhu* – abundantly; *cumbitam* – kissed; *itara* – other; *rāga* – attachments; *vismāraṇam* – causing to forget; *nṛṇām* – men; *vitara* – please spread; *vīra* – O hero; *naḥ* – upon us; *te* – Your; *adhara* – of the lips; *amṛtam* – the nectar.

Translation

O hero, the nectar of Your lips increases the pleasure of amorous meeting, and it eliminates all sorrow due to separation from You. Your ambrosial lips are passionately kissed by Your singing flute, and they cause every human being who drinks that nectar, even once, to forget about all other attachments. O hero, please make us drink the nectar of Your lips.

Bhāva-prakāśika Vṛtti

All the words in this verse have deep significance, with two specific meanings of the word *adharāmṛtam*: 'Your lips (*adhara*) take away death (*a-mṛta*),' and 'the nectar (*amṛta*) of Your lips.' "Your lips have many wonderful qualities," the *gopīs* tell Śrī Kṛṣṇa. "They are nectarean, and their juice is nectarean as well. Please give this nectar to us. Although You left us here and we are dying, when we remember the nectar of Your lips, our desire for *surata* increases."

Surata refers to a particularly exalted state of *prema* in which the *gopīs* desire to meet intimately with Kṛṣṇa (*prema viṣeśa-maya sambhoga-icchā*); they desire a meeting filled with *kāma*. As explained earlier, *su* means 'in a special way,' and *rata* means 'mixing together.' *Surata* refers to Kṛṣṇa and the gopīs meeting together in a special way and relishing great pleasure, and in that meeting Śrī Kṛṣṇa's *adharāmṛta* increases this pleasure to a superlative degree. Regarding the word *surata*, I cannot explain more than this. I have left practically everything hidden.

Śrīla Viśvanātha Cakravartī Ṭhākura says that the *gopīs* address Kṛṣṇa as Dhanvantari, the incarnation of Kṛṣṇa who brought to the world the medical branch of the Vedas known as *Āyur-veda*. "O Dhanvantari," they say, "we are searching for the medicine that will cure the disease of *kāma* from which we are dying, and we have come to You because we know You are the crest-jewel of physicians. Please give us the particular medicine that can save us."

Śrīla Viśvanātha Cakravartī Ṭhākura explains that *surata-vardhana* means 'that which increases *surata*.' Suppose someone has a disease and his doctor has prohibited the intake of certain foods. The doctor may have said, "Do not take tamarind." However, when the diseased person sees tamarind he cannot resist it, and as a result his illness worsens. Similarly, the *gopīs* beseech Kṛṣṇa to give them some medicine to cure their disease of *kāma*, while also acknowledging that the medicine would increase their disease.

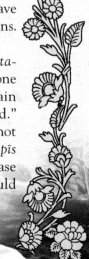

Śoka-nāśanaṁ means 'that which destroys misery.' The *gopīs* say that all their unhappiness will be destroyed by Kṛṣṇa's *adharāmṛta*. How? The taste of His *adharāmṛtam* is so nectarean that it will make them forget everything else.

When a patient is suffering so much that a painful operation must be performed, his doctor may give him an injection of morphine as an anesthetic. Under the influence of this anesthetic, the patient becomes unconscious and cannot feel any pain. Similarly, the *gopīs* say, "Drinking the nectar of Your lips makes us forget everything else, including our body and all sense of the world around us; and thus all our suffering goes away."

"But how will you be able to afford this nectar of Mine?" Kṛṣṇa asks. "It is very precious. I can distribute it to you all, only if you are willing to pay a very high price."

"There is no justification for You to say this," the *gopīs* reply. "You are heroic when it comes to giving in charity. Near a person dying, there may be a compassionate onlooker who knows how to save that person and who wants nothing in return for his help. You are like this onlooker; You are watching us die, You have the medicine that will save us, and You can give it to us freely."

Svarita-veṇunā: Kṛṣṇa fills His flute (*veṇu*) with His *adharāmṛta*. This creates *svara* (*nāda*, or sound vibration), and therefore the sound of the flute is called *veṇu-nāda*. Every word contains a sound vibration, and the word *klīṁ*[1] is the very sound emanating from

1 "The definition of *klīṁ* is understood by this verse in *Śrīmad-Bhāgavatam* (10.29.3): '*vanaṁ ca tat-komala-gobhī rañjitaṁ, jagau kalaṁ vāma-dṛśāṁ manoharam* – Lord Śrī Kṛṣṇa saw the unbroken disk of the full moon glowing with the red effulgence of newly applied vermilion, as if it were the face of the goddess of fortune. He also saw the *kumuda* lotuses opening in response to the moon's presence, and the forest gently illuminated by its rays. Thus the Lord began to play sweetly on His flute, attracting the mind of the beautiful-eyed *gopīs*.'

"It was evening time. The moon was golden and full, and rising on the very reddish eastern horizon. The eastern direction is like the moon's beloved. It was as though by his rays, which are like his hands, the moon had taken a large quantity of red color and was decorating the face of the eastern horizon. Seeing this, Kṛṣṇa at once placed His flute upon His lips and played a very sweet tune (*jagau kalaṁ*). That tune is included in the seed *mantra*, *klīṁ*. Upon hearing it, Rādhā, Lalitā, and all other *gopīs* thought, 'He is calling me alone; no one else.'

Kṛṣṇa's lotus lips through His flute-playing. This sound is non-different from Kṛṣṇa's *adharāmṛta*, and when it emanates from His flute, the nectar of His lips comes through the flute and is heard as *veṇu-nāda*.

This is why the *gopīs* say, "*Svarita-veṇunā* – The nectar of Your lips comes through the sound of Your bamboo flute. The flute is male, which shows that even males do not want to relinquish this taste, what to speak of ladies. That flute is just a piece of bamboo, it is male, and it is without consciousness. Still, it always tries to kiss Your lips and never wants to leave them."

Kṛṣṇa may tell the *gopīs*, "If a lady has contracted the disease of *kāma*, she should avoid a diet which is unfavorable to her condition: her attachments to wealth, husband, sons, sisters, daughters, and other relatives. Give up all of these, and then I can give you what you seek."

The *gopīs* reply, "First give us Your *adharāmṛta*, and that will enable us to give up those attachments. The nectar of Your lips has such extraordinary qualities that if anyone drinks it, all of his or her attachments disappear."

Itara-rāga-vismāraṇaṁ nṛṇām: *Nṛṇām* means 'of mankind' or 'of human beings.' The *gopīs* say, "All those who have tasted this nectar, both men and women, forget all material attachments and think, 'I must always drink the nectar of Kṛṣṇa's lips;' so there is no need for You to worry about our bad diet. This *adharāmṛta* is not only a wonderful medicine; it also removes the inclination for any kind of

---

[1] (continued) "The essence of the *gopāla-mantra* is the seed *klīṁ*. *Kalaṁ*, (translated in this verse as 'sweetly') is a combination of two Sanskrit letters *ka* + *la*. The fourth letter of the Sanskrit alphabet is called *vāma-dṛśāṁ* (translated in this verse as 'the girls who have charming eyes'). As the English alphabet begins with 'a, b, c, d,' the Sanskrit alphabet begins with 'a, ā, i, ī.' The fourth Sanskrit letter, 'ī,' is called *vāma-dṛśāṁ*. So even grammar, the essence of grammar, is in this sound. '*Ka*' and '*la*,' combined with 'ī,' becomes '*klī*'.

"And what is the meaning of the word *manoharam* in this verse? Ultimately *manohara* is Kṛṣṇa, He who attracts the mind. That same Kṛṣṇa gave a portion of His quality of attracting the mind to Candra, the moon-god. The predominating deity of the mind is Candra, and that moon has now taken the shape of *candra-bindu*, a dot. In Sanskrit this dot is called *anusvāra*, and thus the word *klīṁ* is completed. By *klīṁ*, each and every *gopī* thought that Kṛṣṇa was calling her alone, and therefore they all came to Him" (*Secret Truths of the Bhagavatam*, Chapter 4).

bad diet. We realize that we have contracted our disease again, and for this reason we have come to You again to receive the medicine. Because You are most munificent when it comes to giving in charity, we believe that You will give us this nectar just to protect us."

Śrīla Jīva Gosvāmī's commentary is practically the same as Śrīla Viśvanātha Cakravartī Ṭhākura's. There is some speciality, however, in the way he explains the words *itara-rāga-vismāraṇaṁ* with reference to the taste for sense objects in this world.

In this connection, we find a reference to the prayer of Vṛtrāsura in *Śrīmad-Bhāgavatam*:

na nāka-pṛṣṭhaṁ na ca pārameṣṭhyaṁ
na sārva-bhaumaṁ na rasādhipatyam
na yoga-siddhīr apunar-bhavaṁ vā
samañjasa tvā virahayya kāṅkṣe

Śrīmad-Bhāgavatam (6.11.25)

Vṛtrāsura prays, "I have no desire for Svarga, nor do I wish for Dhruva's planet or position. I also do not desire Brahmā's post, even though Brahmā has enormous power; and, beyond that, I am not interested in the cessation of birth and death (liberation). I do not want anything other than service to You with my body, remembrance of You with my mind, and performance of Your *kīrtana* with my words."

The *gopīs* have a similar understanding: "Those who take the medicine of the nectar of Your lips can easily forget their father and mother, dear wife or husband, and everything else of this world. They can easily forget Svarga-loka and Brahma-loka, and everything else up to and including impersonal liberation (*mukti*)."

The nectar of Kṛṣṇa's lips emanates through His flute and then enters the ear of the listener. The ear then becomes like a tongue, tasting nectar, and the listener is able to forget all worldly considerations. How much more blessed is someone who directly tastes the nectar of Kṛṣṇa's lips? One who does not have this extreme good fortune, but just hears that nectar, is still very fortunate. Furthermore, if one cannot hear the sound of Kṛṣṇa's flute, one may be able to hear about His pastimes. That person is also fortunate. The *gopīs* hear Kṛṣṇa's flute melody, and others, such as the deer and the cuckoos, also hear it. When the peacocks hear the flute, they stop all their other activities and begin to dance. And those who see these pastimes can also become free from their taste for anything else.

The deer and cuckoos are indeed fortunate, but the most fortunate are the *gopīs*, who can directly taste Kṛṣṇa's original *adharāmṛta*. The deer and the cuckoos cannot relish this *adharāmṛta* directly, but they can listen to Kṛṣṇa's flute-song. And there are others, who can hear about Kṛṣṇa's pastimes. They hear that Kṛṣṇa is playing His flute and that all human beings, animals, birds, and other creatures in Vṛndāvana are hearing His flute-song. As a result of listening to narrations of His pastimes, these persons, too, develop the ambition to hear His flute. They will certainly give up all desire to taste the forms and qualities of this world. They will never want Svarga or even liberation from birth and death.

The *gopīs* say, "The nectar of Your lips is so relishable that no one can criticize us for desiring to taste it. It is not only the ladies of Vraja who are attracted to that nectar; even a dry, male piece of bamboo called *veṇu* wants it. If a dry bamboo flute cannot give up this desire, what to speak of us?"

The nectar of Kṛṣṇa's lips is not easily obtained. Ordinary devotees cannot have it, whereas Kṛṣṇa's associates can get it through His *mahā-prasāda*, such as the remnants of His betel (*tāmbūla*). He tastes the betel and then, in the form of His remnants, He gives them His *adharāmṛta*. He tastes *purīs*, rice, *dhal*, *pakorās*, and other preparations, and His remnants are distributed as *mahā-prasāda*. These remnants are also called *adharāmṛta*.

Only an advanced, *rasika* devotee can realize that *mahā-prasāda* is Kṛṣṇa's *adharāmṛta*. An ordinary devotee can certainly think in that way, but he cannot realize it. He may be conscious that it is *mahā-prasāda*, but only an advanced devotee can actually relish it as such. The tenth canto of *Śrīmad-Bhāgavatam* is *rasa* itself. It is directly *mahābhāva* and *rasarāja*; that is, it is directly Śrīmatī Rādhikā and Śrī Kṛṣṇa. If, after honoring *mahā-prasāda*, we want to touch *Śrīmad-Bhāgavatam*, which is the very heart of Kṛṣṇa, we first wash our hands. But this rule is only for those practicing *bhakti* in this world. It does not apply to Kṛṣṇa's associates in Goloka-Vṛndāvana. Both

Śrī Kṛṣṇa's book, which narrates His nectarean pastimes, and His *mahā-prasāda*, are He Himself.

As *māhā-prasāda* is Śrī Kṛṣṇa's *adharāmṛta*, His singing or talking to anyone is also His *adharāmṛta*. However, no one except the *gopīs* can taste His original *adharāmṛta*. The *gopīs* are now weeping for this, and they tell Him, "We are dying because we are not getting it."

We may be satisfied by hearing the nectar of Kṛṣṇa's pastimes, because no other type of *adharāmṛtam* is available for us, but the *gopīs* want only the original. Unlike others, they are not satisfied to simply take the remnants of betel leaf and other preparations tasted by Kṛṣṇa. For them, His lips (*adhara*) are the *amṛtam*; nothing else will do.

Śrīla Jīva Gosvāmī explains that the *gopīs*' three phrases: *surata-vardhanaṁ*, *śoka-nāśanaṁ*, and *itara-rāga-vismāraṇaṁ*, are all adjectives that qualify the noun, *adharāmṛtam*.

Surata-vardhanaṁ: This ambrosia increases one's desire to drink it; it makes one hanker to relish it again and again.

Śoka-nāśanaṁ: If this nectar is received, all suffering is destroyed. The suffering it destroys is the suffering of not seeing Kṛṣṇa. If Kṛṣṇa meets the *gopīs*, they will taste nectar and their suffering will immediately disappear.

Itara-rāga-vismāraṇam: Not only is suffering destroyed, but all kinds of worldly attachments disappear immediately.

Śrīla Jīva Gosvāmī further explains that this *adharāmṛtam* is the supreme goal of human life. There are four general goals of life: religiosity, wealth, sense gratification, and liberation. The fifth goal is *kṛṣṇa-prema* (*pañcama-puruṣārtha*), and attaining this *adharāmṛtam* is superior even to that. In other words, it is the final objective for those who hanker for *kṛṣṇa-prema*.

He gives this analogy: If there are many flowers in one place, the combined aroma of those flowers consists of the fragrance of each individual flower; but we cannot distinguish one fragrance from another. Similarly, Śrī Kṛṣṇa's original *adharāmṛta* is very fragrant, as is the fragrance of the flute-song that is the *adharāmṛta* coming through the flute. Both fragrances are mixed so intimately that it is very difficult to distinguish one from another; only a *rasika* Vaiṣṇava can do so.

Another analogy may be given: We cannot separate milk from a mixture of water and milk. We taste both together as a single combined substance, but a swan can differentiate between them. The swan will drink the milk and leave the water. Similarly, *rasika* Vaiṣṇavas have the ability to distinguish between the nectar of Kṛṣṇa's lips (*adharāmṛtam*) and the sound of His flute (*veṇu-nāda*). They will be able to taste both; their enjoyment will double.

Svara means 'tune,' or more specifically, 'trembling tune.' The melodies emanating from Kṛṣṇa's flute sound as if they are trembling, vibrating, and wavering slowly from the high notes to the low notes, and from the low notes to the high notes again. Anyone who hears this tune will faint.

Why does the flute sound like this? It actually has no control over how it sounds. It is maddened by tasting the nectar of Kṛṣṇa's lips and is thus trembling.

The *gopīs* tell Kṛṣṇa, "Your flute-song intoxicates the entire world. If that flute is so maddened by the touch of the nectar of Your lips, what will become of us if we taste it? Actually, we have already tasted it, which is why we are totally maddened. Now You should come and restore our life, for we are dying without that nectar."

Verse Fifteen

If you want to save us,
you must come to
meet with us at once;
otherwise we will die.

Verse 15

अटति यद्भवानह्नि काननं
त्रुटिर्युगायते त्वामपश्यताम्।
कुटिलकुन्तलं श्रीमुखञ्च ते
जड उदीक्षतां पक्ष्मकृद् दृशाम् ॥१५॥

aṭati yad bhavān ahni kānanaṁ
truṭir yugāyate tvām apaśyatām
kuṭila-kuntalaṁ śrī-mukhañ ca te
‘jaḍa udīkṣatāṁ pakṣma-kṛd dṛśām

aṭati – travel; *yat* – when; *bhavān* – You; *ahni* – during the daytime; *kānanam* – to the forest; *truṭih* – about 1/2700 of a second; *yugāyate* – becomes like an entire millennium; *tvām* – You; *apaśyatām* – for those who do not see; *kuṭila* – curling; *kuntalam* – with locks of hair; *śrī* – beautiful; *mukham* – face; *ca* – and; *te* – Your; *jaḍaḥ* – foolish; *udīkṣatām* – for those who are eagerly looking; *pakṣma* – of lids; *kṛt* – the creator; *dṛśām* – of the eyes.

Translation

O beloved, unable to see You as You roam the forest, engaging in pleasure pastimes during the day, we experience every moment as a millennium. Then, upon Your return from the forest at dusk, although we eagerly gaze upon Your exquisitely beautiful lotus face adorned with curly locks, we become greatly perturbed by the occasional blinking of our eyes. At that time, the creator of eyelids appears a fool to us.

Bhāva-prakāśika Vṛtti

The general meaning of this verse is given in the translation. *Aṭati* means 'walks' or 'goes.' *Bhavān* means 'You,' referring here to Śrī Kṛṣṇa because the *gopīs* are speaking. *Ahni* means 'in the daytime,' specifically 'in the morning.' And *kānanam* refers to *vṛndā-kānanam*, the forests and gardens of Vṛndāvana.

The *gopīs* tell Kṛṣṇa, "You look exceedingly beautiful in the morning when, surrounded by many friends, You wander to the pasturing grounds of Vṛndāvana so that Your cows may graze. At that time, You make us suffer from the heart-disease of *kāma*."

Truṭi yugāyate tvām apaśyatām: A *truṭi* is a very short time – a fraction of a second – and a *yuga*[1] is billions of years. The *gopīs* continue, "When You take the cows to graze in Vṛndāvana, we feel so much separation that the very briefest moment, a minute part of a second, becomes millions of millenniums for us."

Kuṭila-kuntalaṁ śrī-mukhaṁ ca te: *Kuntalam* means 'hair,' and *kuṭila-kuntalaṁ* means 'curly hair'. The *gopīs* say, "You also look exquisite when You return home in the evening, Your curly hair falling here and there as it covers part of Your lotus face. At that time also, You give us intense anguish, tormenting us with the affliction of *kāma*."

Jaḍa udīkṣatām: *Udīkṣatām* means 'of those who are looking very carefully and with great eagerness to see.' "We are greatly eager to see Your lotus face," the *gopīs* say. "Everyone in Vṛndāvana, whoever one may be – father, mother, man, woman, or child – says that Brahmā, the creator of eyelids, is certainly dull and foolish (*jaḍa*). He has given us only two eyes, and even those two eyes have lids that interrupt our vision. If we were in Brahmā's place and he was in ours, we would have given him millions of eyes without any lids."

---

1 The Vedas explain that there are four *yugas* or ages: Satya-yuga, Tretā-yuga, Dvāpara-yuga, and Kali-yuga. These four *yugas* rotate, like calendar months. The duration of each *yuga* is different – they are said to be respectively 1,728,000; 1,296,000; 864,000; and 432,000 years.

This is the general meaning of this phrase, and there is another. *Kṛt* means 'the creator,' but it also means 'he who cuts.' *Te jaḍa* can also be understood in two ways, because in Sanskrit, if a word ends with 'e' and it precedes a word beginning with 'a,' the 'a' is omitted. Accordingly, *te jaḍa* can also be understood as *te 'jaḍa*, that is, *te ajaḍa*. In this case, the *gopīs* are saying, "Anyone who can cut off his own eyelids, enabling himself to see forever without any obstacle, is surely very wise (*ajaḍa*). We are not able to do so, but if anyone is so intelligent and expert that he can do so, that person is certainly *rasika* and *bhāvuka*."

Śrīla Viśvanātha Cakravartī Ṭhākura further reveals the *gopīs*' words. Weeping and searching for Kṛṣṇa, they say, "It is not Your fault that we are agonized by separation from You. It is our own misfortune. We suffer unbearable separation in Your absence, and it is the same when we see You in the evening. When You return home from the pastures with all the cows and cowherd boys, we see You for only a moment. We want to relish Your beauty at that time, but we cannot. There is never enough time to see You to our full satisfaction, for as soon as we catch sight of You, You go to Mother Yaśodā's house. Besides that, our eyelids obstruct our vision as we look at You, and sometimes our eyes fill with tears. Sometimes the hooves of the cows raise so much dust that we cannot see You, and at the same time Nanda Bābā, Mother Yaśodā, and all the other elders come to greet You. Furthermore, if Jaṭilā, Kuṭilā, or our husbands were to see us looking at You, a mountain of torment would come upon our heads. So we are not free to gaze upon You. There are numerous problems, and we understand that they are all caused by our own misfortune. This misfortune makes us suffer under all circumstances, both in separation from You and in meeting with You."

Tvām apaśyatām means 'for those who do not see You.' The *gopīs* say, "At nine in the morning, You take the cows out to graze in the pasturing grounds, and at that time we are not the only ones who feel separation from You. Everyone in Vṛndāvana suffers because they can no longer see You. All the Vrajavāsīs suffer, including Nanda Bābā, Yaśodā, and even the calves who cannot go with You. So not only we, but all the Vrajavāsīs are suffering, because time does not want to pass by for us. It seems that it has stopped still.

When we do not see You, time is fixed, and that is why You do not come to us. So many *yugas* pass, but still You do not come."

Suppose someone is very sick and crying from intense pain. At night he cannot sleep. He stares at the clock, which shows the slow passage of time: one o'clock, two o'clock, three o'clock, four o'clock. The patient continually looks at the clock and wonders, "When will morning come? When will morning come?" For that person, a minute, or a second, appears like a month or more.

Similarly, according to the *gopīs*, all the Vrajavāsīs feel that a moment in Kṛṣṇa's absence appears like a *yuga*. Why do the *gopīs* think like this about the other Vrajavāsīs? The cause is their *mahābhāva* for Kṛṣṇa, their attachment to Him. No one else can actually feel as they do. Their *prema* is so elevated that they feel a moment of separation to be like a *yuga*; and conversely, in a *yuga* of meeting, time passes away very quickly for them.

It is not like that for us. This experience is only for those who have crossed the various stages of *prema*. No one else can feel like the *gopīs*, who have not only attained *prema*, but also *sneha*, *māna*, *praṇaya*, *rāga*, *anurāga*, and so on. This advanced stage of separation will only come when one has passed through all these stages. Although only the *gopīs* feel like this, they think, "Everyone else feels more separation than we do and everyone is more elevated than us." They consider that when the cuckoos stop singing, it is because they are weeping in the same mood as they themselves. This is a symptom of *mahābhāva*.

Truṭi yugāyate: One *kṣana* is 32/25 seconds, and a *truṭi* is a 2,700th part of a *kṣana*. A *truṭi* is a very tiny fraction of a second, but whenever the *gopīs* do not see Kṛṣṇa, it becomes like a *yuga*. Kṛṣṇa goes cowherding for three *praharas*[2] of the day, which the other Vrajavāsīs experience as three months, and which the *gopīs* feel as millions of *yugas*. The *gopīs* alone can feel like this, because of their unique attachment for Kṛṣṇa. Their love reaches the stage of *modana*, and Śrīmatī Rādhikā relishes *madana-bhāva* towards Him.[3]

---

2 A *prahara* is a time period of approximately three-hours. Each day consists of eight *praharas*.

3 *Modana* is the first stage of *adhirūḍha-mahābhāva*, some of the symptoms of which are churning the hearts of all those in the presence of the afflicted one, and the

If a man dies, his father, mother, and wife will all weep for him, but the person who has the most attachment to the dead man will cry the most. It may be his wife, but if she has some connection with another man, she may be very satisfied by her husband's death. If a son has caused suffering to his father and mother, they will feel grief for his passing, but perhaps not so much. However, if he was very obedient to them, they will continuously weep for him. The degree of separation a person feels depends on the extent of his love.

The *gopīs* tell Kṛṣṇa, "In the evening, we eagerly wait on the path, thinking, 'When will Kṛṣṇa come? When will Kṛṣṇa come?' Then, when You return, we consider Brahmā, having created eyelids, to be a fool with no wisdom or intelligence. He should have given eyelids to ordinary people only. Why has he given them to us *gopīs*? It is for this reason we say that You give us so much suffering, whether we are in separation from You or we are meeting with You."

Śrīla Jīva Gosvāmī's explanation of the word *pakṣma-kṛta* is similar to that of Śrīla Viśvanātha Cakravartī Ṭhākura, who says that *kṛt* means 'to cut.' The *gopīs* say, "Those who are expert enough to cut off their eyelids are intelligent and very *rasika*, unlike Brahmā. We cannot do this, so we are also unintelligent. We want to see Kṛṣṇa when He returns in the evening, but we cannot do so. We have no chance to see Him sufficiently, either in the morning, daytime, evening, or night."

The *gopīs* are singing their song at night: "If you want to save us, You must come to meet with us at once; otherwise we will die."

---

apprehension that Śrī Kṛṣṇa feels discomfort when He is in fact perfectly satisfied... When *mahābhāva* increases even further, it attains an extremely advanced condition. The paramour emotion, in which it becomes jubilant due to the simultaneous manifestation of all types of transcendental emotions, is called *madana*. This *madana-bhāva* is eternally and splendidly manifest only in Śrī Rādhā, and occurs only at the time of meeting. It is also referred to as *madanākya-mahābhāva*.

Verse Sixteen

Why did You call us in the first place? It was simply pointless. We understand that we have been cheated by You, but in cheating us You have also been cheated.

Verse 16

पति-सुतान्वय-भ्रातृ-बान्धवान्
अतिविलङ्घ्य तेऽन्त्यच्युतागताः।
गतिविदस्तवोद्गीतमोहिताः
कितव योषितः कस्त्यजेन्निशि ॥१६॥

pati-sutānvaya-bhrātṛ-bāndhavān
ativilaṅghya te 'nty acyutāgatāḥ
gati-vidas tavodgīta-mohitāḥ
kitava yoṣitaḥ kas tyajen niśi

pati – husbands; *suta* – children; *anvaya* – lineage (relatives of husband); *bhrātṛ* – brothers; *bāndhavān* – relatives (of *gopīs*); *ativilaṅghya* – completely neglecting; *te* – Your; *anti* – into the presence; *acyuta* – O infallible one; *āgatāḥ* – having come; *gati* – of our movements; *vidaḥ* – who understand the purpose; *tava* – Your; *udgīta* – by the loud flute song; *mohitāḥ* – bewildered; *kitava* – O cheater; *yoṣitaḥ* – young ladies; *kaḥ* – who; *tyajet* – would abandon; *niśi* – in the night.

Translation

O Acyuta, You know very well that, bewitched by the loud song of Your flute, we rejected our husbands, sons, brothers, friends, and our entire family. Disregarding their desires, we disobeyed their orders and came to You. O cheater, who but You would abandon young ladies like us, who have come in this manner to You during the night?

Bhāva-prakāśika Vṛtti

The general meaning of the words in this verse is as follows: *Pati* means 'husband,' *suta* means 'son,' and *anvaya* refers to the relatives of the *gopīs*' husbands. The husband's father becomes the bride's father-in-law, his mother becomes her mother-in-law, his sister becomes her sister-in-law, and so on. All these relationships depend on the husband's relations.

Bhrātṛ-bāndhavān: *Bhrātṛ* means 'brothers' and *bāndhavān* refers to one's own father, mother, brothers and sisters, and all other relatives. They are all *bandhu*, while the husbands' relatives, that is, the *gopīs*' in-laws, are referred to in this verse as *anvaya*.

Those *gopīs* whose relatives had prevented them from leaving the house when Kṛṣṇa first called them with His flute-song are also singing this verse. Some of them were in the homes of their husbands, and were prevented from leaving by their husbands and their husbands' relatives. Others were in their fathers' homes, so they were stopped by their own relatives. Those *gopīs* had been kept in their rooms, but the fire of separation in their hearts burned up any remaining obstacles to their meeting with Kṛṣṇa.[1]

---

1 "Śrīla Śukadeva Gosvāmī hides the confidential desired goal of the *gopīs* from materialistic people. By the words *duḥsaha* etc., he expresses the external meaning, as well as the deep inner meaning that is dear to devotees who have knowledge of confidential devotional service.

"First he speaks for materialistic people: 'Śrī Kṛṣṇa granted liberation to the *gopīs*.' This means that when the *gopīs* experienced the acute pain of separation from their most dearly beloved, the inauspiciousness (*aśubha*) in their beings vanished. The result of their auspicious activity was also destroyed as they experienced the bliss of embracing Acyuta (Kṛṣṇa) in their meditation. Therefore, the bondage of past activity was destroyed, they attained the Supersoul by thinking of Him as their paramour, and they gave up their bodies made of three modes of nature.

"Now he speaks for devotees: At the time of intense meditation, the *gopīs* experienced extreme sorrow due to their fire-like separation from their beloved, and they also attained the unparalleled happiness of meeting with Him. In this way their desire was fulfilled. Furthermore, the immense suffering of separation from their dear most beloved humiliated all inauspiciousness. The intolerable

He entered their hearts, where they tightly embraced Him and then went with Him to *rāsa-līlā*.

Atilaṅghya means 'completely neglecting.' The *gopīs* tell Śrī Kṛṣṇa, "Although it is generally considered very dishonorable for a person to disobey superiors, we neglected our superiors' orders, quarreled with them, and came here to meet with You. They wanted to tie us up by our wrists, but still we came, like deaf or mad persons."

Te 'nty acyutāgatāḥ: The *gopīs* say, "O Acyuta (infallible one), You have disappeared (*cyut*) from our vision. You have failed (*cyut*) in the matter of showing Yourself to us. Thus, is the name Acyuta not contrary to Your deeds?"

Kṛṣṇa may ask, "Why did you come to Me then?"

"It is You who have called us," the *gopīs* reply. "We did not come here of our own accord; we did not desire to come. You are the cause of our coming here."

Śrī Kṛṣṇa says, "No, no, I have not called you."

"Yes, You called us. Do not deny it. *Gati-vidas tavodgīta-mohitāḥ* – It is not that You played Your flute by the will of providence. You did so deliberately, with full knowledge of all the consequences. You knew that we would be irresistibly attracted by Your flute-song and that surely we would be unable to stop ourselves from running to You."

Kṛṣṇa asks, "If you know My intentions and My nature, then why have you come?"

"You called to us with Your flute-song," the *gopīs* repeated. " 'Come on! Come on! Come on!' and we were unable to stop ourselves. We

---

fire of separation from one's beloved exceeds the power of all things that inflict death, beginning from the forest-fire and ending with the *kāla-kūṭa* poison (the severe and fresh poison of a serpent). In this fire, all inauspiciousness renounced its pride in its severity and, conceding defeat, began to tremble.

"As soon as Lord Acyuta came in the *gopīs*' meditation, their transcendental bodies made of *prema* and endowed with appropriate self-conception manifested, and He embraced them. The relief the *gopīs* experienced at that time conquered all material and spiritual auspiciousness. That is, in comparison to the blissful embrace of their beloved who appeared in their meditation, the material happiness of millions of universes as well as the spiritual bliss of thousands of Brahman attainments appeared quite inferior" (*Bhāvānuvāda* of *Sārārtha-darśinī*, Chapter 29, Verse 10).

know about Your nature, but Your flute-song is like a powerful spell; it bewildered us, and we came to You.

"*Kitava yoṣitaḥ* – You are a cheater. What is more, You cheat only for the sake of cheating. One cheats others in order to gain something, but You gain nothing. Such behavior is foolish. You could have gained something from our meeting, but instead You disappeared without gaining anything at all. You cheated us by Your flute-song. Why did You call us in the first place? It was simply pointless. We understand that we have been cheated by You, but in cheating us You have also been cheated."

This is a very important verse. So many moods are hidden here, which cannot be openly discussed.

In *Sarārtha-darśana*, Śrīla Viśvanātha Cakravartī Ṭhākura explains the words of the *gopīs* who tried to leave home to meet with Kṛṣṇa, but were initially prevented from doing so by their relatives. "We were very pleased to be in our homes, with our fathers, mothers, husbands, and other relatives. Why have You called us here? To come here, we disobeyed the orders of our elders and superiors, and now we are ready to take our final breath. We are surely about to die, so what did we gain from disobeying them?"

Acyuta means 'infallible,' or 'one who never fails.' Here the *gopīs* tell Śrī Kṛṣṇa, "You are certainly infallible in Your great obstinacy." Suppose a boy is bitterly weeping for a particular toy, but for some reason his father and mother will not give it to him. They give him a variety of sweetmeats and many other toys, but he will not accept what they offer, maintaining the same stubborn attitude for days.

The *gopīs* are telling Kṛṣṇa that He is like this. "O Kṛṣṇa," they say, "Your mind is single-pointed to the point of obstinacy. We have been weeping continuously due to our longing to see You, and calling You because of our grievous suffering. Still, You are determined not to meet with us. Your determination to make us suffer is relentless, and thus You are Acyuta; You never fail to give us suffering.

"Previously we were under the impression that You are called Acyuta because You never fail to exhibit Your many refined qualities. But now we understand that You are Acyuta because You never fail to exhibit Your cheating."

Kṛṣṇa may say, "O *gopīs*, you say that you know I cannot give up this habit of Mine. Why, then, did you come in the night like this?"

Exasperated, the *gopīs* reply, "We have not come by our own will; You have brought us."

"How did I bring you?"

"We were controlled by the sound of Your flute. The melody of Your flute eagerly called our names. It told us that You were bitterly weeping and on the verge of fainting. It also told us that You cannot live without us. When we understood this, we became like madwomen and came running here. We disobeyed our superiors and did not care about the future consequences of our actions. At that time we could not think about these things at all."

Śrī Kṛṣṇa says, "If your words are true, if that is really how you came, then you are foolish. O ignorant cowherd girls, you will thus have to suffer."

The *gopīs* reply, "O cheater, we have come to You by our own will. Yet, You do not value us. A person must make considerable endeavor to obtain gold, so how much more effort is required to obtain *cintāmaṇi* (a wish-fulfilling gem), which is so rare? You are just like someone who secures a *cintāmaṇi* by extraordinary fortune, and then throws it away. Such a person is completely foolish.

"We are like that *cintāmaṇi*. It is impossible for any male to attain our association. It is impossible even for Nārāyaṇa, what to speak of others. But still we have come here, due to Your good fortune. You have gained *cintāmaṇi* automatically, without making any separate endeavor for it. Furthermore, You have not only attained one *cintāmaṇi*; millions of *cintāmaṇi* gems have come to You. You should understand Your good fortune, but You are Acyuta. You obstinately maintain Your habit of cheating.

"Moreover, You are a coward. You are afraid of society; You are afraid of our husbands and relatives. And what is more, You are cruel and hard-hearted, because now You have left us. You have no mercy at all. You are like a hunter who pursues many beautiful, sweet deer. You have no realization of how precious we are, and therefore You are cheated. You have cheated us, but You have also cheated Yourself."

Kāmadeva (Cupid) speaks about great saintly renunciates like Śrīla Śukadeva Gosvāmī, who do not cut their hair, wear any clothing, cook for themselves, accept luxurious foods, or keep any possessions. Kāmadeva says, "Just look at all these beggars! They hate me, and that is why I have made them like this. They beg here and there without garments or possessions. I have made them like prisoners, and I am making them suffer."

Kāmadeva thinks that by his arrangement such persons are forced to live without possessions. In reality, however, it is by Śrī Kṛṣṇa's mercy that saintly persons have no interest in worldly attractions. Kāmadeva thinks he has cheated the saintly persons, but in fact he is cheated by them. Similarly, the *gopīs* tell Kṛṣṇa that, in the process of cheating them, He has actually cheated Himself.

In *Vaiṣṇava-toṣani*, Śrīla Jīva Gosvāmī explains the words *gati-vidaḥ* in a special way. *Gati-vidaḥ* means 'one who understands another's movements and moods,' and it applies to both Kṛṣṇa and the *gopīs*. The *gopīs* tell Kṛṣṇa, "We understand Your motives. When we hear the melody of Your flute, we at once understand that You are calling for us and cannot live without us. We know that You are very lusty."

The word *gati-vidaḥ* has another meaning when applied to Kṛṣṇa. The *gopīs* continue, "You are also *gati-vidah*, because You know that if the sound of Your flute enters our ears, we can no longer remain in our homes. You know that as deer come to a hunter when they hear the hunter's flute-song, so we come to You. You are so expert at sweetly playing Your flute that all varieties of sounds and melodies blend into its song. Its melody trembles and quivers as it rises from the lower notes to the higher notes, and then falls again. You know many *rāgas* and *rāgiṇīs*, which are so beautiful that everyone is attracted to them. And You are expert in knowing which sound and melody is able to attract different people and creatures. That is why we have come to You, just like deer."

Kṛṣṇa asks, "I know that you are very steady in your chastity and you do not act against your very strict nature. So why have you come?"

"You are fully aware of the influence of the musical arrangements of Your flute-songs," the *gopīs* say. "Even Indra, Śaṅkara, and Brahmā are attracted when they hear those songs. Why, then, would we not respond? After all, You are extremely beautiful and we are young ladies attached to You, so why would we not be attracted? We became maddened and we came."

Kitava yoṣitaḥ kas tyajen niśi: *Kitava* means 'cheater.' The *gopīs* say, "No one but You could leave such beautiful, sweet young ladies on the bank of the Yamunā, on such a cool, enchanting night. O fraud, no cheater in the world cheats as You do – abandoning what You gain by deceit and thus cheating yourself. Your cheating is contemptible even in a society of cheaters. You are truly Acyuta, because You cannot live without cheating. Duplicity is Your favorite quality and therefore Your name is justified."

This verse has many more meanings hidden within it, but I have not touched on them. You will be able to understand them by performing *bhajana*.

There are four kinds of *gopīs*: *svapakṣa*, Śrī Rādhā's own personal party; *vipakṣa*, Her rivals; *taṭasthā*, those who are neutral to Her; and *suhṛd*, those who are friendly to Her. Each of the verses may be spoken by any of these four groups, and each verse has four different meanings, corresponding to the respective moods of the different groups. Our *ācāryas* have not given four different explanations for each verse. The explanations which they have not given, as well as those which they have given, must be realized by the readers themselves.

The *svapakṣa gopīs* are leftist, and they are in Śrīmatī Rādhikā's group. They have a contrary mood, and they express this in the way they speak. The *gopīs* in the *vipakṣa* group are right-wing and are in Candrāvalī's group. They have a submissive mood and express themselves in prayers to Kṛṣṇa. The *suhṛd* and *taṭastha gopīs* are between the *svapakṣa* and the *vipakṣa* groups, with the *suhṛd gopīs*, such as Śyāmalā, being closer to the *svapakṣa* mood and the *taṭastha gopīs*, such as Bhadrā, nearer to the *vipakṣa* mood.

We should understand that a *gopī* who speaks in a contrary mood, with *māna*, is Rādhikā, Lalitā, or Viśākhā, or some other *sakhī* in Rādhikā's party. At other times Candrāvalī is speaking, sometimes

Śyāmalā, and sometimes Bhadrā. Sometimes a *gopī's* mood will also change because, as she sings one verse after another, she experiences many conflicting thoughts and feelings. Sometimes the *gopīs* feel extreme happiness, and sometimes intense sorrow. Their moods are changing like waves in the sea; sometimes those waves are very high, and sometimes rolling in this direction or that.

I hope that you will develop some taste for these topics, which are very profound and difficult to penetrate. Always be careful to avoid lustful thinking, or to consider the *gopīs*' transcendental sentiments as ordinary lust.

Pray to this book, and pray to these verses. These verses are *mantras* containing the words uttered by Śrī Kṛṣṇa and the *gopīs*, given to us so that we may understand and follow them. In their commentaries, Śrīla Jīva Gosvāmī and Śrīla Viśvanātha Cakravartī Ṭhākura have prayed to the *gopīs* for their mercy. Even Śrīla Śukadeva Gosvāmī cannot fully understand all these topics, but he has tasted something of them by their grace and mercy. And we also pray at their lotus feet that we can understand something. Whatever we speak, whatever we think, and whatever we taste is only by their kindness. Without their charitable compassion, no one can realize these topics.

Verse Seventeen

In those conversations You begged something from us, something we are reluctant to openly express.

Verse 17

रहसि संविदं हृच्छयोदयं
प्रहसिताननं प्रेमवीक्षणम्।
बृहदुरःश्रियो वीक्ष्य धाम ते
मुहुरतिस्पृहा मुह्यते मनः ॥१७॥

rahasi saṁvidaṁ hṛc-chayodayaṁ
prahasitānanaṁ prema-vīkṣaṇam
bṛhad-uraḥ-śriyo vīkṣya dhāma te
muhur ati-spṛhā muhyate manaḥ

rahasi – in private; *saṁvidam* – confidential discussions; *hṛt-śaya* – of amorous desires in the heart; *udayam* – the rise; *prahasita* – smiling and laughing; *ānanam* – face; *prema* – loving; *vīkṣaṇam* – glances; *bṛhat* – broad; *uraḥ* – chest; *śriyaḥ* – of the goddess of fortune; *vīkṣya* – seeing; *dhāma* – the abode; *te* – Your; *muhuḥ* – repeatedly; *ati* – excessive; *spṛhā* – hankering; *muhyate* – bewilders; *manaḥ* – the mind.

Translation

O beloved master, having seen You as You conversed intimately with us in secret places – Your smiling face, which acts as a stimulus for our amorous desires, Your glancing at us with love, and Your expansive chest, which is the eternal resting place of the goddess of fortune – our hankering to meet with You has increased manifold and our minds are repeatedly bewildered.

Bhāva-prakāśika Vṛtti

The apparent and most common meaning of this verse is given in its translation, but its deeper significance is explained in the *ācāryas*' commentaries. In his commentary to the previous verse, Śrīla Viśvanātha Cakravartī Ṭhākura quotes the *gopīs* telling Śrī Kṛṣṇa, "You are a cheater, and You have also been cheated. Where in the entire world is there a youth who is as cruel-hearted and merciless as You?

"We teenage *gopīs* are qualified, beautiful, and sweet. We have come to You of our own accord, and yet You have neglected us. We previously thought of You as softhearted and magnanimous, but now we see that You have none of these good qualities. You are simply a cheater.

"We became bewildered by the song of Your flute and have come here. You must have transferred all Your bad qualities to us, and that is why we are now devoid of discrimination and intelligence. In particular, You possess five features, Kāmadeva's five arrows, and You have used these arrows to pierce our hearts. As a result we have lost our minds, our memories, and our intelligence, and we now find ourselves here. Those five arrows entered our hearts through our eyes and wounded us. Now our hearts are burning, and that is why we have come running here. You should free us from this pain.

"Your first arrow," the *gopīs* explain, "is the conversations we previously had with You in solitary places (*rahasi saṁvidam*). In those conversations You begged something from us, something we are reluctant to openly express. Actually, You begged us for our *prema*. Sometimes You begged through the song of Your flute, and sometimes You directly expressed Your prayer in words.

"Your second arrow is the *kāma* in Your heart (*hṛc-chayodayaṁ*). Upon seeing us, You became full of *kāma* and hinted to us to meet with You, trying to persuade us with Your entreaties. You showed us Your heart, and we saw that it was full of desire to meet with us.

"When we saw Your heart burning in this way, we felt great pity for You and came running here to save You; and, on account of seeing the desire in Your heart, our own hearts became filled with such desires. We are now in the same condition as You. However, You should understand that we have not come here because of our own condition, but because of Yours."

By the word *prahasitānanam*, the *gopīs* refer to Śrī Kṛṣṇa's laughing and smiling. He wanted the *gopīs* to meet with Him and, by His laughing and smiling, He inspired in them His desire for *kāma*. The *gopīs* say, "Your third arrow is Your smiling face. A flower can smile, but it cannot speak. On the other hand, Your face not only smiles, but it tells us something. It begs for something with sidelong glances and laughter, which is Your fourth arrow." *Vikṣaṇam* means 'sidelong glances,' and *prema-vīkṣaṇam* refers to Śrī Kṛṣṇa's glancing lovingly at the *gopīs* from the corner of His eyes. He wants something from them, and begs for it by His glance.

The *gopīs* continue, "And the fifth arrow is Your broad chest." When they speak about Kṛṣṇa's chest here, they really mean to say, "We realize that Your chest was burning with desire to meet with us. Your heart was pounding as You considered how to meet us. We know this from Lakṣmī, who sits on Your chest in the form of a tuft of golden hair. Seeing all this and realizing that every part of Your heart is filled with longing to associate with us, we became bewildered and maddened with the desire to protect You and give You what You want."

This mood is called *susakhya-praṇaya-bhāva*, and it is present only in Śrīmatī Rādhikā, who cannot pray in the way that this verse is generally translated. Candrāvalī does not share Rādhikā's mood at all; rather, her words and mood are found in the general meaning, in the translation. While the general meaning of the verse is also correct, Śrīla Viśvanātha Cakravartī Ṭhākura has explained the verse in this particular way. This is because, in his *siddha* form as a *gopī*, he is an associate of Śrī Rūpa Mañjarī, (who is the leader of Śrīmatī Rādhikā's intimate maidservants and is always serving and glorifying Her moods). Not only is Śrīla Viśvanātha Cakravartī Ṭhākura very near and dear to Rūpa Mañjarī, but he is said to be

an incarnation of Śrīla Rūpa Gosvāmī, whose *gopī* form is Śrī Rūpa Mañjarī. Thus, it is Rādhikā's mood that he expresses in his commentary.

In *Vaiṣṇava-toṣaṇī*, Śrīla Jīva Gosvāmī, who, in his *siddha* form as a *gopī* is Śrī Vilāsa Mañjarī, another attendant of Śrī Rūpa Mañjarī, reveals the same sentiments as Viśvanātha Cakravartī Ṭhākura, but with some speciality. He explains that with the words *hṛc-chayodayaṁ* and *muhyate manaḥ*, the *gopīs* tell Śrī Kṛṣṇa, "Your glances (*vīkṣaṇam*) tell us that the disease of *kāma* has arisen in Your heart, and therefore You cannot sit peacefully. That is why You called us. We realized this and, being bewildered, we came here to give You relief from Your disease." *Hṛt* means 'heart,' *saya* means 'disease of love,' and *udayam* means 'rising.'

Kṛṣṇa asks, "How do you know that My heart is full of *kāma?*"

The *gopīs* reply with the words *rahasi saṁvidaṁ*, 'solitary conversations,' referring to their meeting with Him before He disappeared, when He had confided something to them in a solitary place. There are so many ways to express one's ideas: by hints and suggestions (*vyañjana*), by signs and symptoms (*lakṣaṇa*), and by direct statements (*abhidhā*). Those who are expert in *prema* do not express their intentions directly, but with hints and suggestions. For example, when Vṛndā-devī sees Kṛṣṇa placing on His neck a garland made of yellow *campaka* flowers, she tells Śrīmatī Rādhikā, "Kṛṣṇa told me to bring You to Him. He wants to be the garland on Your neck, so please go to Him at once." Another example is that when Kṛṣṇa embraces a cow, it is to be understood that He has some other intention.

The *gopīs* had seen Kṛṣṇa's love-laden glances. They had seen Him looking at them with thirsty eyes, and now they tell Him, "You are thirsty. You wanted to drink nectar and You looked towards us to fulfill that desire, though we had no need for it. You also showed us Your chest, which is the abode of all kinds of beauty because Śrī Lakṣmī-devī lives there. The sight of Your chest caused us to also become full of desire."

Two actions occur in this verse: having seen (*vīkṣya*) Kṛṣṇa, the *gopīs* experience a desire (*spṛhā*). The words *bṛhad uraḥ śriyo vīkṣya* and *ati-spṛhā* denote something very profound. *Bṛhad* indicates that Kṛṣṇa's feeling is extremely deep, and with the words *uraḥ śrīyo*, the *gopīs* imply, "We can see what is in Your heart; we feel it, and Your face affirms it. If Your heart is full of sorrow, Your face expresses it; if You have great *prema* in Your heart, Your face reveals this; and if You are angry, Your face shows that as well. It tells all. We looked at Your face and understood that You have an intense desire (*ati-spṛhā*) for our association. Seeing this desire deep within Your heart, we yearn (*ati-spṛhā*) to satisfy it."

It seems that the *gopīs* are expressing their own desire and begging for it to be fulfilled, but this is the external meaning. According to the general meaning, the *gopīs* are expressing their intense longing: "We want to be held to Your breast." Actually, they are seeing Kṛṣṇa's *ati-spṛha*, His yearning for them, and they consider, "How is it that, although Kṛṣṇa is a male, He is so bewildered? He cannot control His feelings. He tries to attract us with His five arrows of Cupid, but He fails. We want to give Him a remedy for the fire of His desire, but we become completely bewildered when we try to think of what to do."

The general meaning of this verse is that Kṛṣṇa's broad chest is very captivating and is one of His arrows of Cupid. According to this meaning, the word *śrīyo* indicates that His chest is the center of all varieties of sweetness and beauty, in which case the *gopīs* tell Him, "We saw Your chest, and as a result we became bewildered." I have also explained the *gopīs*' inner meaning: "Kṛṣṇa has a deep desire (*ati-spṛhā*). Having seen this, we have a great eagerness (*ati-spṛhā*) to protect Him and fulfill that desire."

Śrīla Viśvanātha Cakravartī Ṭhākura and Śrīla Jīva Gosvāmī both explain that *muhyate manaḥ* has still another meaning. In the previous verse the *gopīs* told Kṛṣṇa, "First You called us, and then we came to You, neglecting the orders of our parents, husbands, and all other relatives (*pati-sutānvaya-bhrātṛ-bāndhavān*). At that time we saw the five arrows of Kāmadeva in Your possession, and we saw how those five arrows are actually You, Yourself.

"But now we see that those five arrows have practically brought You to the point of death. Because of Your *kāma*, You have come to the tenth and last stage – death. That is why we have come running here, bewildered with anxiety as to how to protect You."

The *gopīs* want to serve Kṛṣṇa in all ways.

All these pastimes have several meanings and deep moods. There are many meanings of this verse that have not been discussed in the commentaries, but they cannot be disclosed. To disclose confidential subject matter in the presence of many persons is aptly expressed as "breaking earthen pots in the midst of a market place, where hundreds of thousands of persons are present." When confidential topics are spoken to an unqualified audience, the sprout of *bhakti* in the hearts of the audience is injured and the result is chaos.

In due course, after your *sādhana* and *bhajana* are matured, all details will automatically manifest within your heart. I have given you eyes to see the path required to realize these pastimes. Use them, and think, and be blessed by chanting "Hare Kṛṣṇa, Hare Kṛṣṇa, Kṛṣṇa Kṛṣṇa, Hare Hare, Hare Rāma, Hare Rāma, Rāma Rāma, Hare, Hare."

Verse Eighteen

We have a heart-disease. You are a very expert doctor, so please give us some remedy to counteract and remove it.

Verse 18

व्रजवनौकसां व्यक्तिरङ्ग ते
वृजिनहन्त्र्यलं विश्वमङ्गलम्।
त्यज मनाक् च नस्त्वत्स्पृहात्मनां
स्वजनहृद्रुजां यन्निषूदनम् ॥१८॥

vraja-vanaukasāṁ vyaktir aṅga te
vṛjina-hantry alaṁ viśva-maṅgalam
tyaja manāk ca nas tvat-spṛhātmanāṁ
sva-jana-hṛd-rujāṁ yan niṣūdanam

vraja-vana – in the forests of Vraja; *okasām* – for those who dwell; *vyaktiḥ* – the appearance; *aṅga* – O dear one; *te* – Your; *vṛjina* – of distress; *hantrī* – the killer; *alam* – enough; *viśva-maṅgalam* – auspicious for all; *tyaja* – please release; *manāk* – a little; *ca* – and; *naḥ* – to us; *tvat* – for You; *spṛhā* – with hankering; *ātmanām* – whose minds are filled; *sva* – Your own; *jana* – devotees; *hṛt-rujām* – of the heart disease; *yat* – which; *niṣūdanam* – nullifies.

Translation

O Kṛṣṇa, Your appearance completely destroys the sorrows of Vraja's residents, and in every way brings auspiciousness to the world. Our hearts, which desire You alone, are agonized by our heart-disease, Therefore, giving up all miserliness, kindly give in charity a little bit of that medicine which can cure Your dear ones.

Bhāva-prakāśika Vṛtti

In the previous verse, Śrīla Viśvanātha Cakravartī Ṭhākura explained that Kāmadeva's five arrows are the *gopīs'* confidential discussions with Śrī Kṛṣṇa in solitary places (*rahasi saṁvidaṁ*), the rising of transcendental desire in Kṛṣṇa's heart (*hṛc-chayodayaṁ*), His lotus face when He is smiling in a very special way (*prahasitānanaṁ*), His loving glances (*prema-vīkṣaṇam*), and His broad chest, which is the abode of the goddess of fortune (*bṛhad-uraḥ śriyo vīkṣya*).

In that verse, the *gopīs* told Kṛṣṇa, "We have seen these five symptoms in You, so we know that a desire burns in Your heart."

Śrī Kṛṣṇa asked, "How do you know?"

The *gopīs* replied, "We know this by our confidential discussions in solitary places (*rahasi saṁvidam*); by Your face, smiling in a special way (*prahasitānanaṁ*); and by Your loving glances (*prema-vīkṣaṇam*). That is why we have come here – to give You relief from Your *kāma*. We are bewildered in our concern, and desire to pacify You and give You relief."

The *gopīs* continue to express this mood in the present verse, the common meaning of which is seen in the translation. In order to explore the deeper meaning, I will discuss the points in *Śrī Vaiṣṇava-toṣaṇī*.

Vraja-vanaukasāṁ vyaktir aṅga te. One of the many meanings of the word *vyakti* is as follows: "Your inner condition is manifest (*vyakta*) by these five symptoms, so we know that You are over-whelmed with *kāma* to meet with us. When we see Your desire, this inspires *kāma* in our own hearts as well. For example, if there is a flood in a main river, all the tributaries that flow into the main river also flood; the flood spreads everywhere. Similarly, this flood of *kāma* has entered Your heart and made it burn, and when we recognized this by seeing its many symptoms, it also came into our hearts. Now we always have a burning sensation in our hearts, and we think, 'Alas, how can we devise a way to pacify Your continually inflamed *kāma*?' Our constant absorption in this immerses us in Your mood."

The *gopīs* further explain, "A person will be influenced by the virtues of the people with whom he lives, and he will also be infected with their bad qualities. Similarly, the *kāma* in Your heart has infected our hearts, which are now always ablaze like Yours. Your heart burns with the desire: 'How shall I get the association of the *gopīs*?' and now our hearts burn with longing for You. Each of us burns for the other, and now that You are not here, we are searching for You to give You our association. Our love and affection automatically flows to You.

"It is our very nature to love You, and therefore if any suffering comes to You, we have no peace until we can think of a way to remove it. While searching for You, we think, 'How can we reduce the burning of Your *kāma*?' We have become excessively absorbed in this thought, and thus our affection has increased to such heights that our hearts are breaking in pieces."

This and the next verse explain why the *gopīs*' hearts are breaking, simultaneously with love and sorrow. The *gopīs* tell Kṛṣṇa, "We cannot do anything to help You, because You are not here to meet with us," and they beseech Him to appear before them.

"O *aṅga*! O beloved!" This form of address is full of love and affection. The *gopīs* are also experiencing an intense feeling of separation and also profound humility, and for these reasons they do not address Kṛṣṇa by His name. At other times and in other places they call Him Mukunda and Kṛṣṇa, or other names such as Devakī-suta, Yaśodā-suta, Vrajendra-nandana, and Vrajendra-suta. And sometimes they call Him Kaṁsāri or Aghāri. But here they simply address Him as their beloved *aṅga*. The word *aṅga* actually refers to one's own hand or other limb, so they are saying, "You are part of our body." If a limb is hurt, we tend to hold it close to our body. In this mood the *gopīs* are saying, "You are our *aṅga*, so we want to keep You close to us."

They continue, "Your appearance in this world is only for the Vrajavāsīs, the cowherd community; and for the *vanavāsīs*, those who live in the forest." The words *vraja-vanaukasāṁ* refer not only to men and women, but also to cows, buffalos, peacocks, monkeys; indeed all creatures are included. Kṛṣṇa's appearance is not only to vanquish the sorrow of all the Vrajavāsīs and forest-dwellers. It is the very form of auspiciousness, because He has appeared for the purpose of engaging in sportive pastimes with both the Vrajavāsīs and the forest-dwellers; laughing with them, and satisfying them in every respect. In this way, His appearance is for two purposes: to relieve distress, and to give happiness to the *gopīs* and everyone else.

The *gopīs* say, "Your appearance is auspicious for the entire universe (*viśva-maṅgalam*). It is true that You have appeared to take away everyone's distress and to give everyone happiness. But this is especially for those who live in the forests, more especially for the Vrajavāsīs, and most especially for us, who are here hankering for You. We long to give You relief from the disease of *kāma* in Your heart. We want to please You by singing and dancing, by giving You flowers, garlands, and by doing anything else to make You happy. When we perform these services for You, we will also be so happy."

Vṛjina-hantry alaṁ viśva-maṅgalam: The word *alam*, meaning 'enough,' is used as an adverb to qualify both *vṛjina-hantri* and *viśva-maṅgalam*. Thus, Kṛṣṇa's appearance is sufficient to destroy distress (*vṛjina-hantri*), and to bring auspiciousness to the entire world (*viśva-maṅgalam*). In that case the meaning is: "In the entire world, the Vrajavāsīs are special, and amongst the Vrajavāsīs, we *gopīs* are special. Now we have come here, so kindly remove our sorrows and agony and the raging fire of our *kāma*."

Tyaja manāk ca nas tvat-spṛhātmanāṁ: The *gopīs* say, "Please give us something that can relieve our sorrow and the burning in our hearts." They refer to 'something,' but they do not specify what that 'something' is.

Śrī Kṛṣṇa may say, "You live in Vṛndāvana, in Vraja, and when the demons create some calamity, I kill them and give relief to all the Vrajavāsīs. That naturally includes you, so why are you making a separate case for yourselves? You are already being cared for, so why are you speaking like this?" Kṛṣṇa expresses His desire: "You should say clearly and openly what you want." The words 'clearly and openly' are not written in the *ācāryas*' commentaries, but I am explaining their words. I am taking very good water from the well.[1]

---

1 The previous *ācāryas* are revealing their moods and ideas to the commentator, and he to us.

Nas tvat-spṛhātmanām: *Naḥ* means 'we, all of us *gopīs*;' and *spṛhā* means 'hankering.'

Kṛṣṇa asks the *gopīs*, "What are you hankering for?"

The *gopīs* reply, "You are so beloved to us – to the extreme extent – and therefore we are always thinking about You and how we can make You happy. This is our soul's desire. We cannot be satisfied unless we can see You. We want You very close to us at all times, because otherwise we cannot satisfy You. We want You only; You alone. Nothing else can give us relief. Our only unhappiness is that we are not satisfying You."

The *gopīs* suppose that Kṛṣṇa might say, "All the Vrajavāsīs have love and affection for Me. They always pray to God and to all other great personalities, 'Please make Kṛṣṇa happy.' What is the difference between you and all the other Vrajavāsīs? They all want to see Me near them and they all want to please Me, so what is the difference between you and them? What more do you want?"

The *gopīs* have kept their desire hidden in their hearts. Kṛṣṇa wants to see it openly, but it cannot be seen openly. The *gopīs* say, "The point is that we are not only Vrajavāsīs."

"Then who are you?" Krsna asks.

Sva-jana-hṛd-rujāṁ: *Sva* means 'one's own.' The *gopīs* say, "You are a *gopa* and we are *gopīs*. You are the son of Nanda Bābā, and we are the daughters of Vṛṣabhānu Bābā and all the other *gopas*. We are so near and dear to You that the other Vrajavasis cannot be compared to us. We are Yours and You are ours. You are our life (*jana*). We cannot live without You, just as a body cannot live without consciousness."

This is not the case for all the Vrajavāsīs. When Śrī Kṛṣṇa went to Mathurā and Dvārakā, all the Vrajavāsīs wept in separation, but they could not feel what the *gopīs* felt. They did not come to the brink of death as the *gopīs* did. When Kṛṣṇa sent Uddhava to Vraja, this was especially for these *gopīs*.

Śrī Kṛṣṇa is now pressing them to disclose their specific desire. Therefore they express it to some extent, but then cover it again, without revealing it clearly. They say plaintively, "We have a heart-disease (*hṛd-ruj*). You are a very expert doctor, so please give us some remedy to counteract and remove it (*yan nisūdanam*)."

If a sick person comes to a doctor and says, "I have terrible pain here," he will not tell the doctor what medicine to prescribe. The doctor has to select the medicine according to his own diagnosis. If the patient demands a particular medication, the doctor will be angry at his arrogance, for he is not trained to know what medicine is needed. Accordingly, the *gopīs* tell Kṛṣṇa, "You know what medicine to give us. We know that You know. So give us just a very little (*manāk*) of the medicine that will alleviate our heart-disease (*kāma-roga*)."

In the form of Lord Vāmanadeva, Śrī Kṛṣṇa once went to Bali Mahārāja and said, "I am only asking for three paces of land, the measurement of My steps." Laughing, Bali Mahārāja replied, "Why are You asking for only three steps of land? You can take a kingdom or something else of value. You can have many beautiful *brāhmaṇa* ladies as wives. I can give You elephants, horses, and vast wealth. Why do You ask for only this much?" Lord Vāmanadeva replied, "I am a *brāhmaṇa* boy. I am completely satisfied in all respects, internally and externally. I do not require anything." In the end, however, He took everything away from Bali.

A beggar may approach someone and create sympathy by saying, "Just give me a little something," but actually he does not intend to take just a little. In the same way, the *gopīs* say, "Give us something – just a little." However, this is not their real desire; they do not really think that a little will do. The word *hṛd-rujām*, referring to the heart-disease of the *gopīs*, is a plural noun. There are millions of *gopīs*. If only a drop of medicine is given to millions of *gopīs*, none of them will be able to have even a trace of it; it will not even touch them. The *gopīs* are thinking, "The inferno in our hearts is raging so fiercely that all the water in the world would not be able to put it out. If a dangerous fire is burning and just a little water is put on it, the water works like *ghee*, making the flames flare still higher. The fire in our hearts is like that." The *gopīs*' desire is this: "Kṛṣṇa should always be with us, so that we can always serve Him."

The last words of this verse are *yan niṣūdanam*. *Sūdana* in the word *niṣūdanam* means 'to remove,' and *ni* refers to *niśeṣa-rūpa*. The word *niśeṣa* indicates 'forever,' and implies 'fully, so that which is removed does not return.' The *gopīs* tell Kṛṣṇa, "Please give us a remedy that will fully destroy our distress. And be sure to give plenty of it, because there are millions of us *gopīs*, and this fire of *kāma* in all of our hearts must be extinguished forever. If You only give a little, it will work like *ghee* and the burning will increase."

Śrīla Jīva Gosvāmī infers that the *gopīs*' heart-disease has two aspects. The first is its symptoms and the second is the disease itself. For example, if someone has a cold, the symptoms are that water comes from the nose, there is thick mucus, and there may be a severe headache and fever as well. The second aspect is the disease itself. The *gopīs* tell Kṛṣṇa, "We want You to remove both aspects of the disease. A qualified doctor gives one medicine which dispels both the symptoms and the root of the symptoms."

"What are the symptoms of your heart-disease?"

"Burning. We are always thinking of Your happiness. We cannot live in our homes, and we are greatly distressed. We are always restless; we have no peace at all. These symptoms should be removed."

"How will they be removed?"

"You should give us some antidote in sufficient quantity; otherwise the disease will continue to return in ever-new ways. In other words, if there is still some disease remaining, it will continue to manifest itself in many different features. The symptoms will continue, and we will suffer in newer and newer ways." Although the *gopīs* are not expressing their mood openly, they are in fact saying, "Even though we have only prayed for a very little, You should give the medicine in plenty."

Śrīla Jīva Gosvāmī has not said clearly what medicine should be given. Śrīla Viśvanātha Cakravartī Ṭhākura has given some explanation, and you can read that for yourselves; I am presenting only a part of his commentary. Śrīla Viśvanātha Cakravartī Ṭhākura expresses the subject matter somewhat more openly, whereas Śrīla Jīva Gosvāmī speaks in a more covered way. According to *Sārārtha-darśinī*, the *gopīs* say, "We are innocent, newly married ladies and without offence. With Your flute-song, You have stolen our mind and intelligence, our patience, and our religious principles. You took everything we had, and we became like mad persons. You called us on this very night, and we came here, but then You told us to go away. At that time our eagerness intensified as we asked ourselves,

'When will Kṛṣṇa say, "Stay," instead of telling us to leave and return to our homes?' "

The *gopīs* are thinking that perhaps Kṛṣṇa acted as He did to increase their eagerness, and therefore they tell Him, "We are burning in the fire of intense longing. It was You who set that eagerness ablaze, and then suddenly You went out of our sight. Still, we know that You are our beloved and we are Your beloveds, so You must not have intended to give us this suffering. Surely You must have wanted to give us Your intimate association.

"We know this because Your birth is auspicious for the entire world, and of all the people in the world it is especially true for the Vrajavāsīs. Among the Vrajavāsīs it is especially for the *gopas* and *gopīs*, and amongst them it is especially for the *gopīs*. We know that although You have come for all, You have come especially for us. We know that You are longing to see us, and that is why You called us tonight by Your flute-song. Hearing that You are distressed by the burning in Your heart, we have come to relieve You. But we also want something for ourselves. First pay us our fee, then we will examine You, and then we will give You some medicine. We are not mere third-class doctors. We are highly qualified doctors, so quickly pay us. You can give anything, whatever You have. Perhaps You are too poor to pay; still, You should offer some payment to demonstrate the sincerity of Your desire to be treated. We want to mitigate Your heart-disease of *kāma*, but first You should give up Your miserliness."

"Yes, very good," Kṛṣṇa says. "What should I give you? Tell Me openly what you want."

It is then that the *gopīs* say, "*Sva-jana-hṛd-rujāṁ yan niṣūdanam* – You have the heart-disease of *kāma*, and that disease has entered our hearts as well. So You should give us some medicine that will reduce it."

"What is that medicine?"

"A medicine that will give us some relief."

"But what do you want specifically?"

"Put Your hands on our hearts."

In matters of *prema*, it is inappropriate to speak in a direct manner. For example, it would not be proper to say, "We have brought sweets and many other delicious preparations for you to eat. You told us to bring them, so please enjoy them." Similarly, in matters of *prema*, if one says, "Oh, I love You so much, I will die without You," one's *prema* is diminished. Therefore, this spirit should be kept hidden. If a person's love is of the highest quality, he will keep his love and affection concealed. If it is expressed directly, it will disappear.

Why, then, have the *gopīs* said, "You have *kāma* in Your heart and we have come to pacify You"? Perhaps there is some hidden mystery here, but what is that mystery? It seems that they are expressing themselves openly, but actually they are hiding their feelings and desires. Śrīla Viśvanātha Cakravartī has explained something of their feelings, for the sole purpose of enhancing the *prema* in the hearts of his readers. Actually the *gopīs* cannot express their hearts openly. Their words as explained by Śrīla Cakravartī Ṭhākura are not in the verses. They have either kept their real feelings hidden (*avahittha*), or they have expressed themselves in a joking way. Even then, only bold and outspoken (*prakhara*) *gopīs* can express these words. For example, Lalitā is *prakhara*, but Śrīmatī Rādhikā is not; Rādhikā is *madhya*, moderate, so She cannot directly express Her intentions. Viśākhā is also *madhya*, but she is *mṛdvī*, pliant, at the same time. Lalitā is *prakhara* to the extreme extent, so she can even punish Kṛṣṇa. She can say harsh things, especially when angry. Somehow we should be able to reconcile all these varieties of statements by the *gopīs*.

So here, the *gopīs* are not expressing their real desire directly and openly. Everything has been told, but at the same time everything is still very covered and concealed. When the *gopīs* tell Kṛṣṇa, "Place your hands on our breasts," this is not the meaning. In the verse beginning, "*Yat te sujāta-caraṇāmbu-ruhaṁ* – please place Your lotus feet on our breasts," the *gopīs*' real desire is still hidden, for they cannot speak directly.

Neither Śrīla Jīva Gosvāmī nor Viśvanātha Cakravartī Ṭhākura is fully revealing the *gopīs*' moods. A person can only realize their moods by performing the topmost *rāgānuga bhajana-sādhana*, but even then he will be shy. He will keep his intimate realization in his heart, thinking, "My ears cannot hear this." All the *ācāryas* and Gosvāmīs in our disciplic succession have instructed us not to disclose these topics, and I also do not want to speak much in this regard. I am therefore explaining the topic briefly. That is enough for now. I am not going to disclose any more, for a *sādhaka* who is still unripe in his *bhakti* should not hear more. As Śrīla Jīva Gosvāmī has said, "I will not say more than this. A *bhakta* should perform *sādhana* and *hari-bhajana*, and he will realize everything automatically."

Verse Nineteen

If anything penetrates Your lotus feet, we feel it penetrating our hearts. We want some medicine for this, so please come out of the forest. Do not remain there any longer; please come to us.

Verse 19

यत् ते सुजातचरणाम्बुरुहं स्तनेषु
भीताः शनैः प्रिय दधीमहि कर्कशेषु।
तेनाटवीमटसि तद्व्यथते न किं स्वित्
कूर्पादिभिर्भ्रमति धीर्भवदायुषां नः ॥१९॥

yat te sujāta-caraṇāmburuhaṁ staneṣu
bhītāḥ śanaiḥ priya dadhīmahi karkaśeṣu
tenāṭavīm aṭasi tad vyathate na kiṁ svit
kūrpādibhir bhramati dhīr bhavad-āyuṣāṁ naḥ

yat – which; *te* – Your; *su-jāta* – very fine; *caraṇa-ambu-ruham* – lotus feet; *staneṣu* – on the breasts; *bhītāḥ* – being afraid; *śanaiḥ* – gently; *priya* – O dear one; *dadhīmahi* – we place; *karkaśeṣu* – rough; *tena* – with them; *aṭavīm* – the forest; *aṭasi* – You roam; *tat* – they; *vyathate* – are distressed; *na* – not; *kim svit* – we wonder; *kūrpa-ādibhiḥ* – by small stones and so on; *bhramati* – reels; *dhīḥ* – the mind; *bhavat-āyuṣām* – of those whom Your Lordship is the very life; *naḥ* – of us.

Translation

O beloved, fearing to hurt Your very tender lotus feet, we carefully place them on our hard breasts. Tonight, with those very same soft feet, You are wandering somewhere in this secluded forest. Are Your lotus feet not in pain, being injured by sharp stones, edges of dry grains, and the like? O You who are our very life, our intelligence is bewildered, overwhelmed with thoughts of You.

Bhāva-prakāśika Vṛtti

In his commentary on the previous verse, Śrīla Jīva Gosvāmī explains that the *gopīs* told Kṛṣṇa, "Give a little, a very little of a remedy that will subside our heart-disease and give us pleasure; and it should have two effects: it should remove all kinds of miseries (*vṛjina-hantry alam*) and it should bestow auspiciousness (*viśva-maṅgalam*).

Kṛṣṇa asked, "A little of what?"

The *gopīs* replied, "You are the doctor; the best doctor, in fact. We do not have to tell You what to give us. You certainly have the appropriate medicine to counteract the heart-disease of those who are Your very life and soul."

Kṛṣṇa said, "I cannot understand what heart-disease you refer to."

"You are the doctor, so You should know. We do not have much knowledge about diseases, but You do."

"I still do not understand what you are talking about. You will have to be more specific."

Kṛṣṇa wanted them to state their desire directly, but the *gopīs* would not do so. Rather, they communicated indirectly, by their movements.

He insisted, "I will not give you anything until you plainly tell Me the specific nature of your heart-disease and what medicine you want. Otherwise, how can I remove your disease?"

When He persisted with this point, the *gopīs* began to weep, as described in the verse beginning *yat te sujāta caranāmburuhaṁ staneṣu*. They now say, "O dearly beloved, we will tell You our heart-disease and the medicine we want. We worry that You walk on rough surfaces with Your lotus feet, which are so sweet, tender, soft, and cool."

The word *sujāta* in this verse refers to someone who has been born in a very respectable family. For example, the lotus flower is *sujāta* because it blossoms in pure, clean water; thus it has many natural qualities like softness and a sweet fragrance.

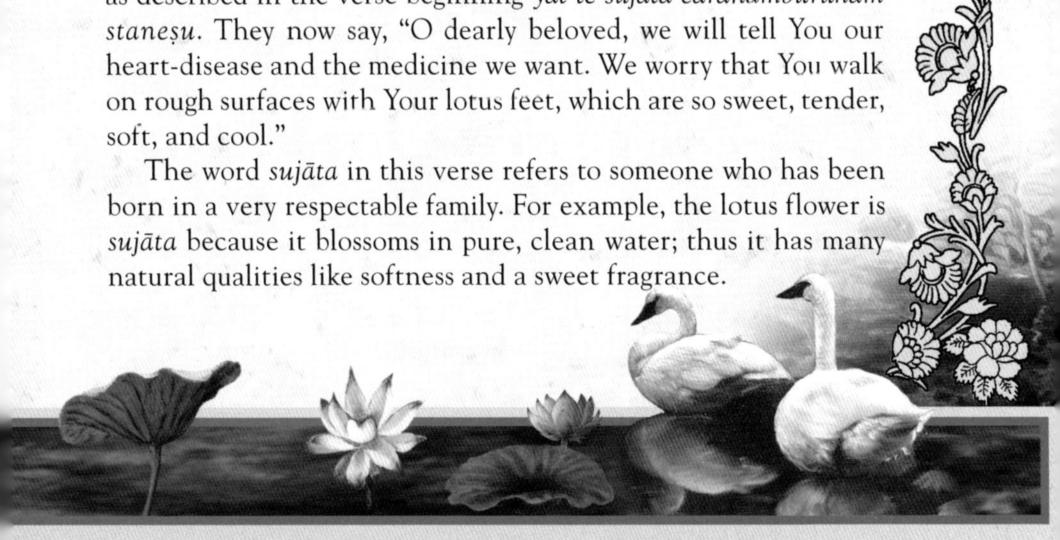

It also gives a cooling effect. The *gopīs* use this word to describe the qualities of Kṛṣṇa's lotus feet, and their anxiety that those feet are pained. Just as they express their anxiety about Kṛṣṇa's walking in the forest in this verse, they had previously done so in Verse Eleven:

> *calasi yad vrajāc cārayan paśūn*
> *nalina-sundaraṁ nātha te padam*
> *śila-tṛṇāṅkuraiḥ sīdatīti naḥ*
> *kalilatāṁ manaḥ kānta gacchati*

> O master, O beloved, when You leave Vraja to take the cows and other animals out to graze, the soles of Your feet, which are more tender than a lotus, must suffer great pain from sharp pebbles, grasses, and the edges of dry grains. When we think about this, our minds become very agitated.

At that time they said, "When You go to the forest to take the cows out for grazing (*yad vrajāc cārayan*), the stones, shoots, and blades of rough grass (*śila-tṛṇāṅkuraiḥ sīdatīti*) prick Your very soft and tender lotus feet."

Actually, when Śrī Kṛṣṇa takes the cows out to graze during the day, He goes to lush green pasturing grounds. The personification of this earth planet, Pṛthivī-devī, is one of His queens. Especially for the comfort of His lotus feet, she grew soft, silken grasses at the time of His appearance in this world. Wherever He goes, Pṛthivī-devī extends her tongue, which is hundreds of thousands of times softer than any carpet, under His lotus feet. Thus, there is no chance of His feet contacting sharp stones, edges of dry grains, or shoots. Moreover, Vṛndāvana is always managed by Vṛndā-devī, who has arranged that not a single stone or other sharp object would be there to hurt His feet.

In this verse, the *gopīs* say, "*yat te sujāta-caraṇāmburuhaṁ staneṣu* – Now it is night, and the ground on the banks of Yamunā is covered with sharp stones. We fear that Your lotus feet are being pricked by stones and sharp, dry grains as You walk in dark and dangerous places."

Why do they speak in this way? They have no need for such concern, but one who has tender feelings for another person always thinks like this. If a man is late in returning home, all his loved ones will think, "Why is he late? What has happened?" His wife may think, "Is he late because his train derailed? Is he seriously injured? What should I do?" She may think, "Maybe he has been attacked by dacoits! Why is he late?" She repeatedly goes to the door to look for him, and she asks her children, "What is the reason he has not returned home? What is the reason?" Her children are young and cannot reply; they can only hear her words, but still she questions them. She again questions herself, although there is really no need for concern. Her husband is peacefully on his way home.

Similarly, the *gopīs* are in anxiety for Śrī Kṛṣṇa's welfare. Why? In the first verse of their *Gopī-gīta* they had said:

jayati te 'dhikaṁ janmanā vrajaḥ
śrayata indirā śaśvad atra hi
dayita dṛśyatāṁ dikṣu tāvakās
tvayi dhṛtāsavas tvāṁ vicinvate

> O most beloved, because of Your birth in this land of Vraja, the entire area has become more glorious than Vaikuṇṭha and other planets. It is for this reason that Lakṣmī, the goddess of beauty and wealth, eternally decorates it with her presence. O beloved, in this most blissful land of Vraja, it is only we *gopīs* who are not happy. We maintain our lives solely for Your sake, being extremely anguished in separation from You, and are wandering from forest to forest in search of You. Therefore, please, appear before us now.

Tvayi dhṛtasavas: *Asavas* means 'life-airs.' They told Kṛṣṇa, "You are our life." Now, in Verse Nineteen, they say the same thing – *dhīr bhavad-āyuṣāṁ naḥ*: The word *asavas* in Verse One has the same meaning as *ayuṣāṁ* in this verse, wherein the *gopīs* now say, "You are our life, You are our soul, You are our everything. If anything hurts Your feet, that pain pierces our soul, because You are our soul. You may not feel the pinching, but we feel it."

The word *aṅga* means 'limb' or 'bodily part.' We carefully tend to different parts of our body, yet the life-air is superior to all these bodily parts. We can remain alive if a limb is amputated, but if the life-air leaves the body, we die at once.

The *gopīs* continue, "When all these sharp things pinch Your feet, we feel this in our heart. Life (*ayus*) lives in the heart, and that is why we want to keep Your soft, fragrant, cooling lotus feet very gently and carefully there. In this way You will not feel any discomfort. Please do not walk in the forest any longer. Return to us. We want to place Your lotus feet here, on our hearts, so that You will not feel any pain. This is our disease: our hearts are pained because we know You are receiving so many injuries while You roam in the forest. This is the scorching fire that burns our hearts."

Kṛṣṇa asks, "Why must you place My feet on your hearts so 'gently and carefully'?"

"Your feet are extremely soft," the *gopīs* reply, "and we fear that our breasts are very hard."

"Why do you want to keep My very soft and tender feet on your hard breasts?"

"Oh, it is because Your lotus feet are so dear to us. We want to serve them on our hearts, because the heart is superior to all the other parts of the body. We do not want to keep them anywhere else."

The *gopīs* are not expressing their mood directly, but in their hearts they are saying, "We keep Your lotus feet on our heart for Your satisfaction. You want this, and that is why we wish to keep them here."

They continue, "But now we see that You are roaming here and there in the dense, dark forest, and we are searching for You."

Kṛṣṇa then inquires, "Why are you so confused and disturbed?"

Again the *gopīs* reply, "You are the life of our lives," just as they had said in the first verse of this *Gopī-gīta*.

In *Śrīmad-Bhāgavatam* and *Bhagavad-gītā*, the same auspicious words are uttered in both the first and last verses. The first verse in *Śrīmad-Bhāgavatam* ends with *dhīmahi*: *satyaṁ paraṁ dhīmahi* – I meditate on the Supreme Absolute Truth, and *dhīmahi* is repeated in *Bhāgavatam*'s final verse (12.13.19):

kasmai yena vibhāsito 'yam atulo jñāna-pradīpaḥ purā
tad-rūpeṇa ca nāradāya munaye kṛṣṇāya tad-rūpiṇā

yogīndrāya tad-ātmanātha bhagavad-rātāya kāruṇyatas
tac chuddhaṁ vimalaṁ viśokam amṛtaṁ satyaṁ paraṁ dhīmahi

I meditate upon that pure and spotless Supreme Absolute Truth, who is free from suffering and death and who in the beginning personally revealed this incomparable torchlight of knowledge to Brahmā. Brahmā then spoke it to the sage Nārada, who narrated it to Kṛṣṇa-dvaipāyana Vyāsa. Śrīla Vyāsa revealed this *Bhāgavatam* to the greatest of sages, Śukadeva Gosvāmī, and Śukadeva mercifully spoke it to Mahārāja Parīkṣit.

In *Bhagavad-gītā* we find the same principle. Śrī Kṛṣṇa began His instructions after hearing Arjuna say, "I surrender myself at Your feet." Arjuna had uttered this verse:

kārpaṇya-doṣopahata-svabhāvaḥ
pṛcchāmi tvāṁ dharma-sammūḍha-cetāḥ
yac chreyaḥ syān niścitaṁ brūhi tan me
śiṣyas te 'haṁ śādhi māṁ tvāṁ prapannam
Bhagavad-gītā (2.7)

Now I am confused about my duty and have lost all composure because of miserly weakness. In this condition I am asking You to tell me for certain what is best for me. Now I am Your disciple, and a soul surrendered unto You. Please instruct me.

In this verse, the word *prapannam*, meaning 'surrendered,' refers to the same tenet of surrender (*śaraṇāgati*) described by Kṛṣṇa in one of the very last verses. There He told Arjuna:

sarva-dharmān parityajya
mām ekaṁ śaraṇaṁ vraja
ahaṁ tvāṁ sarva-pāpebhyo
mokṣayiṣyāmi mā śucaḥ
Bhagavad-gītā (18.66)

Abandon all varieties of religion and just surrender unto Me. I shall deliver you from all sinful reactions. Do not fear.

In the beginning and end of all Vedic scriptures, the same principle is repeated. Important truths and instructions are repeated again and again, and that is why we repeat "Hare Kṛṣṇa, Hare Kṛṣṇa" again and again and again. Chanting and remembering is our *sādhana*, and it is the objective of all scriptures; it is everything. *Hari-nāma* is Śrī Kṛṣṇa and Śrī Rādhā Themselves, and therefore pure chanting is our ultimate goal. Similarly, the fundamental objective of the *gopīs* – "You are our life" – is repeated many times in *Śrīmad-Bhāgavatam*. In particular it appears throughout *Gopī-gīta*, in the beginning, several times in the middle, and also at the end.

The *gopīs* say, "Your happiness, and our love for You, is our very life; and we suffer intolerably if anything threatens our life. This is our heart-disease."

In his commentary, Śrīla Jīva Gosvāmī has given us a very good explanation of some of the meanings of this verse, but still he is concealing something. He has not fully expressed his ideas, and finally he has written, "You will know the full meaning of this verse by practicing *rūpānuga-bhajana*." In order to practice *rūpānuga-bhajana* or *rāgānuga-bhakti*, one needs the mercy of the Lord's associates. In this regard, Śrīla Raghunātha dāsa Gosvāmī prays in his *Stavāvalī* to Śrīla Rūpa Gosvāmī:

gurau mantre nāmni prabhu-vara-śacī-garbhaja-pade
svarūpe śrī-rūpe gaṇa-yuji tadīya-prathamaje
girīndre gāndharvā-sarasi madhu-pūryāṁ vraja-vane
vraje bhakte goṣṭhālāyiṣu param āstāṁ mama ratiḥ
Śrī Svaniyama-daśakam (1)

He says, "I am so much indebted to you, Śrīla Rūpa Gosvāmī. You have given me everything I require for my spiritual perfection in *rāgānuga-bhajana*. You have taught me how to control my mind, how to think, and how to enter into this realm of *rāgānuga*." *Param āstāṁ mama ratiḥ*: Here, the words *mama ratiḥ* imply that one should have great love for one's *guru*, one's *dīkṣā mantra*, *śrī hari-nāma*, Śrī Caitanya Mahāprabhu, Śrī Svarūpa Dāmodara Gosvāmī, and Śrīla Rūpa Gosvāmī, along with Śrīla Rūpa Gosvāmī's followers and his elder brother Śrīla Sanātana Gosvāmī. *Girīndra* means Girirāja-Govardhana; *gāndharvā-sarasi* is Rādhā-kuṇḍa; *madhu-pūryāṁ* refers to Mathurā; *vraja-vane* means Vṛndāvana; and *goṣṭhālayiṣu* refers to all those who dwell in Vraja. Śrīla Raghunātha dāsa Gosvāmī indicates that we should have deep love for the lotus feet of all these divine personalities. He says, "Rūpa Gosvāmī has given me the ability to control my mind and senses. He has given me the power of spiritual discernment, faith in the Supreme Lord, and freedom from sensual and mental transformations (lust) when meditating on the pastimes of Rādhā and Kṛṣṇa."

If, in our early stage of development in *bhakti*, we remember the intimate pastimes of Śrī Śrī Rādhā and Kṛṣṇa in solitary places, a lusty feeling is bound to enter our hearts. It will surely come. If we try to remember the Lord's intimate pastimes without having received the grace or instructions of our Gurudeva, Gaurāṅga Mahāprabhu, and Śrīla Rūpa Gosvāmī, we will certainly go to the lowest of hells. If we try to enter these topics by our own power, we will be ruined. All our *ācāryas*, such as Śrīla Rūpa Gosvāmī and Śrīla Raghunātha dāsa Gosvāmī, Śrīla Viśvanātha Cakravartī Ṭhākura, Śrīla Bhaktivinoda Ṭhākura, and Śrīla Narottama dāsa Ṭhākura can protect us from this, and therefore we first pray for their mercy when beginning our *sādhana-bhajana*.

Śrīla Raghunātha dāsa Gosvāmī surmounted all obstacles by Śrīla Rūpa Gosvāmī's mercy, and he therefore says, "I remember all of Rādhā and Kṛṣṇa's pastimes without experiencing bodily or mental lust." If we are not situated in *bhakti*, as he is, it is essential for us to hear or read these topics very carefully, praying to our *ācāryas* and to the pastimes themselves to protect us from misunderstanding them to be material.

The *gopīs* very clearly tell Kṛṣṇa, "We have understood our disease. If anything penetrates Your lotus feet, we feel it penetrating our hearts. We want some medicine for this, so please come out of the forest. Do not remain there any longer; please come to us. We will then place Your lotus feet on our hearts very gently and carefully, as medicine for the disease that resides there. If You do not do this, we will die. We will only be able to maintain our lives if we can take Your lotus feet in our own hands and, with intense feelings of possessiveness (*mamatā*) towards You, place them on our breasts."

In *Bhakti-rasāmṛta-sindhu* (1.41), *prema* has been described as a deep sense of possessiveness towards Kṛṣṇa:

samyaṅ masṛṇita-svānto mamatvātiśayāṅkitaḥ
bhāvaḥ sa eva sāndrātmā budhaiḥ premā nigadyate

> The advanced stage of *bhāva-bhakti*, which melts the heart much more than in its initial stage, which greatly augments feelings of transcendental bliss, and which bestows a deep sense of *mamatā* (possessiveness) in relation to Kṛṣṇa, is known as *prema* by the learned.

Prema is *bhāva-bhakti* that has become extremely condensed (*sāndrātmā*). The mood 'You are mine and we are Yours,' is known as *mamatā*, and this mood is fully present in the *gopīs*. Śrīla Jīva Gosvāmī says that the *gopīs* are the very embodiments of *prema* in the stage of *mahābhāva*, and that this mood fully lives in them only.

When Śrī Kṛṣṇa hears this prayer of the *gopīs*, their words penetrate His heart. He is their life-breath and their life itself, so when they weep and speak in this way, His heart melts. "I should not conceal Myself any longer," He thinks. "I must appear before them." In *Śrīmad-Bhāgavatam* He says, "I am the heart of My pure devotees, and My pure devotees are My heart:"

sādhavo hṛdayaṁ mahyaṁ
sādhūnāṁ hṛdayaṁ tv aham
mad-anyat te na jānanti
nāhaṁ tebhyo manāg api
Śrīmad-Bhāgavatam (9.4.68)

> The pure devotee is always within the core of My heart, and I am always in the heart of the pure devotee. My devotees do not know anything else but Me, and I do not know anyone else but them.

Kṛṣṇa expresses His heart in this way, and the ladies of Mathurā also explain this fact. When He and Balarāma entered the wrestling arena to fight with Cāṇūra and Muṣṭika, the ladies of Mathurā began discussing how the *gopīs* always remember Kṛṣṇa, no matter what activity they are engaged in:

yā dohane 'vahanane mathanopalepa
preṅkheṅkhanārbha-ruditokṣaṇa-mārjanādau

gāyanti cainam anurakta-dhiyo 'śru-kaṇṭhyo
dhanyā vraja-striya urukrama-citta-yānāḥ
Śrīmad-Bhāgavatam (10.44.15)

The ladies of Vraja are the most fortunate of women because, with their minds fully attached to Kṛṣṇa and their throats always choked up with tears, they constantly sing about Him while milking the cows, winnowing grain, churning butter, gathering cow dung for fuel, riding on swings, taking care of their crying babies, sprinkling the ground with water, cleaning their houses, and so on. By their exalted Kṛṣṇa consciousness they automatically acquire all desirable things.

Urukrama-citta-yānāḥ: The *gopīs*' minds are absorbed in Kṛṣṇa while they make cow-dung patties and prepare cracked wheat (*daliyā*), while they smear the floor of their homes with mud and cow-dung, and while they put their babies to sleep. They do not sing, "O babies, you should sleep." Rather, in very sweet, gentle voices, they sing the names of Kṛṣṇa: "*Govinda dāmodara mādhaveti*." Śrī Kṛṣṇa is always on their minds, and they are always on His. Even while He is away in Mathurā or Dvārakā, they are always thinking of Him.

Now, in this nineteenth verse of *Gopī-gīta*, Śrī Kṛṣṇa hears the *gopīs*' prayer and thinks, "The *gopīs* are weeping and grievously lamenting in the pain of separation from Me. I should not leave them alone any longer. I will appear to them and fully give Myself to them. I hid from them only to see their moods of separation from Me, and having seen that, I am fully satisfied. Never have I seen such exalted sentiments. I can no longer remain hidden from them." The desire to perform varieties of loving pastimes arises in Kṛṣṇa's heart and He thinks: "I shall now engage in sportive pastimes with the *gopīs*, and I shall make their words a reality."

Śrī Kṛṣṇa is *āpta-kāma*, meaning that all His desires are fulfilled automatically. He is also *ātmārāma*, fully satisfied within Himself; He takes pleasure in His own self. He always plays there, free from desires, but when He sees His devotees' desire to serve Him, He immediately desires to accept their service.

Śrīla Jīva Gosvāmī states, "I have not revealed all of the *gopīs*' moods; not all their moods can be told. A Vaiṣṇava should practice *sādhana-bhajana*. Then, all pastimes and devotional sentiments will enter his heart automatically and he can achieve full realization of them." He concludes his commentary by offering utmost respects to all the Lord's amorous pastimes.

Although Śrīla Jīva Gosvāmī is always internally absorbed in the *parakīya* mood (the mood of paramour love between Śrī Kṛṣṇa and the *gopīs*), he remains externally considerate of *maryādā* (etiquette). Therefore, his writings on the Gauḍīya *siddhānta* are often impartial and scholarly, respecting those in the *svakīya* mood (the mood of considering the *gopīs* to be married to Kṛṣṇa) and those in the *parakīya* mood. This created a philosophical platform for Śrīla Viśvanātha Cakravartī Ṭhākura to later openly emphasize the superiority of the *parakīya* mood.

Śrīla Viśvanātha Cakravartī Ṭhākura had no concern for the opinions of others in this world. Everything caught in a swift current becomes immersed in that current, and even an elephant may be carried away. Similarly, unable to check himself, Śrīla Viśvanātha Cakravartī Ṭhākura is caught in such a current. He speaks from his heart, impelled by his own extreme eagerness.

Let us consider which among the *Gopī-gīta* verses expresses the highest degree of transcendental love. During the Ratha-yātrā festival, Mahārāja Pratāparudra, wearing simple attire, approached Śrī Caitanya Mahāprabhu while He rested in a garden, immersed in internal consciousness. Mahārāja Pratāparudra circumambulated Him and bowed down before Him. Then, sitting next to Him, he began to massage His lotus feet, slowly and gently, while reciting the verses of *Gopī-gīta*.

Aroused by the king's singing, Mahāprabhu exclaimed, "What sweet nectar I hear! Where is it coming from?" Captivated by the nectar of *Gopī-gīta*, He listened patiently, enraptured, without breathing or trembling or showing any sign of life. When Pratāparudra Mahārāja came to the verse beginning *tava kathamṛtam tapta-jīvanam*, Mahāprabhu's alertness sharpened and He thought, "Oh, who is this, pouring this supreme nectar into My ears? How is it that, resting in this garden, I have heard such exquisite ambrosia as this?" He arose and told the king, "You are pouring elixir into my ears. Who are you?" He then bestowed His mercy upon the king.

It may seem that this verse, Verse Nine, is the most beautiful in this chapter of *Śrīmad-Bhāgavatam*, but it is not. Our present verse, *yat te sujāta-caraṇāmbu-ruhaṁ staneṣu*, and the two verses preceding it, are far superior.

rahasi saṁvidaṁ hṛc-chayodayaṁ
prahasitānanaṁ prema-vīkṣaṇam
bṛhad-uraḥ śriyo vīkṣya dhāma te
muhur ati-spṛhā muhyate manaḥ
Śrīmad-Bhāgavatām (10.31.17)

O beloved master, having seen You as You conversed intimately with us in secret places – Your smiling face, which acts as a stimulus for our amorous desires, Your glancing at us with love, and Your expansive chest, which is the eternal resting place of the goddess of fortune – our hankering to meet with You has increased manifold and our minds are repeatedly bewildered.

vraja-vanaukasāṁ vyaktir aṅga te
vṛjina-hantry alaṁ viśva-maṅgalam
tyaja manāk ca nas tvat-spṛhātmanāṁ
sva-jana-hṛd-rujāṁ yan niṣūdanam
Śrīmad-Bhāgavatām (10.31.18)

O Kṛṣṇa, Your appearance completely destroys the sorrows of Vraja's residents, and in every way brings auspiciousness to the world. Our hearts, which desire You alone, are agonized by our heart-disease, Therefore, giving up all miserliness, kindly give in charity a little bit of that medicine which can cure Your dear ones.

These three verses are hundreds upon hundreds of times sweeter than *tava kathāmṛtam tapta-jīvanam*, which merely praises Śrī Kṛṣṇa's pastimes. That verse states that *hari-kathā* is nectar (*amṛta*), but these three final verses are actual *hari-kathā*.

I have already explained the verse beginning *rahasi saṁvidam*, wherein the *gopīs* refer to their previous intimate conversations with Kṛṣṇa. Another example of such conversations is in Verse Sixteen, wherein the *gopīs* told Kṛṣṇa, "Give a little."

Kṛṣṇa asked them, "What should I give?"

"Oh, You are certainly a very good doctor," they replied, "the best in the world. You know more about diseases than we do. Place Your fingers on our hearts, and then You will be able to understand the nature of our disease and recommend the required medicine."

As soon as Śrī Kṛṣṇa touched the *gopīs* by placing His fingers on their hearts, something transpired in His own heart. In this way, *rahasi-saṁvidam* refers to their many intimate dialogues.

Here is another example. When the *gopīs* first arrived at Vaṁśī-vaṭa after Kṛṣṇa had called them with His flute, He asked them, nonchalantly, why they had come.

"You called us," they replied.

"No," He said, "I have not called you."

"Oh, yes You did."

"I certainly did not."

"Did You play on Your flute?"

"Yes, I played on My flute."

"So, You called us."

"I was not calling you."

"You were! You called our names, and in so doing, You completely stole our hearts. You stole our valuable and precious wealth and ran away with it, so we have run here to catch You. Please return our wealth, and then we will go."

"I do not have anything of yours."

"That is not true. You do have it, and we will not go home until You return it to us."

This is an instance of *rahasi-saṁvidam*, intimate conversations in solitary places, and the discussion below is an instance of *hṛc-chayodayam*, the disease of *kāma* rising in the heart.

The *gopīs* told Kṛṣṇa, "We see Your heart."

"What do you see?"

"We see that it is palpitating."

"Why is it doing so?"

"It palpitates because of Your desire to associate with us, which is revealed by the display of all Your five arrows."

This is why these last three verses of *Gopī-gīta* are superior to the verse beginning *tava kathāmṛtam*. In fact, all the verses following it are superior. For example, Verse Fourteen (*surata-vardhanam śoka-nāśanaṁ*), and Verse Eleven (*calasi yad vrajāc cārayan paśūn*) especially manifest the moods of the *gopīs* and their specific pastimes with Kṛṣṇa. While beautiful, the eight verses before *tava kathāmṛtam* are not the most exalted; yet, Śrī Caitanya Mahāprabhu became overwhelmed with transcendental ecstasy and experienced the *aṣṭa-sāttvika-bhāvas* when He heard them. All transcendental ecstasies, such as *vyabhicārī*, *vibhāva* and *anubhāva*, blazed in Him. Had He heard the sublime later verses of the *gopīs*' song, especially these last three verses, He would have certainly become still more maddened.

These are all invaluable topics, but our hearts do not value them. We are still not on such a level of *bhakti* that we can remember them and become absorbed in the *gopīs*' moods. If after hundreds upon hundreds of births we become qualified, by the grace of Śrīla Rūpa Gosvāmī, Śrīla Raghunātha dāsa Gosvāmī, and their associates, we will then be able to understand these topics in the right way.

Śrīla Viśvanātha Cakravartī Ṭhākura has offered a thoughtful commentary on this nineteenth verse:

Kṛṣṇa asks, "O *rasika gopīs*, what is it that you are begging?"

They implore Him, "We are begging some medicine for our hearts."

"Do you want to serve My lotus feet by putting them on your breasts? This is not possible. My feet are fully satisfied to walk through the forests of Vṛndāvana, so I will not put them where you want. I have no time at all for such things."

This brings deep sorrow to the *gopīs*' hearts, and as they chant this verse, they begin to weep. In India, women often weep as they express their feelings in very sweet songs, and it cannot be discerned whether they are singing or weeping. It is described in *Bṛhad-Bhāgavatāmṛta* that Gopa Kumāra heard something that sounded like a very beautiful song. He followed the sound, and as he came nearer he could not understand whether the singer was weeping or overjoyed. Following the sound a bit further, he entered a *kuñja*.

There he saw that his *guru* was sweetly singing, and yet at the same time weeping with tears in his eyes, quite unconscious of the external world.

Similarly, the *gopīs* weep as they sing their mellifluous song: "*Yat te sujāta-caraṇāmbu-ruhaṁ staneṣu* – we carefully and gently hold Your lotus feet on our heart." Why on their heart? The heart is the best part of the body. One who has something very valuable and precious keeps that possession close to the heart. As mentioned in our discussion of Śrīla Jīva Gosvāmī's commentary, the *gopīs* tell Kṛṣṇa, "You are our life; everything about You, and each part of You – Your feet, face, hands, head, and everything else – is our life. We want to keep our life in our heart. We want to serve our life very tenderly and gently, but You are running here and there throughout the forests of Vṛndāvana, where there are rough places, full of sharp stones and other things that can hurt Your feet."

As mentioned above, there is no fear of stones and other sharp objects in Vṛndāvana; there exists no imperfection at all. As stated in the first verse of *Gopī-gīta*, Vṛndāvana has been decorated by Śrī Lakṣmi-devī, who is present there: *jayati te 'dhikaṁ janmanā vrajaḥ, śrayata indirā*. Vṛndāvana is not a desert, nor is it a hilly place; on the contrary, its terrain is very gentle and verdant. But the *gopīs* do not acknowledge this; they think just the opposite, as lovers inherently feel apprehension at the time of separation, out of concern for their beloveds.

"Alas! Alas!" the *gopīs* tell Kṛṣṇa, "You are extraordinarily daring."

Kṛṣṇa may say, "Why do you fear My walking in Vṛndāvana?"

There is not just one *gopī*, but millions, and they tell Kṛṣṇa, "Your lotus feet are so soft – much softer than any lotus. We realize this. We take them in our hands and place them on our very soft breasts. However, when we compare Your lotus feet to our breasts, we realize that Your lotus feet are millions of times more tender and soft. We know that in comparison to rough pebbles and stones, our breasts are soft, but they do not have the softness and other good qualities of Your lotus feet. We therefore hold them on our hearts very gently and carefully so that You do not feel any pain. But now You are roaming in the forest."

Kṛṣṇa replies, "If you know that My feet are so soft in comparison to your breasts, why do you try to put them there?"

"O beloved, we know You will feel great happiness if we do this. We become unhappy by doing it, but knowing that it will certainly make You happy, we forget all our own suffering and become immersed in the ocean of happiness. If we know that our behavior or anything about us brings You a little joy, we become filled with ever-increasing bliss."

Śrī Kṛṣṇa is satisfied in Himself (*ātmārāma*) and all His desires are fulfilled (*āpta-kāma*). There is no possibility that His pleasure can increase – it is already unlimited. Nonetheless, even though there is no room for it to increase, it does so when Kṛṣṇa is with Śrīmatī Rādhikā. Kṛṣṇa is beautiful. He is Madana, the transcendental Cupid, the captivator of all. However, when He is with Śrīmatī Rādhikā, He is Madana-mohana, that personality who bewilders even Cupid.

Śrīla Raghunātha dāsa Gosvāmī has said in his *Sva-niyama-daśakam*, "I will not leave Rādhā-kuṇḍa in Vṛndāvana, even to see Śrī Kṛṣṇa personally present in His Deity form at Badri-Nārāyaṇa, Dvārakā, Purī, and other places. *Rasika* Vaiṣṇavas may be speaking *hari-kathā* there, but I will never leave Śrīmatī Rādhikā to go elsewhere. If Rādhikā is not there, I will not go, even if Śrī Kṛṣṇa Himself calls me, saying, 'O dear one, come to Dvārakā and serve My lotus feet here.' Yet, if I hear that Rādhikā is also there, I will go there immediately. Of course She would never normally go there, but if She were to become mad and lose Her senses, and thus go to Dvārakā, I would go there immediately. I would fly there with more speed than Garuḍa, who flies faster than the mind."

This raises a point for discussion. We hear that Śrīmatī Rādhikā left Vṛndāvana and went to Kurukṣetra. We read in *Śrī Bṛhad-bhāgavatāmṛta* that Śrī Kṛṣṇa left Vṛndāvana for Mathurā, and from there went to Dvārakā. *Śrīmad-Bhāgavatam* vividly describes Dvārakādhīśa Kṛṣṇa going to Kurukṣetra and meeting with Rādhikā there. But we also know that Kṛṣṇa of Mathurā, Dvārakā, and

Kurukṣetra is not Nanda-nandana Kṛṣṇa or Rādhā-kānta of Vraja. He is Devakī-nandana or Vasudeva-nandana, the son of Vasudeva and Devakī, a manifestation of Kṛṣṇa.

Śrīla Rūpa Gosvāmī writes in Lalitā-Mādhava that when Kṛṣṇa went to Mathurā and Dvārakā, Śrīmatī Rādhikā was in such a deep state of separation that She went to Khelanvana, where She entered the waters of Yamunā and drowned. Then, through the rays of the sun, She went to the Sun-planet. Śrīla Rūpa Gosvāmī is silent about what transpired between that time and Her arrival as Satyabhāmā in Nava-Vṛndāvana, Dvārakā, but he explains that once there, She met Rukmiṇī.

Rukmiṇī thought, "Oh, this girl is exquisitely beautiful! If Kṛṣṇa sees Her, He will be attracted to Her and will no longer love me as He does now." She tried to keep the new girl from the sun planet hidden from Kṛṣṇa, hoping to prevent Him from seeing Her. Nevertheless, Kṛṣṇa eventually saw Her and fell in love with Her at once. Because Rukmiṇī continued her attempt to stop Kṛṣṇa and Satyabhāmā (Rādhikā) from meeting, Satyabhāmā felt such painful separation from Kṛṣṇa that She went to the Kāliya Lake in Nava-Vṛndāvana with the aim of being bitten by the poisonous serpents there. She jumped into the lake and, unknown to Her, Kṛṣṇa saw Her and jumped in after Her. When He caught hold of Her from behind, Satyabhāmā thought with relief, "Oh, here are two black snakes, full of poison, and they are about to bite Me." She could not imagine that Kṛṣṇa Himself was holding Her until He turned Her around to face Him. Upon seeing Him, She came to her external senses and fell on His chest. Rukmiṇī saw this and thought, "I tried hard to keep them apart, but I was not successful. Now they should be married." Kṛṣṇa then proposed to Satyabhāmā and married Her.

Who is the teenage girl who traveled by the rays of the sun to Nava-Vṛndāvana in Dvārakā? And who went to Kurukṣetra to meet with Kṛṣṇa there? This is a significant point. The explanation is that there are three features of Śrīmatī Rādhikā. One of them, Her complete feature, is the daughter of Vṛṣabhānu Mahārāja and Kīrtidā-devī. Just as Śrī Nanda-nandana, the son of Nanda Mahārāja, is the cause or origin of all His expansions, so Śrīmatī Rādhikā, the daughter of Vṛṣabhānu Mahārāja and Kīrtidā-devī, is the origin of all Her female expansions. Neither Vṛṣabhānu-nandinī nor Kṛṣṇa ever leaves Vṛndāvana. She may think that He has gone somewhere else for a short time and feel separation from Him then, but She never thinks that He has permanently gone anywhere else.

There are different types of separation (*pravāsa*) that occur before the four main types of meeting: *saṅkṣipta*, *saṅkīrṇa*, *sampanna*, and *samṛddhimān*. There is a small separation in the daytime when Kṛṣṇa goes out to herd the cows. Sometimes *māna*, the sulky mood of transcendental loving jealous anger, comes between Rādhikā and Kṛṣṇa like a wall. This is also a kind of separation, because They cannot talk or interact, even though They are together. *Sudūra-pravāsa* takes place when They are separated for many years, as when Śrī Kṛṣṇa leaves Vṛndāvana for Mathurā and Dvārakā. When They meet after such a lengthy separation, They feel supremely blissful.

In Vṛndāvana, Śrī Śrī Rādhā and Kṛṣṇa do not generally think or feel that Their separation lasts for long. Śrīmatī Rādhikā's mood is this: "I am here at Sūrya-kuṇḍa, and Kṛṣṇa is coming from Kusuma-sarovara; we will wait for Him." Or, She is in *māna*. Vṛṣabhānu-nandinī Rādhikā does not think, "Kṛṣṇa has gone to Mathurā and Dvārakā." She embraces the *tamāla* trees, talking and laughing with them, thinking, "Oh, Kṛṣṇa is here!" She decorates Herself and acts as though He were present. In this way, She lives in Vṛndāvana and never goes anywhere else.

There are two manifestations of this complete and original feature of Rādhikā as the daughter of King Vṛṣabhānu and Kīrtidā-devī. One manifestation is *saṁyoginī* Rādhā, who has the mood of meeting Kṛṣṇa at Kurukṣetra, and the other is *viyoginī* Rādhā, who is immersed in a spirit of separation. *Saṁyoginī* Rādhā has a relatively submissive, rightist (*dakṣiṇa*) mood, whereas *viyoginī* Rādhā has a more contrary, leftist (*vāmya*) mood. It is *saṁyoginī* Rādhā who goes to Kurukṣetra and meets Kṛṣṇa there, and *viyoginī* Rādhā who goes to Sūrya-loka.

Everything that I have explained here regarding these three features of Śrīmatī Rādhikā should be remembered when hearing, reading, or recalling any pastime of Śrī Śrī Rādhā and Kṛṣṇa; only in this way is it possible to understand these pastimes.

Vṛṣabhānu-nandinī Rādhikā and Her *sakhīs* speak this verse beginning *yat te sujāta-caraṇām*. Although this verse may be interpreted as the *dakṣiṇa-bhāva* of Candrāvalī and her *sakhīs*, it may also be understood to be extremely leftist in mood.

Kṛṣṇa says to the *gopīs*, "Why do you want to keep My feet on your hearts?"

They reply, "We know that You will be satisfied if we do."

There is so much that cannot be told here, so you can come to know the hidden meanings through your chanting and a mood of pure devotion. The *gopīs*' desires are not understood by material intelligence, but rather by realized experience.

The *gopīs* continue, "We wanted to perform austerities to please Brahmā, but his nature is like Yours; you both want to make us suffer. Suppose we perform austerities to please him, and we beg him to make our hearts soft. We believe that he may comply, but then You would not be at all satisfied. When You place Your lotus feet on our hearts, two things happen. First, we become happy because You are happy, and second, we feel sorry that our breasts are so hard. Still, when we see You a little satisfied, we become so happy that all our sorrows and sufferings disappear."

This is a symptom of *mahābhāva*. In *mahābhāva* there are times when, even though Kṛṣṇa is satisfied, the *gopīs* become very sorrowful, thinking that He is not. Sometimes, when Rādhā and Kṛṣṇa are together, Their love for each other reaches such extreme rapture that They forget They are together. At such times They drown in sorrow, feeling deep separation from each other. Let us take the example of Rādhikā and Kṛṣṇa at Prema-sarovara. They were sitting very happily, side by side, when a bumble-bee came and tried to fly near Rādhikā's lotus face, as if it were a very fragrant lotus flower. Rādhikā became frightened. Madhumaṅgala swiftly drove away the bumble-bee with his stick, and then he returned, saying, "*Madhusūdana* will not come back. I have driven him so far away that he will not return." In Sanskrit, a bumble-bee is called *madhusūdana*, and this was Madhumaṅgala's meaning. However, Śrīmatī Rādhikā thought he was talking about Kṛṣṇa, who is also known as Madhusūdana. Even though She was sitting right beside Kṛṣṇa, She began to weep, and then She fainted.

Rādhikā and all the other *gopīs* singing *Gopī-gīta* are in *mahābhāva*; none of them are below the stage of *mahābhāva*. Now they weep and say, "When Brahmā constructed our bodies, he wrote only misery on our foreheads. We even considered performing austerities to please him so that our hearts would be very soft. Although we understand that You will not be satisfied if our hearts are soft, at the same time we will always be unhappy if they are rough. We are uncertain and bewildered about what to do and what not to do. If we know that Your lotus feet are happy, then our heart-disease will go away as well. So come at once – do not delay."

The word *dhīr* in this nineteenth verse means 'discrimination' or 'intelligence.' The *gopīs* tell Śrī Kṛṣṇa, "Our discrimination sometimes goes one way and sometimes another. Should our hearts be hard or soft? When You roam in Vṛndāvana, we wonder whether or not You are suffering. Sometimes it seems to us that You feel pleasure when You place Your feet on the forest floor, and sometimes we fear it is very painful for You. Our intelligence is caught between these two extremes. We only know that You give us suffering in both meeting and separation."

In our discussion on Verse Fifteen, I explained one reason the *gopīs* feel pain in meeting with Śrī Kṛṣṇa. At that time they said, "When You go to Vṛndāvana forest for herding the cows, one second, or even a tiny part of a second, becomes like a millennium for us. Then, when You return, we become happy, thinking, 'Oh, Kṛṣṇa has returned.' Yet, even then we can only look at You for a moment. The eyelids given to us by Brahmā fall down and make our eyes blink, thus interrupting our vision of You. Sometimes our eyes do not blink for a moment, but then tears come, and again we cannot see You. In this way, being with You becomes even more painful than not being with You, and our unhappiness increases. Hence, You give us suffering in both meeting and separation.

"We are dependent; we are not free. We cannot meet with You because we are under the control of our husbands, in-laws, parents, and so many other persons. But You are quite free, so why must You suffer? Why do You go to the forest where the sharp pebbles and grain sprouts can cause You suffering? Your feet are not suited for walking in the forest."

Kṛṣṇa may reply, "Yes, I am quite free. I do whatever I wish, so why are you telling Me what to do? This has nothing to do with you."

Hearing this, the *gopīs* say, "It may be true that we have nothing to do with Your actions, but how can You say that You do not feel pain while walking? Indeed You feel it. We think You are cruel and merciless to all Your bodily limbs, just as You are cruel to us. It is Your nature to give pain to Yourself as well as to others. You give pain to everyone. In our opinion, Your thinking is like this: 'My nature is to give distress to others, and when I see others' misery, I become elated. However, if I am to give suffering to these *gopīs*, I will have to accept some bodily pain Myself.' You then irresponsibly inflict pain upon Yourself, just so You can give pain to us *gopīs*. This is the reason You walk in the forest and suffer these injuries to Your feet."

Bhramati dhīr bhavad-āyuṣāṁ: The *gopīs* utter the word *bhrama*, meaning 'confusion about many different possibilities.' Considering those possibilities, they tell Kṛṣṇa, "You feel pain, but Your pain is secondary for You. It is necessary for You to feel some pain, because then You can give pain to us. Your heart is so cruel that You feel joy by giving anguish to others, and that is why You willingly accept Your own suffering."

They continue, "A second possibility is that, in seeing our pain and suffering, You feel such abundant pleasure that Your own pain feels like pleasure as well."

Suppose someone acquires a great deal of money and then purchases a building, at which time he receives a registered document that gives him legal ownership. Being the new owner he happily thinks, "What a palatial building I have!" He is a tall man and, opening the door with the key, he hits his head on the top of the door-frame as he enters; and thus injures himself. "Any injury? Any injury?" asks the person with him. "No, no. Nothing of the sort," he replies. In the midst of the happiness he feels upon acquiring such a good property, he takes no notice of any pain. Similarly, the *gopīs* tell Kṛṣṇa, "You become so happy when You give us pain, and in Your happiness, You think that any pain You feel is also very good."

Once, when Śrī Kṛṣṇa met with Śrīmatī Rādhikā and all Her *gopī* companions, He forcibly caught hold of a *mañjarī*'s hand and pulled her towards Him while trying to embrace her. That *mañjarī* began to weep, crying out in submission to Rādhikā, "O Svāminī, Svāminīji! Save me! Save me!" Śrīmatī Rādhikā ran over to Kṛṣṇa and twisted His hand. Now free, the *mañjarī* ran behind Her, gasping for breath. Kṛṣṇa again attempted to catch her, and again Rādhikā twisted His hand. This time Kṛṣṇa felt some pain, but that pain was much more pleasurable for Him than anything else could have been. Overjoyed, He thought, "I have been waiting for this for a long time; waiting for Rādhikā to take hold of My hand."

The third possibility considered by the *gopīs* can be understood in this way. In *Nīti-vākya* it is said, *saṁsargayā doṣa-guṇā bhavanti*. This means that a person will imbibe the good or bad qualities of whomever he comes in contact with. It is a matter of association.

There is a story in this connection: A trapper used to go to the forest to catch parrots and other birds for selling. One day he caught two baby parrots, brought them to a town, and sold them to two different families. After a while, someone visited the house of the owner of one the parrots, and the bird spoke sweetly to him, saying, "Welcome, welcome. Come in, come in," and, "Rāma, Kṛṣṇa, Rāma, Kṛṣṇa." That person then visited the house of the owner of the other parrot, which said, "Who are you?! Who are you?! Get out, you rascal! You stupid, nonsense person!" Each of these birds had begun to mimic the behavior of those around them. Thus, by one type of association one becomes gentle, and by another type of association one becomes rough.

Applying this aphorism, the *gopīs* tell Kṛṣṇa, "At first Your heart was very soft, more soft than a lotus, and consequently Your lotus feet were as soft as Your heart. But Your feet have associated with our hard breasts. Now they have become very hard, and Your heart, by association, has also become hard. As a result, neither Your heart nor Your feet feels any pain when You roam in the forest. Your feet are callous to the stones and Your heart is callous to us."

The *gopīs* then offer a fourth possible explanation, again on the basis of *saṁsargayā doṣa-guṇā bhavanti*: by association, one may become hard or soft. They say, "Your heart is very soft, and by its association, Your lotus feet are also soft. By the touch of Your soft lotus feet, all the sharp stones, shoots, and everything else that might cause pain become soft. It is for this reason that You do not feel any pain when You wander in the forest."

This brings us to another point. The *gopīs* say, "The earth loves You so much that wherever You place Your lotus feet, she extends her soft tongue for You to step on. Perhaps this is why You do not feel any pain. Or perhaps it is this: You are such an ocean of love, that when You observed our feelings of separation from You, You also felt separation from us. You became maddened and bewildered and, thus bewildered, You do not feel any pain."

Rādhikā is recollecting Her own experience. Once She went to a high place on Govardhana Hill to observe Śrī Kṛṣṇa, who was standing below. Even though the stone on which She stood was burning hot, She did not feel its heat at all. She felt as if She were standing in a cool place, under the shade of a tree or in a river. She stood without blinking, feeling so much happiness that the hairs on Her body stood on end and tears flowed from Her eyes. Remembering Her own experience, She now says, "You have become maddened by witnessing our *prema* – our grief in separation from You. As a result You are also feeling separation, and that is why You do not feel pain."

After considering all these arguments, the *gopīs* finally conclude, "There are so many possible explanations that we cannot say definitely why You would not feel pain while roaming in this forest."

They suppose that Kṛṣṇa may say, "Perhaps you are expressing your own suffering, but I do not feel your suffering. When I see your misery, I do not feel any misery; I feel pleasure." He may also tell them, "You say that you feel My pain, and also that I am your life; yet you have not died yet. I see that you are walking and talking and passing your days very nicely."

In reply to this the *gopīs* say, "You are our life. It is for Your welfare that we have kept our life in You. The reason we do not die in spite of such anguish is that You are both our life-air and our life. Because You are feeling pleasure, we do not die. You and Brahmā, who is also known as Vidhātā, the giver of one's destiny, are two friends with the same nature. Brahmā has created us to give us suffering, and Your nature is the same. Perhaps Brahmā is thinking, 'If the *gopīs* die, then the purpose for which I have created them – so that I would become happy by seeing their suffering – will not be accomplished."

According to the *gopīs*, it is for this reason that Brahmā placed their life-airs in Śrī Kṛṣṇa. They continue, "You are very happy to see our agony, and therefore our life-air is also happy in You. That is the reason we have not died yet, in spite of our agony. But now You will see our life-air come out of our bodies as we die."

Kṛṣṇa asks, "How can you die if your life (*ayuṣ*) is still present?"

It is in reply to this question that the *gopīs* say, "*Bhavad-āyuṣāṁ naḥ* – You are our life. Now we will die, but our life will remain in You and You will live joyfully for millions of millenniums. We are going."

Śrī Vaiṣṇava-toṣaṇī explains that Kṛṣṇa's heart melts when He sees the *gopīs* in this condition. He cannot escape. He thinks, "The *gopīs* will surely die, and if they die, I will die. I must go to them at once and satisfy them."

The *gopīs* now fall to the ground unconscious, and at that moment Kṛṣṇa appears before them. When they open their eyes and see Him, it is as if their lives have returned to their bodies.

The following chapter of *Śrīmad-Bhāgavatam* reveals what happened next.

Chapter Thirty-two

Verses One and Two

Just then Śrī Kṛṣṇa, the crest-jewel of the Śūra dynasty, appeared before the weeping *vraja-devīs*. A gentle smile blossomed on His face. He had adorned His neck with a forest garland and His body with a yellow garment. The beauty of such a form bewilders the mind of even Cupid himself, who agitates the minds of all beings.

Verse One

श्रीशुक उवाच—
इति गोप्यः प्रगायन्त्यः
प्रलपन्त्यश्च चित्रधा।
रुरुदुः सुस्वरं राजन्
कृष्णदर्शनलालसाः ॥१॥

śrī-śuka uvāca
iti gopyaḥ pragāyantyaḥ
pralapantyaś ca citradhā
ruruduḥ su-svaraṁ rājan
kṛṣṇa-darśana-lālasāḥ

śrī-śukaḥ uvāca – Śrī Śukadeva Gosvāmī said; *iti* – thus, as related above; *gopyaḥ* – the *gopīs*; *pragāyantyaḥ* – singing forth; *pralapantyaḥ* – speaking forth; *ca* – and; *citradhā* – in various charming ways; *ruruduḥ* – they cried; *su-svaram* – loudly; *rājan* – O King; *kṛṣṇa-darśana* – for the sight of Kṛṣṇa; *lālasāḥ* – hankering.

Translation

Śrīla Śukadeva Gosvāmī said: O Parīkṣit, thus the gopīs of Vraja, brimming with intense eagerness to see their beloved Kṛṣṇa, could no longer contain their feelings. Absorbed in separation and lamenting, they spoke many plaintive words, their voices heart-wrenching and sonorous.

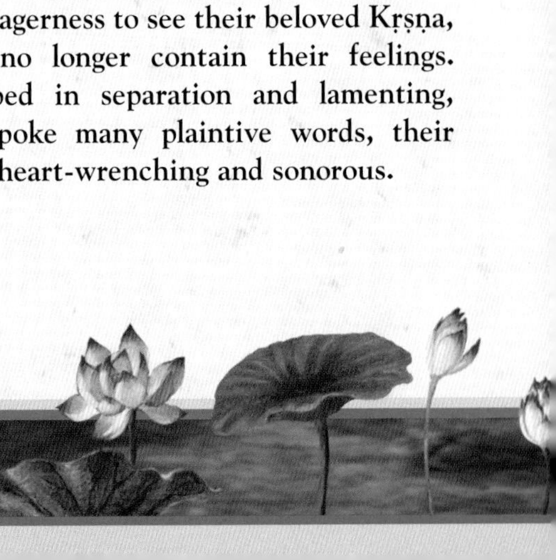

Verse Two

तासामाविरभूच्छौरिः
स्मयमानमुखाम्बुजः ।
पीताम्बरधरः स्रग्वी
साक्षान्मन्मथ मन्मथः ॥२॥

tāsām āvirabhūc chauriḥ
smayamāna-mukhāmbujaḥ
pītāmbara-dharaḥ sragvī
sākṣān manmatha-manmathaḥ

tāsām – before them; *āvirabhūt* – He appeared; *śauriḥ* – Lord Kṛṣṇa; *smayamāna* – smiling; *mukha* – His face; *ambujaḥ* – lotuslike; *pīta* – yellow; *ambara* – a garment; *dharaḥ* – wearing; *srak-vī* – wearing a flower garland; *sākṣāt* – directly; *man-matha* – of Cupid (who bewilders the mind); *man* – of the mind; *mathaḥ* – the bewilderer.

Translation

Just then Śrī Kṛṣṇa, the crest-jewel of the Śūra dynasty, appeared before the weeping *vraja-devīs*. A gentle smile blossomed on His face. He had adorned His neck with a forest garland and His body with a yellow garment. The beauty of such a form bewilders the mind of even Cupid himself, who agitates the minds of all beings.

[When Śrīla Bhaktivedānta Nārāyaṇa Gosvāmī Mahārāja sings the verses of Śrī Gopī-gīta, he includes the first and second verses of Chapter Thirty-two, called "The Reunion." We have therefore included those first two verses herein, along with Śrīla Mahārāja's commentary on Verse Two. – Ed.]

Commentary

[Śrīla Bhaktivedānta Nārāyaṇa Gosvāmī Mahārāja's commentary on Verse Two first appeared in his purport to *Śrī Bhajana-Rahasya*, Chapter Seven, Texts Sixteen and Seventeen. We have excerpted it from there:]

Śrī Kṛṣṇa, who is ever-skillful in increasing His devotees' *prema*, disappeared from the *rāsa-līlā*. Devastated by separation from Him, the *gopīs* arrived, weeping, at the bank of the Yamunā. There, having exhausted all alternatives in their search for Him, they performed *kīrtana*. Their voices were full of extreme feeling and they used metaphors with multiple meanings to express their sentiments. As they were full of *prema* and restless in the pain of separation, their tears flowed freely and continuously from their eyes. Hearing their weeping, Śrī Kṛṣṇacandra, who was in the dense, dark forest, suddenly appeared in their midst, manifesting His luster.

In this text, Śrīla Śukadeva Gosvāmī is thoroughly absorbed in *mañjarī-bhāva*, and therefore he has used the word *śauri* in anger, as an insult. Śrī Kṛṣṇa appeared in a *kṣatriya* family within the Śūra dynasty, the members of whose hearts were deceitful and hard. Śukadeva Gosvāmī was unable to tolerate his Svāminī's agony of separation from Kṛṣṇa, and he therefore saw Śrī Kṛṣṇa's hiding as a defect.

He addressed Kṛṣṇa, "The young girls of Vraja are simple lovers, and You become joyful by making them unhappy. Seeing the *gopīs* afflicted by grief, You display Your prowess (*śaurya*)." Śrīla Śukadeva Gosvāmī felt that such so-called prowess was a disgrace, and said, "If Your heart were truly honest, You would not have done such a thing." This is an example of defamatory remarks used in *prema*; only one whose *prema* is deep can speak in this way.

Śrī Kṛṣṇacandra, the crown-jewel of all those skilled in amorous pastimes, appeared in the midst of the *vraja-devīs*, displaying His unparalleled beauty which is described in this text with three adjectives: *smayamāna*, *sragvī*, and *sākṣān-manmatha-manmathaḥ*.

Smayamāna: Although Śrī Kṛṣṇa's face was radiant and smiling, His heart was remorseful. Smiling is a characteristic of the quality of being the Supreme Personality of Godhead, but Kṛṣṇa's smiling before the *gopīs* was caused by the emotions He experienced upon seeing them. He smiled to remove their distress and console them, for *darśana* of His extremely enchanting lotus face would remove all their sorrow. When Śrī Kṛṣṇa, wearing a *pītāmbara* (golden-yellow garment), heard the distressed cries of the *vraja-devīs*, He came swiftly, holding His *pītāmbara* around His neck so that it would not slip off.

He had charmed the *gopīs* with the sound of His flute, at which time all those *gopīs* had abandoned their families, morality, patience, and shyness to arrive at His side. But on that day He had abandoned them and disappeared. Therefore, upon His return, He held His yellow cloth around His neck as a gesture to show that He was praying for forgiveness. Conscious that He had given great suffering to His dear ones, He was admitting that He was an offender, and He held His *pītāmbara* with His hands.

Sragvī: Kṛṣṇa wore a fresh, radiant garland of forest flowers around His charming neck. He wore this garland of cooling lotuses only to remove the *gopīs*' fire of separation and, in doing so, He expressed the sentiment, "You are the flowers of My garland; you are My very heart. By embracing you, I pray for forgiveness and beg you to soothe the heat of My feelings of separation from you. You strung this very garland yourself and garlanded Me with it. I am displaying My eternal gratitude by wearing it upon My heart."

Sākṣān-manmatha-manmathaḥ: Śrī Kṛṣṇa's extremely charming beauty, embellished by His being in the midst of the *gopīs*, churned the mind of Cupid. Here, the words *vyaṣṭi-kāmadeva* and *samaṣṭi-kāmadeva* are concealed in the words *sākṣāt-manmatha*, who is the original Kāmadeva. The *vyaṣṭi-kāmadevas* are the Kāmadevas who exist in different universes; *samaṣṭi-kāmadeva* is Pradyumna, and the original Kāmadeva is Nanda-nandana Himself. The material Kāmadeva, or Cupid, intoxicates all *jīvas*, but when this material Cupid receives *darśana* of Śrī Kṛṣṇa's form, which enchants the three worlds, he falls unconscious. *Sākṣāt-manmatha-manmatha* Kṛṣṇa, who is the transcendental Kāmadeva, manifested such a form to decrease the *gopīs*' suffering.

Śrīla Jīva Gosvāmī writes in the *Krama-sandarbha* that *manmatha-manmatha* signifies that person who infatuates even Cupid (also known as Madana). Śrī Kṛṣṇacandra displayed His Mohinī-mūrti and bewildered Mahādeva in his form as Rudra, but Śrī Kṛṣṇa's form as *sākṣāt-manmatha-manmatha* is displayed only in the *rāsa-maṇḍala*. This is confirmed in *Śrī Caitanya-caritāmṛta* (*Ādi-līlā* 5.212–3):

vṛndāvana-purandara śrī-madana-gopāla
rāsa-vilāsī sākṣāt brajendra-kumāra
śrī-rādhā-lalitā-saṅge rāsa-vilāsa
manmatha-manmatha-rūpe yāṅhāra prakāśa

Lord Madana-gopāla, the chief Deity of Vṛndāvana, is the enjoyer of the *rāsa* dance and is directly the son of the King of Vraja. He enjoys the *rāsa* dance with Śrīmatī Rādhārāṇī, Śrī Lalitā and others. He manifests Himself as the Cupid of Cupids.

Śauri Śrī Kṛṣṇa, who defeats even Cupid, appeared before the *gopīs*, and upon seeing His beauty, Rādhā became perplexed and wondered, "Is Kṛṣṇa really present before us?" Confused, She said to Her *sakhīs*, "O *sakhīs*, is He who is standing before us Cupid incarnate, whose invisible form attacks everyone?"

Concluding Words

[Below is a summary of Śrīla Bhaktivedānta Nārāyaṇa Gosvāmī Mahārāja's translation[1] of Śrīla Jīva Gosvāmī's commentary on this verse:]

Kṛṣṇa heard the *gopīs*' song of love, full of pathos in their pain of separation from Him. Perceiving that they were suffering for His sake, and not their own, He then appeared in their midst. By doing so, He demonstrated that those who unhesitatingly put His happiness before their own can easily attain Him.

In this connection, Śrī Uddhava has stated in his prayers (*Śrīmad-Bhāgavatam* 10.47.58):

1 Śrīla Mahārāja's translation (*anuvād*) is not a literal one. It is an explanation of the deep meaning and moods (*bhāvas*) hidden in the commentary of Srīla Jīva Gosvāmī, and therefore it is called a *bhāvānuvāda*.

> Among all persons on earth, these cowherd women alone have actually perfected their lives, for they have achieved the most elevated love for Lord Govinda (Śrī Kṛṣṇa), the Supersoul of all embodied beings. Their immaculate love is hankered after by those who fear material existence, by great sages, and by us as well. For one who has relished descriptions of the sweet pastimes of Kṛṣṇa and the *gopīs*, what is the use of taking birth as a high-class *brāhmaṇa*, or even as Lord Brahmā himself?"

Śrīmad-Bhāgavatam (11.2.42) states:

> Devotion, direct experience of the Supreme Lord, and detachment from other things – these three occur simultaneously for one who has taken shelter of the Supreme Personality of Godhead, in the same way that pleasure, nourishment, and relief from hunger come simultaneously and increasingly, with each bite, for a person engaged in eating.

It was in harmony with this *tattva* that Śrī Kṛṣṇa appeared amidst the *gopīs*, exhibiting a form of such unparalleled beauty and sweetness that He enchanted even Cupid himself.

Thus Kṛṣṇa appeared before them. With love and veneration He had placed the garland they had previously given Him, around His neck, and it now rested upon His chest. By this He revealed His desire to be blessed by their embrace and His yearning to be with them only. Śrīla Śukadeva Gosvāmī describes the beauty of Śrī Kṛṣṇa at that moment, in order to bring this enchanting form to the heart of the reader, so that it will ultimately manifest there.

About The Commentators of Gopī-gīta

In his own commentary on *Gopī-gīta*, Śrīla Bhaktivedānta Nārāyaṇa Gosvāmī Mahārāja illuminates the commentaries of Śrīla Jīva Gosvāmī and Śrīla Viśvanātha Cakravartī Ṭhākura, who mercifully revealed the *gopīs'* inner moods as they sang their sublime song of separation. In this section, a brief summary of the life and character of these commentators is presented, along with that of Śrīla Mahārāja himself.

Śrīla Jīva Gosvāmī

Śrīla Jīva Gosvāmī's father, Anupama, was the brother of Śrīla Rūpa Gosvāmī and Śrīla Sanātana Gosvāmī. His exalted father and uncles were employed by the Muslim ruler – Śrīla Sanātana Gosvāmī as prime minister, Śrīla Rūpa Gosvāmī as the private secretary, and Anupama as treasurer. All three of them met Śrī Caitanya Mahāprabhu when He came to Rāmakeli, where they lived.

As the only son of the three brothers, Jīva received abundant affection. Śrīla Rūpa Gosvāmī was always especially affectionate towards him and treated him as if he were his own son. When Jīva was still very young, Śrīla Rūpa Gosvāmī took him to Mahāprabhu, who blessed him by placing His hand on his head.

During childhood, Jīva studied and soon learned all logic, Sanskrit grammar, and theistic philosophy from the books in his father's home. Before Śrīla Rūpa Gosvāmī and Anupama left household life to retire in Vṛndāvana, they divided all the family's wealth and property, allocating sufficient funds for Jīva to continue his studies. All three brothers realized that he was the only son in their dynasty, so they nurtured him with great affection and ensured he had whatever material facility he required.

Jīva had a very soft nature, and as he grew, he gradually began worshipping Deities of Śrī Śrī Rādhā-Kṛṣṇa. Making garlands for Them and offering *pūjā* to Them, he would become immersed in meditation, preferring these activities to playing with other children.

When he was about fourteen years old, he went to Navadvīpa. By then, Mahāprabhu had returned to the spiritual world and all the devotees of Navadvīpa had left and gone elsewhere. Because Navadvīpa now brought them all great sadness, Śrīvāsa Paṇḍita, Advaita Ācārya, and everyone else had left, and Navadvīpa was deserted.

A few days before Jīva's arrival, Nityānanda Prabhu had arrived at Śrīvāsa-aṅgana from Khardaha. When Jīva Gosvāmī arrived, Nityānanda Prabhu was very pleased to meet him. Nityānanda Prabhu placed His feet on Jīva's head and said, "I came here just to meet with you; otherwise I would have stayed in Khardaha." He showed Jīva all the places of Mahāprabhu's pastimes in Navadvīpa, and then showed him great mercy by ordering him to go to Vṛndāvana and stay with Śrīla Rūpa Gosvāmī and Śrīla Sanātana Gosvāmī.

On the way to Vṛndāvana, Jīva stopped in Vārāṇasī, where he met a disciple of Sārvabhauma Bhaṭṭācārya named Madhusūdana Vācaspati who was teaching Vedanta, but not the commentary of Śaṅkarācārya, which was famous at that time. Mahāprabhu had refuted that commentary when Sārvabhauma Bhaṭṭācārya tried to teach it to Him. Madhusūdana Vācaspati was a great scholar and, having studied and understood everything which Mahāprabhu had taught to Sārvabhauma Bhaṭṭācārya and Śrīla Rūpa and Sanātana Gosvāmīs, was teaching it there. Jīva Gosvāmī went to his home and learned all *bhakti-vedānta* from him. He also learned Śaṅkarācārya's commentary, because without learning it he would have been unable to refute it. After studying all of this and fully understanding it, he proceeded to Vṛndāvana. There in Vṛndāvana, Sanātana Gosvāmī placed him in the care of Rūpa Gosvāmī, and he stayed near Rūpa Gosvāmī's hut at the Rādhā-Dāmodara temple.

Rūpa Gosvāmī would read everything he was writing to Jīva Gosvāmī. One day while they were in the midst of reading together, an effulgent, elderly *brāhmaṇa* arrived there. Most likely, judging from his age and his scholarship, this was Śrī Vallabhācārya, who knew Rūpa Gosvāmī from the time Mahāprabhu was in Prayāga. He was approximately the same age as Advaita Ācārya, so Rūpa Gosvāmī would have been the appropriate age to have been his son. He asked, "Rūpa, what are you writing these days?"

Hesitating a little, Śrīla Rūpa Gosvāmī replied, "I am writing a book entitled *Bhakti-rasāmṛta-sindhu*." Vallabhācārya then picked up the book and, turning the pages, said, "Very good, I will look through it and correct any errors."

At that time Jīva Gosvāmī was fanning Rūpa Gosvāmī with a leaf from the *tāla* tree. When he heard Vallabhācārya say this, he felt disturbed, considering that his Gurudeva was being criticized. Later when he went to the river to fetch water, he met Vallabhācārya, who was just finishing his midday bath. Jīva Gosvāmī said, "Gosāi, you said before that you would proofread the *Bhakti-rasāmṛta-sindhu* which Rūpa Gosvāmī is writing. If you have found any errors, precisely where are they?"

Vallabhācārya replied, "How can you understand, child? Have you studied Sanskrit grammar?"

"Yes, a little."

"Then what could you possibly understand?"

"Still, please just show me any errors you have detected." When Vallabhācārya showed him an apparent error, a fierce debate commenced between them. Eventually Jīva Gosvāmī established the point so convincingly that Vallabhācārya could neither refute it nor give any answer.

When Vallabhācārya returned to Rūpa Gosvāmī's hut, he asked, "Who was that boy who was fanning you? He is very intelligent and extremely learned in the scriptures."

Very humbly and with folded hands Rūpa Gosvāmī replied, "He is the son of my younger brother and is also my disciple. He does not know how to behave."

"No, he is a genius, and in the future he will be very famous."

Soon afterwards, Vallabhācārya left. When Jīva Gosvāmī arrived with the water, Śrīla Rūpa Gosvāmī said to him, "You are so intolerant that you quarrel with an elderly, scholarly *brāhmaṇa* who kindly proofread something for my own good? Your behavior is unacceptable; leave now."

Being obliged to obey his *guru*, Jīva Gosvāmī left Vṛndāvana. He went to the village of Bhayagaon to live in a cave infested with crocodiles. There, for some days, he remained in the cave doing *bhajana* and crying, feeling bereft of his *guru*'s affection. He stopped eating and taking water, and within a short time he became emaciated. After some time, Śrīla Sanātana Gosvāmī happened to visit that village as he was wandering around Vraja. The local people said to him, "Baba, we always considered you to be a great *bhajanānandī* (one who is absorbed in *bhajana*), but a young boy who is even more of a *bhajanānandī* than you has come to our village. Day and night he calls out the names of Rādhā-Kṛṣṇa and weeps. We take him *prasādam* but he refuses it, and he never sleeps either. Day and night he remains immersed in *bhajana*; we have never seen anything like it."

Śrīla Sanātana Gosvāmī could understand that this was Jīva, and immediately went to him. Reunited, they both wept. Sanātana

Gosvāmī then took him back to Vṛndāvana, where he said to Rūpa Gosvāmī, "The duty of Vaiṣṇavas is to be compassionate to others, yet you renounced this young disciple of yours who is adorned with so many extraordinary qualities. You should be merciful to Jīva, but instead you banished him. This was a mistake and you should correct it. I order you to quickly call him back."

Hearing this, Rūpa Gosvāmī began crying for Jīva, whom he loved so much. When Sanātana Gosvāmī brought Jīva there and placed him in the lap of Rūpa Gosvāmī, both *guru* and disciple wept. Rūpa Gosvāmī arranged for Jīva to be treated by the best doctors from Mathurā, and gradually Jīva became strong again. From then on their former practice resumed, with Rūpa Gosvāmī giving whatever he wrote to Jīva for proofreading.

Śrīla Jīva Gosvāmī did the right thing when he defeated the arguments of Śrī Vallabhācārya and defended his Gurudeva. And Śrīla Rūpa Gosvāmī was also right. How is it possible that both were right? The answer is that Śrīla Rūpa Gosvāmī wanted to show respect to Śrī Vallabhācārya, but Jīva Gosvāmī, his disciple, appeared to disrespect him. Śrīla Rūpa Gosvāmī considered, "Śrī Vallabhācārya may think, 'Openly Rūpa Gosvāmī is respecting me, but he is disrespecting me through his disciple.'" For this, some blame might come to Rūpa Gosvāmī. By acting as though he were punishing his disciple, Śrīla Rūpa Gosvāmī was showing respect towards Śrī Vallabhācārya.

Śrīla Rūpa Gosvāmī was right, and Śrīla Jīva Gosvāmī was also right. A disciple should not tolerate any offence to his *guru*. Jīva Gosvāmī considered it an offence that Vallabhācārya wanted to 'correct' Rūpa Gosvāmī's understanding of *siddhānta*.

Years later, Śrīla Jīva Gosvāmī became well-known for expanding upon and enhancing the writings of other great *ācāryas*. One such *ācārya*, Śrīla Gopāla Bhaṭṭa Gosvāmī, had heard *hari-kathā* directly from Śrīla Rūpa Gosvāmī and Śrīla Sanātana Gosvāmī, whom he considered to be his *śikṣā-gurus*. While studying the writings of ancient Vaiṣṇava *ācāryas* such as Madhva and Rāmānuja, Gopāla Bhaṭṭa Gosvāmī selected different points in relation to *sambandha* (establishing one's relationship with Kṛṣṇa), *abhidheya* (acting in the dealings of that relationship), and *prayojana* (achieving life's ultimate goal), and compiled everything in a notebook.

Śrīla Jīva Gosvāmī learned all these established truths from Gopāla Bhaṭṭa Gosvāmī. Then, he took the volume which contained all the information on *sambandha* and enlarged it. He also took from the conceptions given in *Bhakti-rasāmṛta-sindhu*, *Ujjvala-nīlamaṇi*, *Bṛhad-bhāgavatāmṛta*, and the other books composed by Rūpa and Sanātana Gosvāmīs, and composed the first Sandarbha.

The word *sandarbha* means 'a chest of valuable jewels.' Of Śrīla Jīva Gosvāmī's Six Sandarbhas, the first four – *Tattva-sandarbha*, *Bhagavat-sandarbha*, *Paramātma-sandarbha*, and *Kṛṣṇa-sandarbha* – all expound *sambandha-jñāna*. They include knowledge of the *jīva*, the illusory energy, and the objective of the *jīva*; all of this was explained in the first four Sandarbhas.

In the *Tattva-sandarbha*, the conception of *pramāṇa* (the body of evidence) and *prameya* (evidence) is given. What is the meaning of *pramāṇa*? In any issue, whose words will we accept as authoritative? Suppose a young boy reports that a large fire has ravaged a holy place and everything has been burned. An elderly gentleman, however, reports that a small fire started in a tea shop there, but was easily contained. From these conflicting stories, whose words will we accept as authoritative? Certainly, the man's words are more authoritative because he is older and more mature than the boy.

This conception of *pramāṇa* relates to many things. Different people may assert their beliefs that this world is real, their status as human beings or *brāhmaṇas* is real, or that they are masters of their property. All this false identification and proprietorship causes so much fighting and quarreling. Another man will say, "These things are all temporary, so do not bother fighting over them. Instead, do something for your soul and for the Supreme Personality of Godhead; they are permanent." Which of these two opinions will we accept? Analyzing the relationships between the Supreme Lord, the *jīva*, and material existence, Śrīla Jīva Gosvāmī explained where we should place our faith. He wrote that the Vedas are the sole authority, and that any other, so-called authority lacks credibility. That which we perceive with our limited senses and mind may be defective, but the words of the Vedas cannot be so.

In his *Bhagavat-sandarbha*, Śrīla Jīva Gosvāmī writes that everything we see has the same source. The Absolute Truth is one, and He is naturally endowed with inconceivable potency. By the power of this potency, He exists within four forms: *svarūpa*, His original form; *tad-rūpa-vaibhava*, all incarnations, beginning with Baladeva Prabhu; *jīva*, the living entity; and *pradhāna*, the illusory energy. He is like the sun which also exists in four forms: its original form, the sun disc, its rays, and its reflected light which is compared to *māyā*.

Jīva Gosvāmī took parts from *Brahma-sandarbha* and wrote his own *Bhagavat-sandarbha*, in which he analyzes *brahma-tattva*, the established truth about the Supreme Spirit Whole, and refutes the opinions of Śaṅkarācārya. The *jīva* is not *brahma*, an impersonal God. If *brahma* is the Absolute Truth, which is full in knowledge, then how did it separate into billions of living entities and become bound within material existence? Śaṅkarācārya states that it was covered over by *māyā*, but then where did this separate entity he calls *māyā* come from? If there is no separate entity known as *māyā* and all is the one *brahma*, where could this other object known as ignorance have come from? Refuting all of Śaṅkarācārya's concepts, Śrīla Jīva Gosvāmī proved that Kṛṣṇa is Parabrahma, the Supreme Personality of Godhead, the source of *brahma*.

He also analyzed *paramātma-tattva*, and in the *Kṛṣṇa-sandarbha* he explained how Kṛṣṇa alone is the original Personality of Godhead. He explained how Kṛṣṇa is all-powerful (*sarva-śaktimān*), how He is an ocean of *rasa*, how from Him the *jīvas* and all else emerge, and how the *jīvas* can achieve His eternal association. He refuted the concept that Kṛṣṇa is an incarnation of Nārāyaṇa. Using evidence from the Vedas, Upaniṣads, and Purāṇas, he established that Kṛṣṇa is the original Absolute Truth, the Supreme Personality of Godhead, and that all other incarnations are His plenary or partial expansions. On the basis of scriptural evidence, he reinforced Mahāprabhu's conception, which had been established in the literatures of Rūpa Gosvāmī and Sanātana Gosvāmī. In doing so, he established our *sampradāya* upon a firm philosophical foundation. He protected the flowing river of *rasa* by placing large rocks of *siddhānta* on both its banks; in that way no contaminated water of misconceptions could ever enter it.

In his *Bhakti-sandarbha*, he explained many subtle aspects of *bhakti*. He delineated the sixty-four types of *bhakti*, and he expertly explained *guru-tattva*. He also described *guru-pādāśraya*, the process of taking exclusive shelter of the *guru*, how it should be done, what are its rules and regulations, and so on. If the *guru* carefully evaluates the prospective disciple and the disciple carefully considers the *guru*, then a circumstance will never arise where the disciple will have to abandon his *guru*. He taught that one should not accept a *guru* whimsically; one should accept a *guru* in whom he will never lose faith, otherwise there will be a problem. One should ensure that he only accepts a *sad-guru*, who is detached from sense enjoyment, who is conversant with all *tattva* and *siddhānta*, who is *rasika*, who is spiritually realized, and who is affectionate towards him. One should examine the *guru* carefully, even if this process takes as long as a year.

Śrīla Jīva Gosvāmī also explained that all *bhakti* is not the same, just as all varieties of water are not one and the same – there is clean water, purified water, contaminated water, sewage water, and so forth. Jīva Gosvāmī examined all these topics in depth in his Sandarbhas, which one must read in order to understand the true nature of *bhakti*. Thus, by regularly hearing the knowledge delineated in these books and by associating with advanced Vaiṣṇavas, one's *bhakti* will gradually become *uttama-bhakti*. Śrīla Jīva Gosvāmī described at length the five types of *prema: śānta* (neutrality), *dāsya* (servitorship), *sākhya* (friendship), *vātsalya* (parental love), and *mādhurya* (amorous love), especially emphasizing *gopī-prema* and explaining the *sādhana* for achieving it.

Much of this can be found in his *Gopāla-campū*, which is a very philosophical book. Śrīla Jīva Gosvāmī wrote that book in Goloka Vṛndāvana and then gave it to this world. He composed so many literatures that we could spend this entire birth immersed in reading them. Moreover, in practicing the *sādhana* prescribed by them, who knows how many lives we could spend? If we endeavor to enter into these books, and if we examine both the personal conduct and conceptions of Jīva Gosvāmī and try to personally follow them, our spiritual lives will certainly be successful. May Śrīla Jīva Gosvāmī be merciful upon us so that we can learn all the instructions he gave, in order to perform *bhajana* purely.

Śrīla Viśvanātha Cakravartī Ṭhākura

Following in the footsteps of Śrīla Rūpa Gosvāmī, Śrīla Viśvanātha Cakravartī Ṭhākura composed abundant transcendental literatures on *bhakti* and thus established in this world Śrīman Mahāprabhu's innermost heart's desire. He also refuted various faulty conclusions opposed to the genuine following of Śrī Rūpa Gosvāmī (*rūpānuga-bhakti*)[1]. He is thus revered in the Gauḍīya Vaiṣṇava society as an illustrious *ācārya* and as an authoritative *mahājana*, or self-realised soul. He is renowned as a great transcendental philosopher and poet, and a *rasika* devotee.

The Vaiṣṇava poet, Kṛṣṇa dāsa, has written the following lines at the conclusion of his translation of Śrīla Cakravartī Ṭhākura's *Mādhurya-kādambinī*: "Śrīla Viśvanātha Cakravartī Ṭhākura has benedicted the world by writing *Mādhurya-kādambinī*. In reality, Śrī Kṛṣṇa Caitanya Mahāprabhu is the speaker of this book through the mouth of Śrīla Cakravartī Ṭhākura. Some say that Śrīla Cakravartī Ṭhākura is an incarnation of Śrīla Rūpa Gosvāmī. He is expert in the art of describing extremely complex truths in a way that is easy to understand. O ocean of mercy, Śrīla Viśvanātha Cakravartī Ṭhākura, I am a very foolish person. Kindly reveal the mystery of your transcendental qualities in my heart. This is my prayer at your lotus feet."

After the disappearance of the Six Gosvāmīs of Vṛndavana, when there was a slight decline in their influence, a controversy arose regarding the doctrines of wedded love (*svakīyāvāda*) and paramour love (*parakīyāvāda*) in the Lord's pastimes. To dispel the misconceptions regarding *svakīyāvāda*, Śrīla Viśvanātha Cakravartī Ṭhākura wrote two books, *Rāga-vartma-candrikā* and *Gopī-premāmṛta*, both of which are filled with all the conclusions of the scriptures. Thereafter, in his *Ānanda-candrikā* commentary of *Ujjvala-nīlamaṇi* (1.21), he soundly refuted the theory of *svakīyāvāda* with scriptural evidence and irrefutable arguments, and established the conception of *parakīyā*. Additionally, in his *Sārārtha-darśinī* commentary on *Śrīmad-Bhāgavatam*, he gave strong support to *parakīyā-bhāva*.

---

1 Please turn to the glossary for a more elaborate definition of *rūpānuga-bhakti*.

At the time, there were some scholars who opposed Śrīla Viśvanātha Cakravartī Ṭhākura's conclusions regarding worship in the mood of *parakīyā*, but he defeated them with his deep scholarship and irrefutable logic. Resentful, these envious scholars resolved to kill him. Knowing his daily habit of performing *parikramā* around Śrī Vṛndāvana in the very early morning, they made a plan to kill him in a dark, hidden grove. As he approached the assigned spot where his adversaries lay in wait, he suddenly disappeared. In his place, they saw a beautiful young girl of Vraja picking flowers with some of her friends.

Bewildered, the scholars asked the girl, "Dear child, just a moment ago a great devotee was coming this way. Did you see where he went?" The girl replied that she had seen him, but that she did not know where he had gone. Her astonishing beauty, shy glances, gentle smile and graceful manner melted the hearts of the scholars, and purged all the impurities from their minds. Asked her identity, she replied, "I am a maidservant of Śrīmatī Rādhikā, who is presently at Her in-law's house at Yāvaṭa. She sent me here to pick flowers."

Saying this, the girl disappeared, and in her place the scholars saw once again Śrīla Viśvanātha Cakravartī Ṭhākura. They fell at his feet and prayed for forgiveness, and he forgave them all.

In this way he refuted the theory of *svakīyāvāda* and established the truth of pure *parakīyā*, an achievement which is very important for the Gauḍīya Vaiṣṇavas. There were many such astonishing events in the life of Śrī Cakravartī Ṭhākura.

Śrīla Viśvanātha Cakravartī Ṭhākura possessed uncommon genius, and not only protected the integrity of the Śrī Gauḍīya Vaiṣṇava *dharma*, but he also re-established its influence in Śrī Vṛndāvana. The Gauḍīya Vaiṣṇava *ācāryas* have composed the following verse in praise of his extraordinary work:

viśvasya nātha-rupo 'sau
bhakti-vartma-pradarśanāt
bhakta-cakre vartitatvāt
cakravarty ākhyayābhavat

"He is known by the name Viśvanātha, lord of the universe, because he indicates the path of *bhakti*; and he is known by the name Cakravartī, or he around whom the circle or assembly turns, because he always remains in the assembly (*cakra*) of pure devotees. Therefore, his name is Viśvanātha Cakravartī."

Very few Gauḍīya Vaiṣṇava *ācāryas* wrote as many books as Śrīla Cakravartī Ṭhākura. Even today, the following aphorism regarding three of his books is quoted in the general Vaiṣṇava community: "*kiraṇa-bindu-kaṇā, ei tina niya vaiṣṇava-panā* – the Vaiṣṇavas take these three books, namely *Ujjvala-nīlamaṇi-kiraṇa*, *Bhakti-rasāmṛta-sindhu-bindu*, and *Bhāgavatāmṛta-kaṇā*, as their wealth."

Below is a list of his other books, commentaries and prayers, which comprise an incomparably rich storehouse of Gauḍīya Vaiṣṇava devotional literature: *Vraja-rīti-cintāmaṇi*, *Śrī Camatkāra-candrikā*, *Śrī Prema-samputa*, *Gītāvalī*, *Subodhinī*, (commentary on *Alaṅkāra-kaustubha*), commmentary on *Śrī Gopāla-tāpanī*, *Stavāmṛta-laharī*, *Śrī Kṛṣṇa-bhāvanāmṛtam Mahākāvyam*, *Aiśvarya-kādambinī*, *Śrī Mādhurya-kādambinī*, and also commentaries on *Srī Bhakti-rasāmṛta-sindhu*, *Śrī Ānanda-vṛndāvana-campūḥ*, *Dāna-keli-kaumudī*, *Śrī Lalita-mādhava-nāṭaka*, *Śrī Caitanya-caritāmṛta*, *Brahma-saṁhitā*, as well as his *Sārārtha-varṣiṇī* commentary on *Śrīmad Bhagavad-gītā*.

In his old age, Śrīla Viśvanātha Cakravartī Ṭhākura spent most of his time in a semi-conscious or internal state, deeply absorbed in *bhajana*. During that time, a debate broke out in Jaipur between the Gauḍīya Vaiṣṇavas and the Vaiṣṇavas who supported the doctrine of *svakīyāvāda*, or wedded love in the Lord's pastimes.

The Vaiṣṇavas of the antagonistic camp had led King Jaya Singh II of Jaipur to believe that the worship of Śrīmatī Rādhikā along with Śrī Govindadeva is not supported by the scriptures. Their contention was that Śrīmatī Rādhikā's name is not mentioned anywhere in *Śrīmad-Bhāgavatam* or the *Viṣṇu Purāṇa*, and that She was never married to Śrī Kṛṣṇa according to Vedic ritual. Another objection was that Gauḍīya Vaiṣṇavas did not belong to a recognised line of disciplic succession (*sampradāya*).

Since time immemorial there have been four Vaiṣṇava *sampradāyas*: the Śrī *sampradāya*, the Brahma *sampradāya*, the Rudra *sampradāya* and the Sanaka (Kumāra) *sampradāya*. In the age of Kali, the principal *ācāryas* of these four *sampradāyas* are respectively Śrī Rāmānuja, Śrī Madhva, Śrī Viṣṇusvāmī, and Śrī Nimbāditya. The Gauḍīya Vaiṣṇavas were thought to be outside these four *sampradāyas* and were not accepted as having a pure lineage. In particular, the Gauḍīya Vaiṣṇavas were not accepted as a bona fide line of Vaiṣṇava disciplic succession because they did not have their own commentary on the *Brahma-sūtra* (also known as *Vedānta-sūtra*).

Mahārāja Jaya Singh knew that the prominent Gauḍīya Vaiṣṇava *ācāryas* of Vṛndāvana were followers of Śrīla Rūpa Gosvāmī, so he summoned them to Jaipur to take up the challenge with the Vaiṣṇavas from the line of Śrī Rāmānuja. As Śrīla Cakravartī Ṭhākura was quite aged and fully absorbed in the transcendental bliss of *bhajana*, he sent his student, Śrīla Baladeva Vidyābhūṣaṇa, to address the assembly in Jaipur on behalf of the Gauḍīya Vaiṣṇavas. Śrīla Baladeva Vidyābhūṣaṇa was the greatest among the exalted teachers of Vedānta and was therefore known as the Gauḍīya Vaiṣṇava *vedāntācārya mahā-mahopādhyāya*. He was accompanied by Śrīla Cakravartī Ṭhākura's disciple Śrī Kṛṣṇadeva.

The caste *gosvāmīs* had already forgotten their own connection with the Madhva *sampradāya*. Furthermore they were disrespectful of the Gauḍīya Vaiṣṇavas' viewpoint of Vedānta and created a great disturbance for the true Gauḍīya Vaiṣṇavas. Śrīla Baladeva Vidyābhūṣaṇa used irrefutable logic and powerful scriptural evidence to prove that the Gauḍīya *sampradāya* is a pure Vaiṣṇava *sampradāya* coming in the line of Madhva.

This *sampradāya* is called the Śrī Brahma-Madhva-Gauḍīya-Vaiṣṇava *sampradāya*. Śrīla Jīva Gosvāmī, Śrīla Kavi Karṇapūra and other previous *ācāryas* accepted this fact. The Gauḍīya Vaiṣṇavas accept *Śrīmad-Bhāgavatam* as the genuine commentary on the *Vedānta-sūtra*, and for this reason no separate commentary of *Vedānta-sūtra* had been written in the Gauḍīya Vaiṣṇava *sampradāya*. All this was shown to the assembled Vaiṣṇavas.

Śrīla Baladeva Vidyābhūṣaṇa then put forward the scriptural evidence for the worship of Śrīmatī Rādhikā. The name of Śrīmatī Rādhikā, the personification of the pleasure-giving potency (*hlādinī-śakti*) and the eternal beloved of Śrī Kṛṣṇa, is mentioned in various

Purāṇas. Throughout *Śrīmad-Bhāgavatam*, specifically in the Tenth Canto in connection with the description of the Lord's Vṛndāvana pastimes, Śrīmatī Rādhikā is referred to in a way that is highly concealed and indirect. Only *rasika* and *bhāvuka* devotees, who are conversant with the conclusions of the scriptures, can understand this confidential mystery.

In the learned assembly in Jaipur, Śrīla Baladeva Vidyābhūṣaṇa refuted all the arguments and doubts of the opposing party, who was silenced by his presentation. He solidly established the position of the Gauḍīya Vaiṣṇavas as following in the line of disciplic succession descending from Madhva. Nonetheless, the contesting party did not accept the Gauḍīya Vaiṣṇava *sampradāya* as being a pure line of Vaiṣṇava disciplic succession because they did not have a commentary on *Vedānta-sūtra*. So Śrīla Baladeva Vidyābhūṣaṇa then and there composed the famous Gauḍīya commentary on the *Vedānta-sūtra* named *Śrī Govinda-bhāṣya*. Consequently, the worship of Śrī Rādhā-Govinda recommenced in the temple of Śrī Govindadeva, and the validity of the Śrī Brahma-Madhva-Gauḍīya *sampradāya* was accepted.

It was only on the authority of Śrīla Viśvanātha Cakravartī Ṭhākura that Śrī Baladeva Vidyābhūṣaṇa was able to write the *Śrī Govinda-bhāṣya* and prove the connection of the Gauḍīya Vaiṣṇavas with the Madhva *sampradāya*. There should be no doubt in this regard. This accomplishment of Śrīla Viśvanātha Cakravartī Ṭhākura, performed on behalf of the *sampradāya*, will be recorded in golden letters in the history of Gauḍīya Vaiṣṇavism.

In 1754, on the fifth day of the light phase of the moon of the month of Māgha (January–February), when Śrīla Viśvanātha Cakravartī Ṭhākura was about a hundred years old, he left this material world in Vṛndāvana while deeply absorbed in internal consciousness. Today his *samādhi* can be found next to the temple of Śrī Rādhā-Gokulānanda in Śrīdhāma Vṛndāvana.

Śrī Śrīmad Bhaktivedānta Nārāyaṇa Gosvāmī Mahārāja

Śrī Śrīmad Bhaktivedānta Nārāyaṇa Gosvāmī Mahārāja is the disciple of *oṁ viṣṇupāda* Śrī Śrīmad Bhakti Prajñāna Keśava Gosvāmī Mahārāja, who is one of the foremost leading disciples of *oṁ viṣṇupāda* Śrī Śrīmad Bhaktisiddhānta Sarasvatī Prabhupāda.

On February 16, 1921, Śrīla Nārāyaṇa Gosvāmī Mahārāja took his divine birth in the village of Tewaripur, located near the bank of the sacred Ganges River in Bihar, India. It was here that Lord Rāmacandra killed the Taraka demon. Śrīla Mahārāja appeared in this world on the *amāvasyā* (new moon) day. His birth name was Śrīman Nārāyaṇa Tiwari. He was born in a very religious Trivedi *brāhmaṇa* family, and throughout his childhood he had many opportunities to regularly accompany his father to *kīrtanas* and lecture assemblies.

In February of 1946, he had his first meeting with his Gurudeva, in Śrī Navadvīpa Dhāma, West Bengal. He had traveled there from his village after meeting a disciple of Śrīla Bhaktisiddhānta Sarasvatī Thakura named Śrīla Narottamānanda Brahmacārī, who had been touring in the area, preaching the message of Śrī Caitanya Mahāprabhu. After some discussions with him, Śrīla Mahārāja had become convinced of the paramount position of the philosophy disseminated by the *ācāryas* in the line of Śrīla Rūpa Gosvāmī. Within days, he had left home to join the mission of his spiritual master and surrender his life to him.

Arriving in Śrī Navadvīpa Dhāma, Śrīla Mahārāja enthusiastically joined the annual *parikramā*. At the end of the *parikramā*, on Gaura-pūrṇimā, he was given both *harināma* and *dīkṣā mantras* by Śrīla Bhakti Prajñāna Keśava Gosvāmī Mahārāja, receiving the name Śrī Gaura Nārāyaṇa Brahmacārī. Soon afterward, his Gurudeva also awarded him the title 'Bhakta-bāndhava,' which means 'friend of the devotees,' as he was always serving the Vaiṣṇavas in a very pleasing manner.

Over the next seven years, He traveled extensively with his Gurudeva on preaching tours throughout India. In 1952, again on Gaura-pūrṇimā, his beloved Gurudeva awarded him initiation into the sacred order of *sannyāsa*. In 1954, his Gurudeva gave him charge of the newly opened temple in Mathurā, Śrī Keśavajī Gauḍīya Maṭha. Śrīla Mahārāja then began to spend part of the year in Mathurā and the other part in Bengal, serving extensively in both areas. This continued for the next fourteen years.

His responsibility further increased when Śrīla Bhakti Prajñāna Keśava Gosvāmī Mahārāja appointed him vice-president of his institution, the Śrī Gauḍīya Vedānta Samiti, as well as editor-in-chief of its Hindi publications and monthly magazine, *Śrī Bhāgavat Patrikā*. In 1968, his Gurudeva departed from this world and Śrīla Mahārāja personally performed all the necessary ceremonial rituals for his *samādhi*. During this time period, as a humble servitor of the Śrī Gauḍīya Vedānta Samiti, he began to organize the annual Kārtika Vraja-maṇḍala *parikramā*, which he continues to carry on up to this present day.

Śrīla Mahārāja was requested by his Gurudeva to translate the books of Śrīla Bhaktivinoda Thakura from Bengali into his native language, Hindi. He has carried out this request by translating some of the Ṭhākura's most prominent books, such as *Jaiva-dharma*, *Caitanya-Śikṣāmṛta*, *Bhakti-tattva-viveka*, *Vaiṣṇava-siddhānta-mālā*, to name only a few. All these books, as well as his translations and commentaries of other prominent *ācāryas* of the *guru-paramparā*, are presently being translated into English and other languages by his followers. To date, he has translated and published over eighty books in Hindi, and over fifty books in English. In addition, many of his English books have now been translated into other languages, including Spanish, French, German, Italian, Russian, Portuguese, Chinese, and several Indian languages.

He continues to lecture in Hindi, Bengali, and English throughout India and internationally, and all of his discourses are recorded. Several Hindi lectures have been transcribed, as well as translated into English and other languages for publication. Additionally, thousands of his English lectures have been recorded and filmed, and, they are also being sent as transcriptions, audios, and videos over the internet to reach hundreds of thousands of fortunate souls.

A significant relationship in the life of Śrīla Nārāyaṇa Gosvāmī Mahārāja is his association with Śrīla Bhaktivedānta Swāmī Mahārāja, known throughout the world as Śrīla Prabhupāda, the famous preacher of Gauḍīya Vaiṣṇavism and Founder-Ācārya of ISKCON, the International Society for Kṛṣṇa Consciousness. They first met in Calcutta, in 1946, on the occasion of the inauguration of a new branch of the Gauḍīya Vedānta Samiti when they had both come to render their services. Śrīla Bhaktivedānta Swāmī Mahārāja is one of its founding members.

Śrīla Nārāyaṇa Gosvāmī Mahārāja accompanied his Gurudeva to Jhansi, where Śrīla Bhaktivedānta Swāmī Mahārāja, or Abhaya Caraṇāravinda Prabhu, as he was formerly known, had been trying to start a Vaiṣṇava society named The League of Devotees. A few years later, in the early Fifties, Śrīla Bhaktivedānta Swāmī Mahārāja came to reside in Mathurā at Śrī Keśavajī Gauḍīya Maṭha, on the invitation of his god-brother, Śrīla Bhakti Prajñāna Keśava Gosvāmī Mahārāja, and he remained there for some months. Sharing regular devotional exchanges and deep discussions of Vaiṣṇava *siddhānta* with him, Śrīla Nārāyaṇa Gosvāmī Mahārāja developed a still further intimate relationship with Śrīla Bhaktivedānta Swāmī Mahārāja during this time period, regarding him both as his *śikṣā-guru* and bosom friend.

In 1959 Śrīla Bhakti Prajñāna Keśava Gosvāmī Mahārāja initiated Abhaya Caraṇāravinda Prabhu into the sacred *sannyāsa* order, giving him the *sannyāsī* name and title Śrī Śrīmad Bhaktivedānta Swāmī Mahārāja, and the ceremony of Vedic fire *yajña* and all the rituals were personally performed by Śrīla Nārāyaṇa Gosvāmī Mahārāja. Śrīla Bhaktivedānta Swāmī Mahārāja was already residing in Vṛndāvana during this period, first at the Vaṁśī Gopāla Mandira and a few years later at the Śrī Śrī Rādhā-Dāmodara Mandira, and Śrīla Mahārāja would often go there to visit him. He would cook for him and honor the *prasāda* with him, and they would exchange intimate discussions on Vaiṣṇava philosophy.

When Śrīla Bhaktivedānta Swāmī Mahārāja went to preach in the West and succeeded in starting the first Rādhā-Kṛṣṇa temple in America, Śrīla Nārāyaṇa Gosvāmī Mahārāja sent him the first *mṛdaṅga* drums and *karatālas* that he would be using for *saṅkīrtana*.

Śrīla Bhaktivedānta Swāmī Mahārāja maintained regular correspondence every month or two with Śrīla Bhakti Prajñāna Keśava Gosvāmī Mahārāja and Śrīla Nārāyaṇa Gosvāmī Mahārāja up until 1968, when Śrīla Keśava Gosvāmī Mahārāja entered *nitya-līlā*. After that, he continued to write Śrīla Nārāyaṇa Gosvāmī Mahārāja, until his own divine departure in 1977.

Toward the end of his manifest stay in this world, he requested Śrīla Nārāyaṇa Gosvāmī Mahārāja several times to kindly give his association to his western disciples and help them to understand the deep truths of the Vaiṣṇava philosophy in the line of Śrīla Rūpa Gosvāmī. Śrīla Nārāyaṇa Gosvāmī Mahārāja humbly agreed to honor his request, considering him to be one of his worshipable *śikṣā-gurus*. Śrīla Bhaktivedānta Swāmī Mahārāja also requested Śrīla Nārāyaṇa Gosvāmī Mahārāja to take complete charge of performing all the rituals for his *samādhi* after his departure. Both of these requests clearly demonstrated his firm and utter confidence in Śrīla Nārāyaṇa Gosvāmī Mahārāja.

For three decades since Śrīla Bhaktivedānta Swāmī Mahārāja's departure from the vision of this world in November 1977, Śrīla Mahārāja has been unwaveringly carrying out this final request, by providing insightful guidance and loving shelter to all who come to him seeking it. Through the medium of his English books and extensive world touring, he is now giving his association and divine realizations to Śrīla Bhaktivedānta Swāmī Mahārāja's followers and all other sincere searchers of truth throughout the globe. Although he is over 88 years of age, he regularly travels throughout India and abroad, preaching the glories of Śrī Caitanya Mahāprabhu and Śrī Śrī Rādhā-Kṛṣṇa, and the true glory of ISKCON's Founder-Ācārya Śrīla Bhaktivedānta Swāmī Mahārāja and his entire *guru-paramparā*.

In 2009, the year of the publication of his *Gopī-gīta* discourses, Śrīla Nārāyaṇa Gosvāmī Mahārāja completed his thirtieth world preaching tour. In many countries, he is invited to prominent Hindu temples to give lectures on India's Vedic *sanātana-dharma*. When he is in India, he is regularly invited by dignitaries to speak at their spiritual programs. A prominent member of the Brahma-Madhva-Gauḍīya disciplic succession, he is highly acclaimed throughout India as a spiritual scholar and teacher, and as a pure devotee of Lord Śrī Kṛṣṇa in the line of Śrī Caitanya Mahāprabhu. He is recognized as a strict follower of Vedic culture, Hindu *sanātana-dharma*, Vaiṣṇava etiquette, *daivī-varṇāśrama*, and *bhāgavat-bhajana*. Most of the notable spiritual scholars of Mathurā and Vṛndāvana invite him to speak at their assemblies, and he also invites them to attend programs at his Maṭha.

Many Indian government officials, like the DCP (Deputy Commissioner of Police) and also many court judges, in Delhi, Bombay, Calcutta, Mathurā, and elsewhere are his disciples. Many renowned industrialists and businessmen regularly come to him to inquire about spiritual life and receive his blessings. Many head *pūjārīs* throughout Vraja-maṇḍala visit him. The head *pūjārī* of the well-known Rādhā-Govinda Mandira in Jaipur regularly arranges to bring garlands and *mahā-prasāda* from the Deities, especially on the occasions of Śrīla Mahārāja's commencement of another world tour. This is also true of the *pūjārī* of Śrī Jagannātha Mandira in Purī. The leader of all Lord Jagannātha's servants, the Dayitā-pati of Purī, also attends Śrīla Mahārāja's classes when he is in Purī.

Śrīla Mahārāja has been conducting Vraja-maṇḍala Parikramā for over 50 years, and, during that time, the heads of all the villages come to him and pay their respects. He has also been engaged for several years in organizing the renovation of many holy places in Vṛndāvana, such as Bhāṇḍīravaṭa in Bhāṇḍīravana, Kadamba-kyārī near Nandagrāma, Brahma-kuṇḍa and Surabhi-kuṇḍa in Govardhana, and Kāliya-ghāṭa in Vṛndāvana. His work in this regard is recognized by the public, the government and the press. For this and his other spiritual achievements, he was awarded the title Yuga-Ācārya by the heads of the various villages throughout Vraja-maṇḍala.

He also leads a Navadvīpa-dhāma *parikramā* every year at the time of Gaura-pūrṇimā. At that time he and his *sannyāsīs* are followed by over 20,000 pilgrims from Bengal, and over 2,000 other Indian and Western pilgrims. Most of the devotees from Bengal are poor village people, and they are given free facilities and *prasādam* throughout the week-long festival.

Śrīla Bhaktivedānta Nārāyaṇa Gosvāmī Mahārāja has demonstrated and exemplified the unadulterated life of utter dedication and pure loving service to his Gurudeva, his *guru-paramparā*, Śrī Caitanya Mahāprabhu, and the Divine Couple, Śrī Śrī Rādhā-Kṛṣṇa. As Their intimate servitor, he continues to illuminate the path for those who wish to discover and dive deeply into the ecstatic ocean of *rādhā-dāsyam*, service to the radiantly beautiful lotus feet of Śrī Kṛṣṇa's dearly beloved, Śrīmatī Rādhikā.

Appendix

A recording of Śrīla Mahārāja singing the nineteen verses of Gopī-gīta, as well as the first two verses of the next chapter that describe Śrī Kṛṣṇa reappearing to the gopīs, is available at https://soundcloud.com/srila-bv-narayan-maharaja/gopi-geet. Before singing, Śrīla Mahārāja speaks three sanskrit verses as an auspicious invocation (maṅgalācaraṇa) and gives a short Hindi introduction to the song. The translation of both is given here.

Invocation

oṁ ajñāna-timirāndhasya jñānāñjana-śalākayā
cakṣur unmīlitaṁ yena tasmai śrī-gurave namaḥ

O Gurudeva, you are so merciful. I offer my humble pranāma to you and am praying from the core of my heart that, with the torchlight of divine knowledge, you open my eyes which have been blinded by the darkness of ignorance.

vāñchā-kalpa-tarubhyaś ca kṛpā-sindhubhya eva ca
patitānāṁ pāvanebhyo vaiṣṇavebhyo namo namaḥ

I offer pranāma unto the Vaiṣṇavas, who are just like wish-fulfilling desire trees, who are an ocean of mercy, and who deliver the fallen, conditioned souls.

namo mahā-vadānyāya kṛṣṇa-prema-pradāya te
kṛṣṇāya kṛṣṇa-caitanya-nāmne gaura-tviṣe namaḥ

I offer pranāma unto śrī Kṛṣṇa-Caitanya, who is śrī Kṛṣṇa Himself. Having assumed the golden hue of śrīmatī Rādhikā, He is munificently bestowing kṛṣṇa-prema, the rarest of all gifts.

A few words...

(English translation of the Hindi introduction)

When Śrī Kṛṣṇa disappeared from the rāsa-sthalī, the gopīs of Vraja sang a song, weeping in separation from Him. As the song reached His ears, His heart melted. He could no longer hide Himself. At once He manifested His enchanting form, which steals even the mind of Cupid, and humbly stood before them like an offender.

Glossary

A

Ācārya – spiritual preceptor; one who teaches by example.

Adhirūḍha-mahābhāva – the extremely high state of mahābhāva, found only in the gopīs of Vraja.

Anubhāva – one of the five essential ingredients of rasa; the thirteen actions which display or reveal the spiritual emotions situated within the heart of the pure devotee: dancing, rolling on the ground, singing, loud crying, writhing of the body, roaring, yawning, breathing heavily, neglecting others, drooling, loud laughter, staggering about, and hiccups.

Anurāga – (1) attachment, affection, or love; (2) an intensified stage of prema, which comes just prior to mahābhāva. Ujjvala-nīlamaṇi (14.146) states: "Although one regularly meets with the beloved and is well-acquainted with the beloved, the ever-fresh sentiments of intense attachment cause the beloved to be newly experienced at every moment, as if one has never before had any experience of such a person."

Arcana – Deity worship; one of the nine primary processes of devotional service.

Āsakti – deep attachment for the Lord and His associates. It occurs when one's liking for bhajana leads to a direct attachment for the person who is the object of bhajana. It is the seventh stage in the development of the creeper of devotion, and it is awakened upon the maturing of one's taste for bhajana.

Aṣṭa-sāttvika-bhāvas – eight symptoms of spiritual ecstacy: becoming stunned, perspiring, bodily hairs standing on end, faltering of the voice, trembling, loss of bodily color, tears, and fainting.

B

Bhajana – spiritual practices, especially the process of hearing, chanting, and meditating upon the holy name, form, qualities and pastimes of Śrī Kṛṣṇa.

Bhakta – a devotee; one who performs bhakti or devotional service.

Bhakti – the performance of activities which are meant to satisfy or please the Supreme Lord Śrī Kṛṣṇa, which are executed in a favorable spirit saturated with love, which is devoid of all desires other than the desire for the Lord's benefit and pleasure, and which is not covered by reward-seeking activity and the speculation that God is impersonal.

Bhakti-yoga – the path of spiritual realization through devotional service to Lord Kṛṣṇa.

Bhāva – spiritual emotions or sentiments

Bhāva-bhakti – the initial stage of perfection in devotion. The stage of bhakti in which śuddha-sattva, the essence of the Lord's internal potency consisting of spiritual knowledge and bliss, is transmitted into the heart of the practising devotee from the heart of the Lord's eternal associates. It is like a ray of the sun of prema and it softens the heart by various tastes. It is the sprout of prema, and it is also known as rati. It is the eighth stage of the creeper of devotion.

Brahma-vimohana-līlā – The following summary of this pastime (līlā) is presented by Śrīla Bhaktivedānta Swāmī Mahārāja in his English translation of Śrīmad-Bhāgavatam (10.13): "After killing Aghāsura, Kṛṣṇa, along with His associates the cowherd boys, went for a picnic in the forest. The calves, being allured by green grasses, gradually went far away, and therefore Kṛṣṇa's associates became a little agitated and wanted to bring back the calves. Kṛṣṇa, however, encouraged the boys by saying, "Take your lunch without being agitated. I shall go find the calves." And thus the Lord departed.

Then, just to examine the potency of Kṛṣṇa, Lord Brahmā took away all the calves and cowherd boys and kept them in a secluded place. When Kṛṣṇa was unable to find the calves and boys, He could understand that this was a trick performed by Brahmā. Then the Supreme Personality of Godhead, the cause of all causes, in order to please Lord Brahmā as well as His own associates and their mothers, expanded Himself to become the calves and boys, exactly as they were before being taken by Brahmā.

In this way, He discovered another pastime. A special feature of this pastime was that the mothers of the cowherd boys became more attached to their respective sons, and the cows became more attached to their calves. After nearly a year, Baladeva observed that all the cowherd boys and calves were expansions of Kṛṣṇa. Thus He inquired from Kṛṣṇa and was informed of what had happened.

When one full year had passed, Brahmā returned and saw that Kṛṣṇa was still engaged as usual with His friends and the calves and cows. Then Kṛṣṇa exhibited all the calves and cowherd boys as four-armed forms of Nārāyaṇa. Brahmā could then understand Kṛṣṇa's potency, and he was astonished by the pastimes of Kṛṣṇa, his worshipful Lord."

G

Gopa – (1) a cowherd boy who serves Kṛṣṇa in a mood of intimate friendship; (2) an elderly associate of Nanda Mahārāja who serves Kṛṣṇa in a mood of parental affection.

Gopāla-mantra – a sacred verse that is repeated by Gauḍīya Vaiṣṇava brāhmaṇas at the three junctions of the day. It is one of the mantras given by the guru at the time of initiation.

Gopī – (1) one of the young cowherd maidens of Vraja, headed by Śrīmatī

Rādhikā, who serve Kṛṣṇa in a mood of amorous love; (2) an elderly associate of Mother Yaśodā, who serves Kṛṣṇa in a mood of parental affection.

Gosvāmī – one who is the master of his senses; a title for those in the renounced order of life. This often refers to the renowned followers of Śrī Caitanya Mahāprabhu who adopted the lifestyle of mendicants.

J

Jñāni-bhakta – a devotee who worships the Supreme Lord in the mood of opulence and, due to that sense of the Lord's all-pervasiveness and completeness, does not render personal services.

K

Kajjala – an eye ointment made from lampblack, which is used to darken the edges of the eyelids.

Kāma – (1) lust to gratify the urges of the material senses; (2) the gopīs' transcendental desire to enjoy amorous pastimes with Śrī Kṛṣṇa.

Kāma-gāyatrī – a sacred verse that is repeated by Gauḍīya Vaiṣṇava brāhmaṇas at the three junctions of the day. It is one of the mantras given by the guru at the time of dīkṣā-initiation.

"The kāma-gāyatrī mantra is just like a Vedic hymn, but it is the Supreme Personality of Godhead Himself. There is no difference between the kāma-gāyatrī and Kṛṣṇa. Both are composed of twenty-four and a half transcendental syllables (see Madhya 21.125–29). The mantra depicted in letters is also Kṛṣṇa, and the mantra rises just like the moon. Due to this, there is a perverted reflection of desire in human society and among all kinds of living entities. In the mantra, klīṁ kāma-devāya vidmahe puṣpa-bāṇāya dhīmahi tan no 'naṅgaḥ pracodayāt, Kṛṣṇa is called Kāma-deva, Puṣpa-bāṇa and Anaṅga. Kāma-deva is Madana-mohana, the Deity who establishes our relationship with Kṛṣṇa; Puṣpa-bāṇa (He who carries an arrow made of flowers) is Govinda, the Personality of Godhead who accepts our devotional service; and Anaṅga is Gopījana-vallabha, who satisfies all the gopīs and is the ultimate goal of life. This kāma-gāyatrī (klīṁ kāma-devāya vidmahe puṣpa-bāṇāya dhīmahi tan no 'naṅgaḥ pracodayāt) simply does not belong to this material world. When one is advanced in spiritual understanding, he can worship the Supreme Personality of Godhead with his spiritually purified senses and fulfill the desires of the Lord" (Caitanya-caritāmṛta, Madhya-līlā 8.138, purport by Śrīla Bhaktivedānta Swāmī Mahārāja).

Kaniṣṭha-adhikārī – a novice devotee or neophyte practitioner of bhakti.

Karma – (1) any activity performed in the course of material existence; (2) reward-seeking activities; pious activities leading to material gain in this world or in the heavenly planets after death; (3) fate; previous actions which yield inevitable reactions.

Kuṅkuma – a reddish powder or liquid applied by married women on the part in their hair, to signify their marriage.

Kuñja – a secluded forest grove; a natural, shady retreat with a roof and walls formed by flowering trees, vines, creepers, and other climbing plants.

M

Mādana-bhāva or *mādanākhya-mahābhāva* – the highest spontaneous stage of mahābhāva, which is characterized by the simultaneous manifestation of all types of transcendental emotions. It is eternally and splendidly manifest only in Śrī Rādhā, and it occurs only at the time of meeting.

Madhyama-adhikārī – a practitioner of bhakti who has reached the intermediate stage of spiritual development.

Mahābhāva – the highest stage of prema or divine love. In Ujjvala-nīlamaṇi (14.154) mahābhāva is defined thus: "When anurāga reaches a special state of intensity, it is known as bhāva or mahābhāva. This state of intensity has three characteristics: (1) anurāga reaches the state of sva-samvedya, which means that it becomes the object of its own experience, (2) it becomes prakāśita, radiantly manifest, which means that all eight sāttvika-bhāvas become prominently displayed, and (3) it attains the state of yāvad āśraya-vṛtti, which means that the active ingredient of this intensified state of anurāga transmits the experience of Rādhā's and Kṛṣṇa's bhāva to whomever may be present and qualified to receive it.

Mahā-prasāda – literally means 'great mercy,' and especially refers to the remnants of food offered to the Deity; may also refer to the remnants of other articles offered to the Deity, such as incense, flowers, garlands, and clothing.

Māna – the sentiment that prevents the lover and beloved from meeting freely, although they are together and are attracted to each other. Māna gives rise to transient emotions like transcendental anger, despondency, doubt, restlessness, pride, and jealousy.

Mañjarī – (1) bud of a flower; (2) a maidservant of Śrīmatī Rādhikā.

Māyā – the Lord's deluding potency; illusion; that which is not; the Lord's external potency, which influences the living entities to accept the false egoism of being independent enjoyers of this material world; also called mahāmāyā or māyā-śakti.

N

Niṣṭhā – firm faith; steadiness in one's devotional practices. The fifth stage in the development of the creeper of devotion.

P

Praṇaya – an intensified stage of prema; a stage in the development of prema up to mahābhāva. It is described in Ujjvala-nīlamaṇi (14.108): "When māna assumes a feature of unrestrained intimacy, learned authorities refer to it as praṇaya." The word viśrambha used in this verse means complete confidence, devoid of any restraint or formality. This confidence causes one to consider one's life, mind, intelligence, body, and possessions to be one in all respects with the life, mind, intelligence, and body of the beloved.

Prema – "Love for Kṛṣṇa which is extremely concentrated, which completely melts the heart, and which gives rise to a deep sense of mamatā or possessiveness in relation to the Lord" (Bhakti-rasāmṛta-sindhu 1.4.1).

Prema-bhakti – the stage of bhakti which is characterised by the appearance of prema (see above); the perfectional stage of devotion; the eighth and fully blossomed state of the bhakti-latā, or creeper of devotion.

Pūjā – offering of worship; worship of the Deity in the temple or of respected personalities such as one's guru, by which different paraphernalia like incense, a lighted ghee-lamp, and flowers are offered.

Pūrva-rāga – "When attachment produced in the lover and beloved before their meeting by seeing, hearing, and so on becomes very palatable by the mixture of four ingredients such as vibhāva and anubhāva, this is called pūrva-raga" (Ujjvala-nilamani, Vipralambha-prakarana 5).

R

Rāga – (1) deep attachment for the object of one's affection; "That stage at which affection for the beloved converts unhappiness into happiness is called rāga, or attachment. When one has such attachment for Kṛṣṇa, he can give up his own life to satisfy his beloved Kṛṣṇa (Caitanya-caritāmṛta, Madhya-līlā 19.178, purport by Śrīla Bhaktivedānta Swāmī Mahārāja);" (2) a musical mode or sequence (e.g., malhāra rāga)

Rāgānuga or *rāgānuga-bhakti* – bhakti that follows in the wake of Śrī Kṛṣṇa's eternal associates in Vraja, whose hearts are permeated with rāga, which is an unquenchable loving thirst for Kṛṣṇa that gives rise to spontaneous and intense absorption.

Rasa – (1) the spiritual transformation of the heart which takes place when the perfectional state of love for Śrī Kṛṣṇa, known as rati, is converted into 'liquid' emotions by combining with various types of transcendental ecstasies; (2) taste, favor.

Rāsa-līlā – Śrī Kṛṣṇa's dance with the vraja-gopīs, which is a pure exchange of spiritual love between Kṛṣṇa and the gopīs, His most confidential servitors.

Rasika or *rasika-bhakta* – one who is able to relish bhakti-rasa within his heart. At the stage of bhāva, a bhakta's heart becomes infused with śuddha-sattva from the heart of one of Kṛṣṇa's eternal associates in Vraja. This śuddha-sattva is then known as kṛṣṇa-rati, the first dawning of divine love. When this permanent sentiment of love combines with other ecstatic emotions, it generates the unique experience of bhakti-rasa. One who is eligible to taste this rasa is known as a rasika-bhakta.

Ratha-yātrā – a festival of chariots, held yearly at Jagannātha Purī in Orissa, which celebrates Śrī Kṛṣṇa's return to Vṛndāvana from Dvārakā. On the Ratha-yātrā day, the Deities of Lord Jagannātha, Baladeva and Subhadrā are placed on three huge decorated chariots. In Purī, the devotees pull these chariots from the Jagannātha temple to the Guṇḍicā temple. The Jagannātha temple represents Dvārakā and the Guṇḍicā temple represents Vṛndāvana. Śrī Caitanya Mahāprabhu and His associates gathered every year to observe this celebration with a great festival of saṅkīrtana.

Ruci – taste; this is the sixth stage in the development of the creeper of devotion. At this stage, with the awakening of actual taste, one's attraction to spiritual matters, such as hearing, chanting, and other devotional practices exceeds one's attraction to any type of material activity.

Rūpānuga – "Rūpa Gosvāmī and Sanātana Gosvāmī are the most exalted servitors of Śrīmatī Rādhārāṇī and Lord Śrī Caitanya Mahāprabhu. Those who adhere to their service are known as rūpānuga devotees" (Caitanya-caritāmṛta, Madhya-līlā 8.246, purport by Śrīla Bhaktivedānta Swāmī Mahārāja).

"We Gauḍīya Vaiṣṇavas, we are known as rūpānuga. Rūpānuga means the followers of Rūpa Gosvāmī. Why we should become followers of Rūpa Gosvāmī? Śrī-caitanya-mano 'bhīṣṭaṁ sthāpitaṁ yena bhū-tale – he wanted to establish the mission of Śrī Caitanya Mahāprabhu" (Śrīla Bhaktivedānta Swāmī Mahārāja. Lecture on Śrīmad-Bhāgavatam 5.5.2, Hyderabad, April 13, 1975).

"Rūpānuga-bhaktas are only those who follow the same manner and mood in which Śrī Rūpa Mañjarī serves Rādhā and Kṛṣṇa. Although Śrī Rūpa Mañjarī serves both Rādhā and Kṛṣṇa, she is more inclined to-wards Śrīmatī Rādhikā – happy in the happiness of Śrīmatī Rādhikā and suffering like Her when She suffers. Internally, in their constitutional forms,

ENGLISH TITLES PUBLISHED BY
ŚRĪ ŚRĪMAD BHAKTIVEDĀNTA NĀRĀYAṆA GOSVĀMĪ MAHĀRĀJA

A Life of Humble Service
Arcana-dīpikā
Beyond Nīrvāṇa
Bhagavad-gītā
Bhajana-rahasya
Bhakti-rasāmṛta-sindu-bindu
Bhakti-rasāyana
Bhakti-tattva-viveka
Brahma-saṁhitā
Bṛhad-bhāgavatāmṛta (Vol. 2.1)
Butter Thief
Caitanya Mahāprabhu – The Original Form of Godhead
Camatkāra-candrikā – A Moonbeam of Complete Astonishment
Controlled by Love
Dāmodarāṣṭakam
Discerning the True Sentiments of the Soul
Distinctive Contribution of Śrī Rūpa Gosvāmī
Essence of All Advice
Essence of Bhagavad-gītā
Fearless Prince
Five Essential Essays
Gauḍīya Gītī-guccha
Gaura-vāṇī-pracāriṇe
Gift of Śrī Caitanya Mahāprabhu
Gīta-govinda
Going Beyond Vaikuṇṭha
Gopī-gīta
Guru-devatātmā
Happiness in a Fool's Paradise
Harināma Mahā-mantra
Harmony
Hidden Path of Devotion
Impressions of Bhakti
Jagannātha Ratha-yātrā
Jaiva-dharma
Journey of the Soul
Kṛṣṇa – the Lord of Sweetness
Letters From America
Maharṣi Durvasā and Śrī Durvāsā-āśrama
Manaḥ-śikṣā
My Śikṣā-guru and Priya-bandhu
Navadvīpa-dhāma-māhātmya
Navadvīpa-dhāma
Nectar of Govinda-līlā
Our Eternal Nature
Our Gurus: One in Siddhanta, One at Heart
Our Lasting Relationship
Pinnacle of Devotion
Prabandhāvalī
Prema-sampuṭa
Rādhā-kṛṣṇa-gaṇoddeśa-dīpikā
Rāga-vartma-candrikā
Rāya Rāmānanda Saṁvāda
Saṅkalpa-kalpadrumaḥ
Secrets of the Undiscovered Self
Secret Truths of the Bhāgavatam
Shower of Love
Śikṣāṣṭaka
Śiva-tattva
Ślokāmṛtam
Ślokāmṛtam-bindu
Soul of Book Distribution
Śrī Śrīmad Bhakti Prajñāna Keśava Gosvāmī – His Life and Teachings
To Be Controlled by Love
True Conception of Guru-tattva
Ujjvala-nīlamaṇi-kiraṇa
Upadeśāmṛta
Utkalikā-vallarī
Vaiṣṇava-siddhānta-mālā
Veṇu-gīta
Śrī Vraja-maṇḍala Parikramā
Walking with a Saint (2007, 2008, 2009, 2010)
Way of Love
When Kindness and Compassion Take a Form
Rays of The Harmonist (periodical)

WORLDWIDE CENTRES & CONTACTS

www.purebhakti.com/contact-us/centers-mainmenu-60.html

INDIA

Mathura: Shri Keshavaji Gaudiya Math – Jawahar Hata, U.P. 281001 (Opp. Dist. Hospital), Email: mathuramath@gmail.com • **New Delhi**: Shri Raman-vihari Gaudiya Math – Block B-3, Janakpuri, New Delhi 110058 (Near musical fountain park), Tel: 9810192540; Karol Bagh Centre: Rohini-nandana dasa, 9A/39 Channa Market, WEA, Karol Bagh, Tel: 9810398406, 9810636370, Email: purebhakti.kb@gmail.com • **Vrindavan**: Shri Rupa-Sanatana Gaudiya Math – Dan Gali, U.P. Tel: 09760952435; Gopinath Bhavan – Parikrama Marga (next to Imli-tala), Seva Kunja, Vrindavan 281121, U.P., Email: vasantidasi@gmail.com • **Puri**: Jay Shri Damodar Gaudiya Math – Sea Palace, Chakratirtha Road. Tel: 06752-223375 • **Bangalore**: Shri Madan Mohan Gaudiya Math – 245/1 29th Cross, Kaggadasa pura Balaji layout, Bangalore-93, Tel: 08904427754, Email: bvvaikhanas@gmail.com; Shri Ranganath Gaudiya Math – Hesaraghatta, Bangalore, Tel: 09379447895, 07829378386 • **Faridabad**: Shri Radha Madhav Gaudiya Math – 293, Sector-14, Hariyana, Tel: 09911283869 • **Navadvipa**: Shri Shri Keshavaji Gaudiya Math – Kolerdanga Lane, Nadiya, Bengal, Tel: 09153125442

AUSTRALIA

Garden Ashram – Akhileshvari dasi, Tel: 612 66795916, Email: akhileshvari.dasi@gmail.com • Shri Gaura Narayan Gaudiya Math – Brisbane, Queensland, Tel: +61 403 993 746, Email: bhaktibrisbane2010@gmail.com

CHINA / HONG KONG

15A, Hillview Court, 30 Hillwood Road, Tsim Sha Tsui, Kowloon, Tel: +85223774603

UNITED KINGDOM & IRELAND

Birmingham: Shri Gour Govinda Gaudiya Math – 9 Clarence Road, Handsworth, Birmingham, B21 0ED, U. K., Tel: (44) 121551-7729, Email: bvashram108@gmail.com • **London**: Shri Gangamata Gaudiya Math – 631 Forest Road, E17 4NE London, Tel: 02080578406, Email: gangamatas@hotmail.com • **Galway**: Family Centre – Tel: 353 85-1548200, Email: jagannathchild@gmail.com

USA

Gaudiya Vedanta Publications Offices – Tel: (800) 681-3040 ext. 108, Email: orders@bhaktiprojects.org • **Alachua:** Shri Shri Radha-Govinda Mandir – Tel: (1) 386-462-2682. Email: yourbvgi@gmail.com, Website: www.bvgi.org • **Houston:** Shri Govindaji Gaudiya Math – Tel: (1) 281-650-8689. Email: info@sggm.org, Website: www.sggm.org